Donated
In Loving Memory of

BY:

© DEMCO, INC. 1990 PRINTED IN U.S.A.

DISCARD

PRESERVING AMERICAN

Mansions and Estates

PRESERVING AMERICAN

Mansions and Estates

William C. Shopsin, AIA

with

research assistance by

Nora Lucas

McGraw-Hill, Inc.

New York San Francisco Washington, D.C. Auckland Bogotá
Caracas Lisbon London Madrid Mexico City Milan
Montreal New Delhi San Juan Singapore
Sydney Tokyo Toronto

Library of Congress Cataloging-in-Publication Data

Shopsin, William C.
    Preserving American mansions and estates / William C. Shopsin.
        p.   cm.
    Includes bibliographical references and index.
    ISBN 0-07-057041-8
    1. Mansions—United States—Conservation and restoration—Case
studies.   2. Country homes—United States—Conservation and
restoration—Case studies.   3. Mansions—United States—Remodeling
for other use—Case studies.   4. Country homes—United States
—Remodeling for other use—Case studies.   I. Title.
    NA7511.S53   1994
    363.6'9'0973—dc20   93-46157
                                                                                        CIP

1 2 3 4 5 6 7 8 9 0   KGP/KGP   9 0 9 8 7 6 5 4

ISBN 0-07-057041-8

The sponsoring editor for this book was JOEL STEIN,
the editing supervisor was JANE PALMIERI,
the designer was SILVERS DESIGN,
and the production supervisor was SUZANNE BABEUF.
It was set in Perpetua by SILVERS DESIGN.

Printed and bound by KINGSPORT PRESS, INC.

*To Nora and Tony whose cheerful assistance and encouragement
made this project possible*

CONTENTS ❧

PREFACE

In December 1992 the Athenaeum of Philadelphia sponsored an exhibition and symposium with the theme of "Three American Country Houses, the Architectural Patronage of Mr. and Mrs. Edward T. Stotesbury." All three palatial mansions commissioned by this rich and socially prominent Philadelphia couple—Whitemarsh Hall in Chestnut Hill, Pennsylvania (Trumbauer, 1916 to 1919); El Mirasol in Palm Beach, Florida (Mizner, 1919); and Wingwood in Bar Harbor, Maine (Magaziner, Eberhard, and Harris, 1926)—have been demolished in the less than 50 years that have passed since their construction. The widely scattered geographic distribution of these residences, located in prestigious communities that retain their fashionable status today, provides a distressing reminder of the plight of the great American country house. Typically, all the presentations at the Philadelphia Athenaeum were redolent of nostalgic black-and-white photographic recollections of the golden age of American country life with only an occasional reference to the surviving legacy and no mention at all of possible strategies for preserving what is left.

It is the intention of this book to examine both successes and failures, in recent years, of those concerned with the perpetual struggle to rescue and preserve the dwindling inventory of remaining significant American mansions and large estates of the golden age. These extravagant properties represent a unique chapter of affluence in American life that is not likely to repeat itself amidst the grim economic realities confronting our society as the twentieth century draws to a close.

ACKNOWLEDGMENTS

I owe a great debt of gratitude to McGraw-Hill sponsoring editor Joel Stein who had the foresight and confidence to shepherd my book through its long period of gestation. It was also my good fortune to have a wonderful, experienced, and supportive production team, including production supervisor Suzanne Babeuf, my very patient and thorough editing supervisor Jane Palmieri, and Caryl and Scott Silvers of Silvers Design who have been very understanding and produced a most handsome layout. Throughout the complex and sometimes frustrating and pressured modern process of producing a book, everyone involved has been truly amiable and cooperative.

In the course of the preparation of this book, both Nora Lucas and I have been in contact with many individuals from various organizations. Ultimately, limitations of space have not permitted us to include all the projects we researched. We have tried to acknowledge the assistance of many whose cooperation has been invaluable, and we apologize to anyone whom we may have overlooked.

Alex Antonelli, Alan Wanzenberg Architects, *Conyers Farm;* Robert P. Bergman, Director, Walters Art Gallery/*Hackerman House;* Arthur Bernadon, Architect-Planner, *Kaolin Commons;* Alistair Bevington, Edward Larrabee Barnes/John M. Y. Lee Architects, *Hyde Collection;* Cindy Blais, Mansion Manager, *Tarrywile Park;* Claire Bogaard, Executive Director, *Pasadena Heritage;* James R. Brady, Jr., Developer, *The Maples*; Arthur Brown, General Manager, *Canyon Ranch at Bellefontaine;* Brenda L. Burdick, *Swift River Inn*; Jim Cassidy, Jeter Cook & Jepson Architects, *Ensign House*; Frederick D. Cawley, Preservation League of New York State, *Adirondack Camps*; Msgr. Eugene V. Clark, Homeland Foundation, *Wethersfield*; Kathy Connor, Curator, *George Eastman House*; Robert S. Conte, Historian, *The Greenbrier*; Jewel Cornell, *Carriage House at Lyndhurst*; Angelo Corva, Historic District Commission, *North Hempstead*; Nancy Curtis, SPNEA, *Gropius House*; John Dale, Hartman-Cox Architects, *Dumbarton Oaks*; David DeLucia, Westchester County Parks Department, *Lasdon*; Brent diGiorgio, Shaumut Bank, Simsbury Branch, *Ensign House*; John Downs, Do Chung Architect, *Constitution Hill*; John Dryfhout, Superintendent, *Saint-Gaudens National Historic Site*; Henry Duffy, Curator, *Carriage House at Lyndhurst*; Stephen Ray Fellman, Architect, *McDonald's at Denton House*; Phil Finklea, Hewitt Associates, *Rockledge*; Frank Fish, Buckhurst, Fish, Hutton, Katz & Jackuemart, Inc.; Tim Frank, Planner, City of Palm Beach, *Mar-a-Lago*; Katie Garber, Public Relations Director, *Canyon Ranch*; Glen Gardiner, AIA, Architect, *The Newport Collaborative*; Christie and David Garrett, Owners, *The Point*; Tobias Guggenheimer, Architect, *Frank Lloyd Wright contacts*; John V. H. Halsey, President Peconic Land Trust, *Farmlands Preservation*; Barbara Hammond, Westchester Preservation League, *Squire House*; Robert Hart, Robert Lamb Hart Planners and Architects, *Conyer's Farm*; Wilbert R. Hasbrouck, FAIA, HPZS Architects, *Martin, Robie, and Dana Houses*; Todd Henkels, Architect, *Adirondack Camps*; Nicholas Holmes, FAIA, Architect, *Bragg-Mitchell Mansion*; Paul Ivory, Director, *Chesterwood, The National Trust for Historic Preservation*; Andrew L. Johnson, President, Conservation Advisors, *Preserving Estates, Land, and Open Space*; Bruce Johnson, Jung/Brannen Architects, *Bellefontaine*; Walker Johnson, Architect, *Ragdale Foundation*; Ross Kimmel, Supervisor, Cultural Resources Management, Maryland Department of Natural Resources, *Curatorship Program*; Richard Kinch, The Johnson Foundation, *Wingspread*; Rick Klein, The Berkshire Design Group Inc., *Swift River Inn*; Michael Laspia, Director, *Mashomack Preserve*; Robert Lavchek, Allied Signal Corporation, *Pleasantdale Farms*; Eugene Lawrence, Architect, *Mar-a-Lago*; James Leven, Assistant Archivist, *Chesterwood*; Gay Mackintosh, Assistant Director, *Dumbarton Oaks*; Therese Mambuca, *Ronald McDonald House, Philadelphia*; Doris Masten, *Delamater House*; Robert McKay, Director, SPLIA; Bill and Claudia McNamee, Managers, *The Point*; Peter Mineo, Attorney, *McDonald's at Denton House*; Perry Morgan, Holt & Morgan Architects, *Constitution Hill*; Jim Mullen, Mullen Advertising, *Penguin Hall*; Carrie Osborn, R.T.&E., *Brantwyn*; Michael Ogle, historic architecture of *Annapolis;* David H. O'Sullivan, Miquelle MZO Architectural Group, *The Maples*; Susan Brendel Pandich, Director, *Lyndhurst, Carriage House*; Judy Pascucci, McDonald's Corporation, *Denton House*; Roland Reiser, *Frank Lloyd Wright Conservancy*; Chris Riddle, Kuhn/Riddle Architects, *Swift River Inn*; Lyn Riddle, Southern Plantations, *The New York Times*; Charles Raskob Robinson, *Kaolin Commons*; Sharon Rowe, *Colonnade House, The Greenbrier*; Ted Sanderson, Rhode Island Preservation Commission; Doris Sterner, *Ronald McDonald House, Philadelphia;* Wanda Styka, Archivist, *Chesterwood*, The National Trust for Historic Preservation; David Tansey, The Landmark Trust, *Naulakha*; Loren Taylor, The Du Pont Country Club, *Brantwyn*; Susan Gerwe Tripp, former director of museums and collections at Johns Hopkins University (Baltimore), *Evergreen*, currently executive director Old Westbury Gardens; Kurt VanEss, Steelcase Inc., *Meyer May House*; Bartholomew Voorsanger, FAIA, Voorsanger & Associates Architects, *Morgan Library*; Alec Webb, President, *Shelburne Farms*; Julia Weede, The Biltmore Company, *Biltmore Estate*; Roger Pitt Whitcomb, Architect, *Tarrywile*; Rick Widman, Low-Country Hospitality, *John Rutledge House*; David Wright, Grieves Worrall Wright & O'Hatnick Architects, *Hackerman House*; Richard Youngken, *The Newport Collaborative*; Frederick J. Zivic, Owner, *Tollgate Hill Inn*

INTRODUCTION

General Background

The great age of mansion and estate building spans the period from 1890 to 1940. Before then, in the eighteenth and early nineteenth centuries, many large houses were constructed in various parts of the country. For example, upriver from New York City the gracious estates and working farms of the landed gentry were built several decades before the industrialization of the East began. Usually established by old mercantile and patroon families, the estate lands that overlook the Hudson River, particularly in Dutchess County, were all in existence by the mid-nineteenth century, a number of them having been built by the end of the eighteenth century. The dramatic scenery captured by the Hudson River school of painters was dubbed "the American Rhine" as Gothic Revival castles, more English than German in derivation, could be glimpsed from the riverfront.

In the mid-1850s Llewellyn Park, New Jersey, was the first of the walled exclusive landscaped garden suburbs with planning by architect Alexander Jackson Davis. Llewellyn Park was followed by Tuxedo Park, developed in the 1880s by Pierre Lorillard IV, heir to a tobacco empire, on 5000 acres including a large lake, carved out of his landholdings of several hundred thousand acres in the Ramapo Mountains, north of New York City. Organized as an exclusive club, Lorillard invited his friends to join. The designs of the earliest houses were relatively modest Shingle Style cottages designed by architect Bruce Price. The club provided golf, hunting, and fishing, a racetrack, and tennis and raquet courts. By the 1890s the original rustic style was replaced by increasingly grander houses in eclectic revival styles. Exclusive "parks" were developed in other parts of the country, for example, Roland Park in Baltimore and Elkins Park in Philadelphia.

In Tidewater, Virginia, and the eastern shore of Maryland, great eighteenth-century plantations were created.

The summer places began to appear in old New England coastal towns already possessing impressive eighteenth-century captain's houses, and the elegant homes of merchants and those in the China trade in the 1870s.

At first many well-to-do city people, seeking to escape from summer in the city, preferred to congregate at enormous wooden hotels with long verandahs, which were developed in many regions of the country. As the railroad network expanded, greater access to wilderness areas became more comfortable and practical. Resort hotels flourished at spas such as Saratoga Springs and Richfield Springs in New York, mountain resorts in New Hampshire and in the Adirondacks, in Asheville, North Carolina, and

Overleaf The Chalet (1866), Newport, Rhode Island, was designed by architect Richard Morris Hunt as an "avowed reproduction of the Swiss chalet in vernacular clapboard." It has been converted to 12 condominum apartments.

George Washington's 1760 wooden mansion, Mount Vernon, Virginia, now greets 1 million visitors a year.

on the coast at Newport and Naragansett in Rhode Island, Manchester by the Sea and Marblehead in Massachusetts, Bar Harbor in Maine, and Elberon and Long Branch in New Jersey. Most people sought the congeniality and social life of the resorts. Many seemed unwilling to isolate themselves on a rural estate. In many of the resorts large Queen Anne and Shingle Style seasonal houses were constructed.

Since America's wealthy did not evolve from a hereditary landed gentry, they could choose their favorite resort. Even as prosperity spread further westward and mansions were built near major American cities, the prestige of the established eastern resorts attracted wealthy seasonal visitors from the hinterlands. Some stayed at hotels or rented houses, but many eventually built elaborate mansions.

Following the Civil War many great fortunes were made as the freewheeling unrestricted atmosphere of the marketplace created new fortunes for traders, industrialists, and manufacturers. Without unions, the massive waves of immigration provided cheap factory labor, construction workers, skilled artisans, and domestic help.

Often self-made, the captains of industry and finance who amassed these vast fortunes could now live like kings and acquire the trappings of royalty. In their desire for social acceptance by the established old guard, there was a great deal of rivalry, lavish entertaining, and flaunting of great houses, newly acquired antiques and art collections, and the creation of mature landscapes with exotic plantings and dazzling flower gardens.

Joseph Duveen was a master at exploiting and manipulating the competitiveness and grandiosity of the newly rich, first by selling them European art, antiques, and decorative objects and then influencing them in selecting decorators and architects to create settings for their newly acquired masterpieces.

Some great estates and rustic retreats such as those in the Adirondack Great Camps, the Rockefeller's Kykuit, and the Pratt estate Dosoris were developed as family compounds. It is doubtful that many of these successful industrialists ever considered their showplace estates as good investments or pondered much about their future disposition. Duveen observes that after building these formal and elaborate mansions, the owners did not derive much pleasure from them.

The introduction of income taxes in 1913 was in many ways the beginning of the end for the extravagances of the American country house and large estate. Unlike the

southern plantations, which were profitable agricultural operations in part due to slave labor, these gentlemen's estates, even those with "experimental" breeding farms, rarely produced enough income to meet the cost of their operations. So in a sense the future seeds of the destruction of these superb mansions and landscapes were present from the start.

During the depression country houses were built on a smaller and less pretentious scale, and many continue in private use. World War II was the closing chapter of a glorious era that lasted barely 60 years. The housing shortages following the war and the building of new road networks leading out of major cities led to an explosion of suburban sprawl into communities with few sophisticated planning or zoning controls. Many of the formerly desirable estate areas were compromised by the introduction of subdivisions of more modest houses. This left many wealthy estate owners with few options other than to sell out to developers. This process further accelerated the demolition of mansions and the subdivision of their estate lands. This is particularly evident on New York's Long Island, where estates once numbered almost a thousand, the largest concentration of mansions in the whole country.

American life and society have changed considerably as we approach the end of the twentieth century. American mansions and their estate lands have become an endangered species, and their future survival is similar to the struggle of the growing nationwide conservation movement.

CHAPTER 1

Planning for the Future: Government and Private Owners

First and foremost of the difficulties facing the preservation of mansions and large estates is the lack of effective protective legislation on federal, state, and local levels. In order to promote more effective legislation, there needs to be a greater constituency for the preservation movement in general. The protection of wilderness, natural areas, open space, and the habitat of unique species in the wild continues to attract broad public support. The Nature Conservancy and similar groups have achieved enough political clout to pressure legislators and government policy makers to respond to their demands. Unfortunately, in our troubled times with so many pressing social and economic problems, the arts and historic preservation are viewed by many as elitist concerns. In most urban areas that have established successful landmark preservation ordinances, the process of reclaiming historic districts from neglect and abandonment have resulted in gentrification. The displacement of poor and minority communities from their former neighborhoods has caused great resentment. Much of this urban malaise has spread to the suburban, rural, and resort communities, where local residents and individual small-home owners resent supporting additional tax burdens or otherwise giving favorable treatment to the owners of extravagant mansions or estates in their midst.

Survival

The patchwork pattern of the survival of most American mansions and great estates has been determined by complex factors and varies from one location to another. The Massachusetts Trustees of Reservations, described more fully in the section on Naumkeag, was founded in 1891. This group did not wait for government legislation to come to the rescue; from the beginning it acquired historic houses, mansions, estates, and scenic areas. In other parts of the country, many mansions and estates still in private ownership are well maintained even if mounting costs have forced a reduction in size of the household staff. Where groundskeepers have been reduced, this work is now provided on a contracted basis by outside landscaping services.

Once the mansion and estate goes out of family ownership, the preservation dilemma begins. The most successful mansion preservation efforts have been those where wealthy families have planned for and endowed the transition to museum or institutional use. But even in some of these cases, what seemed initially to be reasonable long-term solutions have foundered in less than a few decades. The popular trend for estate owners in the period following World War II was to donate their properties to church groups, charitable organizations, schools, and universities. Most of these donations were not made with preservation restrictions, which might have impacted the value of their owner's charitable gift and federal estate taxes. The lack of restrictions has caused many problems in recent years as the recipients have felt no obligation to preserve the mansions and estates they were given.

The Anglo-American Connection

Since the eighteenth century Americans have been influenced by the architectural heritage of Europe, borrowing and adapting these styles to a different way of life, terrain, and climate. It is interesting to explore the motivating force behind the development of the great estates and their suburban equivalents.

Though the Philadelphia Centennial Fair of 1876 is considered to have sparked the interest in Colonial Revival, the British Pavillion influenced Richard Norman Shaw, who subsequently set off the vogue for the Queen Anne Style. The Queen Anne was an eclectic mix of many traditional architectural elements, materials, and details. Both H. H. Richardson and Stanford White were intrigued by the picturesque massing of the roofs, gables, and massive chimneys as well as the English concept of the great hall. All of these influences, including their earlier preoccupation with the Romanesque, were incorporated in the Shingle Style, which is a distinctive American idiom. This trend

Overleaf The Hillwood facade facing the garden, with the vista directly on an axis with the Washington Monument 6 miles away.

coincided with the development of the large country houses of the 1870s, especially in the Northeast. The abundance of wood and the American tradition of wooden shingles often set on a stone or brick base that could be adapted to dramatic or steep sites and the abundant, porches, or "piazzas," allowed for sprawling asymmetrical layouts and typically three stories incorporating a massive roof with many gables dormers, and round towers. These Shingle Style houses were dark in their color schemes and blended into the landscape.

There were regional variations on the architectural character of country houses even if they had the same common English derivation. The Midwest lake-shore resorts and the Northwest, as well as California, also had their own adaptations.

Philadelphia already had a predilection for English and Welsh place names, such as Bryn Mawr, along the main line of the Pennsylvania Railroad. For example, the Merion Cricket Club was established in 1865. The regional tradition of whitewashed plaster over fieldstone walls may have influenced Philadelphia architect Wilson Eyre's preference for stucco, and consequently his country houses looked more like the English prototypes.

Similarly, early estates along the Hudson River were named Rokeby and Lyndhurst, which was a Gothic Revival mock castle by Alexander Jackson Davis.

Although many long-established American families lived in large houses on rural agricultural estates, often plantations as on Maryland's eastern shore, these houses were austere by comparison to the sumptuousness of the mansions of the golden age. There is a paradox in Americans' concept of a "cozy" home and the formal palatial homes that they began to build.

Starting in the 1890s, wealthy Americans began to cultivate the image of the English country gentleman. This ideal continued through the great depression into the late 1930s. It has been suggested that the wish of wealthy Americans to associate themselves with old English tradition may have been influenced by the desire to distinguish themselves from the waves of immigrants. The image of this bucolic way of life was popularized by the publication of *Country Life in America,* which began in 1901 and which was clearly copied from the successful British journal *Country Life.* However they might try to mimic the great English country house, the American situation is essentially different. Lacking the hereditary nobility and generations of landed gentry settled on their ancestral agricultural estates, which is the essence of the English country life, successful American merchants and industrialists had to establish their own "domains," which they transformed into imitation "manors" and "parks" created from humble farmland and virgin forests. Usually located within a reasonable travel time from major American cities or industrial centers, these estates allowed the urban rich to cultivate the image of the English country gentleman.

In the fulfillment of this ideal, the privileged few of the new American "noblesse" would achieve such wealth that they no longer needed to be engaged in the routine pursuit of earning money, so they could devote themselves to their leisure pursuits. Thus additional estates and properties were needed to provide for seasonal sports and recreation. The complex social calendar of the "arrived" and fashionable defined the "season," in town, at the shore, in the mountains, and by the sea. In a pre-air-conditioned world tied to steam locomotives and steamships, life was more gracious and slower-paced. Multigenerationed households were common, and families were less mobile and less dispersed. It was inconceivable to these tycoons, who felt so secure in their new-found wealth, that the wonderful world of mansions and estates they created would not be perpetuated for generations to come.

Sadly, rather than realizing their fantasies of establishing their own dynastic homesteads, the several decades it has taken for these extravagant confections to acquire the picturesque "antique" patina their eclectic architects sought and the maturing of the landscape nurtured by legions of gardeners, almost all have been sold or abandoned by the descendants of the original owners. Obviously many social, economic, and technological factors have transformed the world as well as the lifestyles of the wealthy in ways that they could have hardly imagined.

The nostalgic yearning for permanence and tradition is still with us amidst today's high-tech environment. Successful purveyors of style and fashion, such as Ralph Lauren, Laura Ashley, and Smith & Hawkin, try to seduce us with their lush flower-filled chintz and mellowed-wood panelled, illustrated catalog settings into believing that we too can achieve an idyllic, old-money ambiance.

MARJORIE MERRIWEATHER POST'S TROUBLED LEGACY

The fate of Marjorie Merriweather Post's (1887 to 1973) legendary acquisitions offers vivid testimony to the vicissitudes of estate planning. Despite her best intentions and careful instructions to her executors, much of her extraordinary legacy was ultimately rejected by her designated recipients and remains in flux since her death in 1973. Mrs. Post expected not only to preserve the buildings and artifacts she assembled but also her special flair for the good life. Ultimately, however, her extravagant lifestyle could not be perpetuated by either governmental or institutional owners. Perhaps her preference for donating her properties to institutions, even when accompanied by endowments, was the main source of the difficulties that later ensued. It is fascinating to follow the stories of the various properties Mrs. Post once cherished. Certainly these stories serve as cautionary tales for others who may have unrealistic expectations for the preservation of their own personal legacies.

Already sole heiress to the Postum Cereal Empire, Marjorie Merriweather Post further increased her wealth after her second marriage in 1920 to Edward F. Hutton in New York City. Hutton was the head of the stock brokerage firm that bears his name, and he managed her vast wealth by skillfully consolidating her diverse holdings to form the General Foods Corporation.

In 1926 she consented to sell her New York townhouse property site on Fifth Avenue and 92nd Street if the apartment house builder would re-create her town house atop the new structure. This resulted in a 54-room triplex occupying the twelfth, thirteenth, and penthouse floors. The apartment had a private elevator and its own entrance and concierge's quarters at the street level. This was a rental apartment with a 15-year lease. After the Huttons vacated the triplex, it remained vacant for 10 years and eventually was split up into six smaller but still luxurious 9-room apartments.

One of the most dashing of smart "society" couples in the roaring twenties, they soon augmented their posh triplex penthouse apartment on Fifth Avenue, overlooking Central Park, by extending their domain to include Hillwood (a Long Island estate), a rustic mountain retreat Camp Topridge in the Adirondacks, Mar-a-Lago (a tropical hacienda in fashionable Palm Beach), and the *Sea Cloud* (a luxurious ocean-going, fully rigged motor yacht).

Hillwood, Brookville, New York

SITE

Between 1920 and 1922 the Huttons developed an elaborate estate in Greenvale, Long Island, which they named Hillwood. They commissioned architects Hart and Shape to design a half-timbered picturesque Elizabethan Tudor manor house surrounded by several hundred rolling acres of English landscape gardens planned by Marian Coffin, a pioneer American landscape architect.

PRESERVATION ISSUE

As a tribute to her father, in 1953 Mrs. Post donated her Brookville, Long Island, estate Hillwood to be used as the campus of C. W. Post College of Long Island University. The mansion now houses the college administrative offices. Of all of the recipients of her properties, Long Island University seems to have carried out her intentions most

successfully, and the college is thriving in the nineties with 8000 students. However, the conditions of the gift did not provide adequate provision for the integration of the original mansion and its outbuildings into the campus plan.

SIGNIFICANCE

Perhaps the most significant factor in the transition of Hillwood from private residence to institutional use is that the gift was made during Mrs. Post's lifetime. Although Hillwood survives, much of the original character of the mansion and its majestic landscaped surroundings have been compromised by the expansion of the school to meet its own needs.

Camp Topridge, Brighton, New York

SITE

Topridge, a turn-of-the-century Adirondack rustic log "camp" in the grand manner, was considerably redesigned for Mrs. Post in the 1920s. It was approachable only by water—by seaplane or boat—and then by a short incline railroad. The main lodge was decorated with a pastiche of Native American paraphernalia, stuffed animals, and rustic furniture. Although much of the original furnishings and decor was left at Topridge, much of its valuable collection of Native American artifacts was donated to the Smithsonian. Some of these artifacts are now on loan from the Smithsonian and shown in a specially built rustic Adirondack Style log building on the grounds of Hillwood in Washington, D.C.

PRESERVATION ISSUE

At the time of its donation "to the people of the State of New York" in 1974, many of the best of the genuine Native American artifacts were donated to the Smithsonian. In addition, there was considerable local debate at the time of the state's acceptance because the donation made the 207-acre property tax-exempt, and the rural town of Brighton lost more than 5 percent of its school and municipal tax base. There was further complaint because it was closed to public visitation. New York State constructed a new entry road and a helicopter pad and refurbished Topridge for use as a retreat for the governor and as an occasional conference center during the Carey administration.

Additional investments were made by the state to winterize Topridge for use during the 1980 Winter Olympics in Lake Placid. It was operated by the New York State Department of General Services for 10 years, but they found they could not justify the cost of its upkeep when confronted with frequent criticism by the legislature because of its restrictive access policy. The state first offered to donate Topridge to the local hamlet of Brighton and Franklin County, but this offer was rebuffed by them citing high maintenance costs. During the administration of Governor Cuomo, it was put up for sale by public bidding with preservation covenants and restrictions in 1984 to a private owner. After an initial unsuccessful offering, the reserve price of $900,000 was lowered to $750,000, and it was eventually purchased for $911,000 in 1985, after some of the preservation covenants and restrictions were removed, by the low bidder, a 42-year-old self-made New Jersey boardwalk entrepreneur for his personal use. By 1992 this owner experienced financial distress, and the property has been seized by a New Jersey bank. It has now been offered for sale again.

SIGNIFICANCE

Less than 20 years after Mrs. Post's death, Camp Topridge faces an uncertain future. What is most discouraging is that a landmark property that was well maintained and donated to the public with most of its original furnishings and contents intact has been removed from the stewardship of the state of New York and transferred to an irresponsible private owner who has abandoned it, leaving its fate in limbo.

Mar-a-Lago, Palm Beach, Florida

SITE

The Huttons also built an extravaganza in Palm Beach, located between the oceanfront drive and the inland waterway (Lake Worth).

PRESERVATION ISSUE

Mar-a-Lago, was given to the U.S. government as a winter retreat for the president, but security concerns and difficulties coping with other conditions of the bequest eventually led to its being returned to the Post Foundation who resold it to Donald Trump in 1985. The Palm Beach community initially breathed a sigh of relief when the flamboyant Trump promised to restore the house to its former glory. The major economic downturn of the nineties curtailed Donald Trump's fling and brought him into conflict with his Palm Beach neighbors and the local Landmarks Commission, which brought suit to halt his subdivision of Mar-a-Lago's lush tropical gardens. Once again Mar-a-Lago's fate is uncertain.

Hillwood, Washington, D.C.

SITE

Hillwood (named after her earlier estate on Long Island) is located in the Rock Creek Park section of Washington, D.C., and was acquired by Mrs. Post in 1955. Originally named Abremont, it was built in the 1920s for Mrs. Henry Parsons Erwin. The Georgian Revival Style house was extensively reconstructed and enlarged under the direction of New York architect Alexander McIlvaine and was designed for eventual museum use.

PRESERVATION ISSUE

It was originally assumed during Mrs. Post's lifetime that the house and its extensive Imperial Russian decorative arts collections, which she began gathering in Moscow

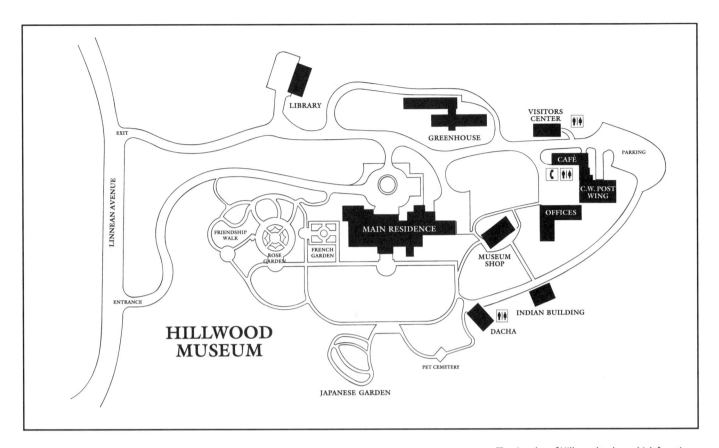

during her marriage to Joseph E. Davies who was appointed by Roosevelt as U.S. Ambassador to Russia from 1936 to 1938, would be willed to the Smithsonian. Convinced that it would one day be the custodian of Hillwood, the Smithsonian advised on display techniques and actually performed conservation work on many objects. The arrangement was later rejected, and Hillwood is now quite successfully run as a private family foundation museum with an elaborate gift shop and an elegant restaurant.

The site plan of Hillwood today, which functions as a house museum.

The *dacha*, a romantic wooden cottage reminiscent of Mrs. Post's stay in Moscow as the wife of the American ambassador, now houses a collection of Russian objets d'art assembled by a former Italian ambassador to Russia.

Sea Cloud

SITE

In 1931 the Huttons commissioned a yacht in Kiel, Germany, now known as the *Sea Cloud*. It was a square-rigged, four-masted barque, the largest private yacht in its day. With its elegantly furnished staterooms paneled in French boiserie, the *Sea Cloud* is a floating "country house." During World War II, it was leased to the U.S. government and lost its masts and rigging. After the war she was refitted as Mrs. Post's private yacht. The *Sea Cloud* is now booked as an exclusive charter cruise ship in Europe and the Caribbean.

PRESERVATION ISSUE

The future of the 60-year-old *Sea Cloud* is not necessarily secure. Maritime preservation of functioning seaworthy vessels is highly problematic since eventually it becomes too costly and possibly too risky to keep them afloat. Enormous oceangoing yachts and passenger liners cannot be displayed indoors. Once stationary they are not always easily adapted to new uses. The one advantage of large boats is that they are generally more easily transferred to a distant new site than large old buildings.

CHAPTER 2

Rustic and Wilderness Preservation

Perhaps one of the most amazing phenomena of the great age of estate building was the development of rustic retreats. Just as New York's Long Island saw the growth of the largest concentration of mansions and estates in the United States, the Adirondack region also saw the largest number of "great camps," as they came to be known. The Adirondack mountain region in northern New York State was largely inaccessible until the post-Civil War period when railroads reached these wilderness areas. Early explorers, campers, and adventurers had to make the arduous journey by stage coach and canoe. Early travelers, artists, and guidebook writers romanticized the lure of the undiscovered wilderness.

Great Camps

In 1869 a young clergyman, Rev. Murray, wrote a book entitled *Adventures in the Wilderness: or Camp-Life in the Adirondacks.* "The wilderness," he suggested, "provides that perfect relaxation which all jaded minds require." This appeal encouraged hoardes of visitors. At first, visitors stayed at boarding houses and later at hotels, Paul Smith's one of the most renowned.

In the 1860s Thomas Clark Durant, a railroad builder, through his Adirondack Company railroad, secured control over 100,000 square miles of wilderness lands in the south central Adirondacks. By 1871 the railroad was operating, but much of the vast Adirondack region was still unserved. The first railroad to cross the Adirondacks was built between 1891 and 1892 by Dr. William Seward Webb, who sold it to the New York Central Railroad soon after. Webb, who created his own domain at Shelburne Farms in Vermont, also built his own great camp called Ne-Ha-Sa-Ne in the midst of his private hunting preserve.

In order to attract the visitors, Durant envisioned building a network of hotels, lodges, and clubs. His son William West Durant, who had lived abroad and had seen Swiss chalets and European hunting lodges, is credited with the development of the "artistic" great camp. At Camp Pine Knot (1876 to 1888) on Raquette Lake, he developed the basic pattern for the more elaborate camps he would later construct. Pine Knot consisted of a lodge, cabins, a dining room, a kitchen building, and platforms for tents. Durant designed rustic log cabins, picturesquely ornamented, with various textures of birch bark and patterned with bent twigs. Pine Knot was sold in 1895 to Collis P. Huntington who further enlarged it. Durant's camps were self-sufficient compounds with one set of buildings for the owners and the other for their retainers. Large boulders and stones were transported to form foundations, massive chimneys, and fireplaces.

Durant's ingenuity was continued on the interior where he developed a whole genre of rustic furniture and built-in banquettes made of rough hewn and shapely twigs and branches. Hunting trophies and stuffed animal heads were an essential element of the decor. The log cabin had long been part of America's pioneering past, and there was a great deal of nostalgia for frontier life. Combined with a nineteenth-century love of hunting, boating, and fishing, the wilderness had great appeal. Durant went on to develop three even grander great camps that were sold to millionaires and still exist today. For the very rich, "roughing it" in luxury was the greatest challenge, for few could afford to indulge in the cost of building, staffing, and maintaining a seasonal retreat. The sporting life in the wilderness required boat houses, a covered bowling alley, ice houses, service buildings, and often a farm group to supply food. Local residents were employed as farmers, guides, and carpenters for logging, building, and caretaking. At the more elaborate camps the caretakers lived on the property.

At some of the camps the expectation was to re-create the lavish lifestyle the families were accustomed to in town. Chefs were brought in, and delicacies were imported so the dinners and picnics were quite elaborate. Once the railroads were operating, vacationers arrived in droves and hundreds of thousands of logs were transported. Prior to the tourist rush there had always been exploitation of the

Overleaf The main lodge of Santanoni, a great camp in the Adirondack wilderness, was the focus of the camp.

Adirondacks resources; trapping and bounty hunting led to the disappearance of the wolf, lynx, and panther by 1910. Another vanished industry was ice harvesting, which was stored for local consumption at hotels and camps and shipped to New York and other cities. There was mining for iron ore and other minerals such as garnet. But by far the greatest tragedy was commercial logging, which was not scientifically managed and spurred on by the timber and paper industries, laid waste to vast wilderness areas. Finally, the public outcry was so great that in 1894 the New York State constitution was amended by Article 14 so that the state's own landholdings "shall forever be kept as wild forest lands. They shall not be leased, sold or exchanged, or be taken by any corporation, public or private, nor shall the timber thereon be sold, removed or destroyed." This was a courageous step at the time, but no thought was ever given to the preservation of any of the existing structures. The owners of the great camps, which were being built at this time, were very sensitive to the rustic ethic, and Durant's camps strove to blend comfortably into the forest and wilderness settings. Most of the families who created these sylvan retreats did not plan for their future any more than they did their mansions and estates.

Current Threat

In recent years the greatest threat to the survival of the great camps, as well as the thousands of acres of forests and wilderness, is that of land speculation and the growing popularity of the region for vacation home sites. It is no longer the railroads but the automobile and an excellent highway system that now make the Adirondacks more accessible then ever before. The Adirondack Forest Preserve managed by New York State's Department of Environmental Conservation (DEC) is still the only major purchaser who will preserve the wilderness character of the region. Just as in other parts of the nation, timbering interests and paper manufacturers have held vast tracts of virgin forest for future exploitation. As the environmental movement has grown in popularity and gained political clout, they have forced federal and state forestry administrators to protect endangered species on both government and privately held land. This has unsettled the government's existing land management programs and reduced revenues.

Business pressures and the worldwide economic recession of the 1990s have convinced many large wilderness landowners to put their properties up for sale, fearing that further governmental restrictions will devalue their holdings. This matter resembles the predicament of owners of designated historic landmark structures, whose property development rights have been diminished without any compensation, tax relief, or other form of government assistance. About 35 of the great camps survive, and many are well maintained and still in private ownership.

The state and federal governments are also facing budget crunches and staggering under the demands for a wide variety of public needs. In this climate it has been difficult for government, which is barely able to sustain the existing burdens of wilderness management, to allocate the funds for further land acquisition. A recent bond issue that would have provided for acquisition of wilderness and scenic areas, as well as historic preservation, was defeated by the voters of New York State. As a result, long carefully orchestrated negotiations for the acquisition of a large environmentally sensitive wilderness tract to be added to the Adirondack Preserve fell apart, and the perplexed private owner is forced to seek other alternatives. Once missed, some of these opportunities never materialize again.

Compounding these matters is the relative inaccessibility of most of the great camps, as well as the shortness of the summer season when they could accommodate visitors. The use of commercial concessionaires in the national parks has resulted in insensitivity to the rustic structures and has been much criticized. In a June 1993 article, *New York Times* reporter Patricia Lee Brown describes a visit to the Old Faithful Inn in Yellowstone National Park.

This inn is a massive log-framed structure with a seven-story-high lobby in which an enormous free-standing, lava stone fireplace chimney reaches up through the rafters, designed by architect Robert C. Reamer in 1908. The inn narrowly missed destruction in a major forest fire in 1988 and continues to serve guests. The writer comments that although the management has preserved much of the original character of the very old hotel, only 90 rustic cabinlike rooms, out of the total of 327, are still used; the others are located in two undistinguished modern wings. She stayed in both accommodations, the former having greater charm, the latter more convenience. She has scant praise for the dining room or the hotel concessionaire who operates it. Unlike many other states that have tremendous national parks and national forests, New York's wilderness areas and parkland is state owned and supported.

The local communities of year-round residents within the Adirondack region are economically hard-pressed, and unemployment is chronically high. There has always been friction between the Adirondack Park Agency and private owners within the forest preserve areas. As logging operations are more curtailed, only tourism and recreation prosper. The tackiness of the motel, fast-food, and roadside signage is difficult to control.

Preserving American Camps

The developing of adaptive-use strategies for several of the great camps is illustrative of both the possibilities and difficulties of achieving a satisfactory solution. It is evident that one generation's solution may not be practical for the next. The same difficulties that faced the owners of mansions and great estates during World War II exacerbated the problems of the owners of the great camps in the Adirondacks. The wartime rationing of food and gasoline made distant travel difficult, and the draft diminished the labor pool to staff and maintain these extravagant wilderness outposts of luxury. The severe winter climate of the Adirondacks requires seasonal maintenance, and during this period much of the routine care was deferred, and the cycle of neglect began.

In many cases the same families who owned the great camps also owned other mansions and estates in other resort areas so that they faced similar problems and were forced to make difficult choices in directing their priorities. One major factor that postponed determining the fate of many of the camps was the inability of Americans to travel abroad during the war.

In the post-World War II period the enlarged and improved highway network across the country made formerly remote areas much more accessible to a much larger cross section of our society and consequently less exclusive for the wealthy camp owners. They too had the opportunity to seek out new retreats, and the advent of the jet age and the development of air conditioning also made people less dependent on the traditional seasonal pattern of moving from resort to resort.

American society had greatly changed in the postwar period; Mobility was far greater, and the idea of the great family gatherings of all the generations' vacationing together annually at the same resort lost its popularity. Family members tended to be more dispersed in various parts of the country. Even the very rich who had built and sustained the great camps had modified and simplified their lives. The exuberant ostentation and extravagance of the turn of the century had mellowed. When they inherited the camps, many of the children of the original owners were not eager to take on the burdens and expenses of maintaining these remote outposts.

One notable exception was Marjorie Merriweather Post who continued to operate her camp Topridge in the grand manner until her death in 1973. Mrs. Post purchased an existing camp on upper Saint Regis Lake, and in the 1920s architect Ted Blake transformed it into one of the largest of the Adirondack Great Camps. The relatively small site of 207 acres contained 68 buildings. Mrs. Post wanted to preserve some of the spirit of adventure in traveling to Topridge. Guests were flown up in her private plane to the local airport, met by limousine, and driven to a boat that crossed the lake. The camp was built on top of a steep bluff and a funicular was built to take

The dining hall at J. P. Morgan's camp, Uncas.

guests to the top. Although a land-side road did exist for service, Mrs. Post insisted on the more dramatic arrival by water. Mrs. Post provided numerous individual cabins for her guests and separate cabins for the staff.

The main lodge was decorated theatrically like Mrs. Post's other homes: A wilderness stage set with rustic furniture, animal hides, and stuffed animals and hung with antler chandeliers, a birch bark canoe, and an exceptional collection of genuine Native American artifacts. As was the case with the decoration of many of the camps, the animal trophies and other furnishings, as well as the Native American artifacts, were not from the Adirondack region but an artistically gathered pastiche of rustic and primitive objects. Mrs. Post's collections included pottery, basketry, and silver from the Southwest, Navajo weaving, and an Eskimo kayak. Some of the most valuable of these artifacts were donated to the Smithsonian at her death. But enough remained to capture the flavor of the original atmosphere.

As mentioned in the section on Mrs. Post's legacy, she left Camp Topridge to the state of New York as a retreat for the governor in 1973. Sadly a decade later the state put Topridge and its acreage on the market. The state of New York has not had a much better track record with regard to preservation of camp structures located on properties it has acquired for wilderness conservation over the years. It must be said that private initiative has been a major factor in the struggle to protect and restore the great camps.

In 1976 and 1977, at the time of the publication of my *Saving Large Estates*, commissioned by the New York State Council on the Arts, I included comments by two knowledgeable observers of the Adirondack region by Graig Gilborn, director at the Adirondack Museum at Blue Mountain Lake, and Paul Malo, an architect and professor at Syracuse University. The Adirondack Museum, founded in the 1950s by Harold K. Hochschild, is unique in its sophistication considering its isolation. The museum collects and displays materials and artifacts reflecting the history of the region. Fortunately many of the artifacts were acquired long before the popularity of rustic furniture. Prices are now very high since their discovery by antiques dealers and private collectors. Gilborn expressed his concern that if the museum tried to acquire and operate one of the great camps in situ, as an extension of its existing operations, that managing an annex might well stretch its resources too thin and overwhelm the entire operation.

Miscellaneous log outbuildings at Camp Uncas.

Paul Malo discusses the future of several of the great camps. Malo made some interesting observations on the status of the three adjoining great camps. Kamp Kill Kare, begun in 1918 for the Garvan family, was designed by architect John Russell Pope (architect for the National Gallery in Washington in the 1930s). Kill Kare was still owned by the Garvan family. Camp Sagamore was begun by Durant in 1897 for Alfred Gwynn Vanderbilt. His widow donated it to Syracuse University in 1954, which used it as a conference center for two decades, after which it was offered for sale to New York

The Vanderbilt's massive log chalet at Camp Sagamore was the center of an elaborate group of lakefront guest houses, a boathouse, and a bowling alley.

The farm group and service buildings at Camp Sagamore were mistakenly excluded from the original survey of the historic structures. It took several years and a public ballot referendum to restore this functional element to the complex.

State in 1974. The third camp, Uncas, was begun by Durant in 1895, and was completed by J. P. Morgan after 1901 and remained in the family until 1947. After a series of owners, it functioned as a Boy Scout camp in the 1960s. It too was offered to New York State about the same time as Sagamore.

The newly formed Preservation League of New York State, based in Albany, of which Paul Malo and the author are founders, took on as one of its first missions to spare the destruction of Camp Sagamore. This was not a simple process, especially for a new nonprofit organization. In 1975 an agreement was worked out with the state to find a third party to purchase Sagamore's historic buildings, with preservation covenants written into the deed. The agreement included a proviso that in the event of a future sale, it could be repurchased by the Preservation League at its original price; this point was meant to discourage speculative proposals. The league agreed to make periodic inspections, giving notice if the maintenance was unsatisfactory. It also required that Sagamore would be open to public viewing at regular scheduled times. Other stipulations prevented the sale of alcoholic beverages and the use of motorboats on the lake.

Only one of the eight prospective buyers agreed to all the restrictions. The league thereupon agreed to sell Sagamore to the National Humanistic Education Center, Inc. The Sagamore Institute was a nonprofit education center of which Dr. Howard Kirschenbaum, an author and educational consultant from Rochester, was then codirector. For almost two decades it has offered programs to the public focused on Adirondack culture and outdoor recreational and environmental issues.

Due to an error in the surveying, the state did not incorporate the portion of the site that contained the farm complex and other support service structures. It took years of wrangling and public ballot initiative to add these ordinary buildings to the Sagamore site.

At the time of the Sagamore purchase, Dr. Kirschenbaum also acquired Camp Uncas as his residence, which he now owns with two friends. It has taken years of hard work to restore and refurbish the numerous structures on the site.

After the late Anthony Garvan's many efforts to preserve his family's camp, Kill Kare, including offering it to the National Trust for Historic Preservation, it was sold privately in the late 1980s and is no longer accessible for visitation.

At the time of the Adirondack Park Centennial in 1992, Dr. Kirschenbaum was the president of Adirondack Architectural Heritage, which, together with the Preservation League and other Adirondack groups, is trying to convince the New York State

Mrs. Garvan's bedroom at Kamp Kill Kare was a rustic fantasy with a stuffed owl perched on a branch sprouting from the headboard.

Wilderness, comfort, and the living room at Kamp Kill Kare.

Kitchen service quarters in Camp Santanoni are linked by roofed passages well suited to the Adirondack climate.

Department of Environmental Preservation (DEC) to restore Camp Santanoni and open it to the public. Owned by the state since 1972, as part of the 12,500-acre Santanoni Preserve, it is an extraordinary camp designed by New York architect Robert H. Robertson in 1888.

It is disappointing that the preservation of these exceptional rustic structures still is not a priority in either the national or the state park systems at a time when the public is clamoring for greater recreational facilities.

Great camps at the turn of the century had to be self-sufficient, and included a barn complex, as at Santanoni.

The Point, Saranac Lake, New York

SITE

During the period between the Civil War and the great depression, northern New York State experienced a unique building phase, that of the Adirondack great camps. Numerous wealthy Americans who had made their money in industry, finance, and transportation, amassed large landholdings and built vacation escapes in the Adirondacks. Originally their inaccessibility guaranteed a certain exclusiveness.

Built as rural retreats, the architecture of the camps took inspiration from nature and were rustic, rambling creations of natural materials including logs, native stone, twigs, and branches. Generally the living spaces were flanked by open porches to allow as much outdoor living as possible.

The Point is one such Adirondack great camp in Saranac Lake, New York, which survives in its new use as a luxury resort. The camp was originally named Camp Wonundra when completed in 1933 for William Avery Rockefeller, a great-nephew of John D. Rockefeller. The last of three camps designed by prominent Adirondack camp architect William Distin, The Point stands on Whitney Point on the western shore of upper Saranac Lake. The original estate consisted of an informal complex of nine buildings situated on a 10-acre peninsula that The Point currently encompasses.

Built at the height of the depression, Camp Wonundra was one of the last of America's great camps and was luxurious, even by millionaires' standards. Unlike the earlier camps, it was designed for year-round use, and the house was fully insulated when built. *Camp*, the colloquial term applied to these Adirondack retreats, is analogous to the 30-room Newport or Berkshire "cottage." Rockefeller employed 50 servants, 4 per house guest. Even in the wilderness, a full day's journey from New York City, black tie was the appropriate dinner garb.

The camp's original nine buildings—the main lodge, the boathouse, the guest house, a garage-maintenance building, a one-car garage, a garage-woodshed, a small sap house, a lean-to, and a stone pumphouse—all designed in the rustic, Adirondack style still survive.

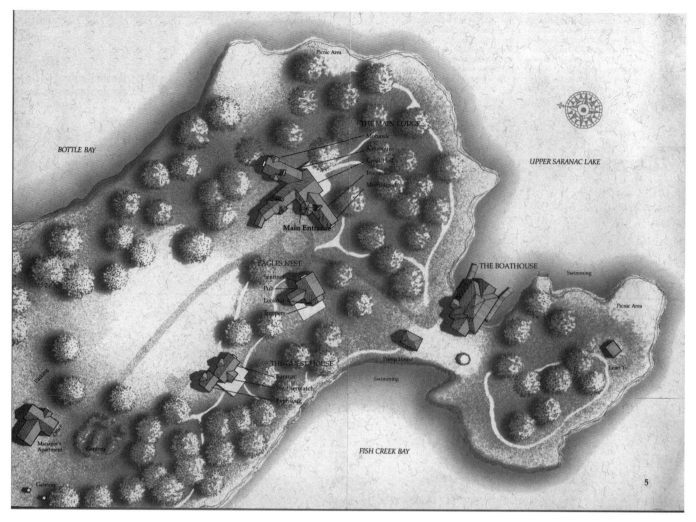

The site plan for The Point illustrates the dramatic siting of the log structures on a small peninsula projecting into upper Saranac Lake.

The exterior of the buildings is articulated with horizontally laid pine log walls and metal window sashes and roofed with muted, multicolored slates. The interiors are characterized by fieldstone chimneys, wide-board pine wainscoting on the walls and ceilings, and pegged flooring.

PRESERVATION ISSUE

The camp, which served as Rockefeller's primary residence, was a holdover from an era of private wealth and luxury. Although its rural setting made it an ideal vacation spot for both winter and summer sports lovers, its isolation and size limited its appeal to many private owners.

Its massive walls, rustic interior, large rooms, and layout dictated a residential use of some sort. Built of natural materials to accommodate its setting, additional construction would have compromised the rural nature of the camp.

Near Lake Placid, Camp Wonundra was still a private house until owner Ted Carter opened it to paying guests during the 1980 Winter Olympics. He renamed it The Point for its location on a peninsula of land that juts out into Saranac Lake. Carter associated The Point with the Relais et Chateaux, an association of exclusive, unique European hotels and restaurants, and subsequently moved to Europe. Early guests Christie and David Garrett were enamored of the camp and purchased it in 1986; they have owned it since.

The use of the property is compatible with the building, with Rockefeller's house guests simply being replaced by inn guests. Since the Garretts reside in Vermont, their on-site managers Claudia and Bill McNamee serve as hosts.

The modest entrance of the main lodge at The Point belies the luxurious ambiance within.

The rustic ambiance of the sumptuously furnished main lodge at The Point creates a cozy spot before a roaring fire in the massive stone fireplace.

Compact and rather isolated well off the road and containing only 11 guest rooms, the property has been converted to an exclusive, expensive, retreat at which visitors can truly experience life as a guest of one of America's richest families. The site is kept private until reservations are confirmed. Breakfast is served in bed, and dining is family style, with each day's gourmet fare the discretion of the chef. Dinners are served in the main dining room, but lunch is served at various locations, depending on the season and weather, including the boathouse or the terrace. The room rate includes all meals, snacks, drinks, and equipment rental so that guests are never confronted with a bill during their stay, and inn staff are said to be solicitous and invisible.

The main lodge, boathouse, guest house, and the garage-maintenance building now contain the 11 unique and individually decorated guest rooms. The garage-woodshed has been converted to an office and management's quarters, and the stone pump house is still a working part of The Point's water system. Through offering first-class hotel service in a unique setting, the owners of The Point are able to maintain the building much as W. A. Rockefeller did in its heyday as a private retreat. Although expensive, a stay at The Point is quite reasonable when compared with owning and maintaining such a property. Its few guest rooms and elegant service offer the visitor the experience of a prewar Adirondack Camp house party, if only for a few days.

SIGNIFICANCE

Many of the turn-of-the-century camps were much more elaborate and had to be self-sustaining, with functioning stables, carriage houses, and farms. They also had to generate their own electric power. Although many remain in private ownership, following the pattern of other estate owners, they were donated to schools and other institutions. At one point Syracuse University owned about 10 camps. Beginning in the 1970s it began divesting itself of these properties. Many others have been acquired by the Adirondack Park Agency along with vast acreage and have fallen into neglect.

CHAPTER 3

Preservation of Open Land

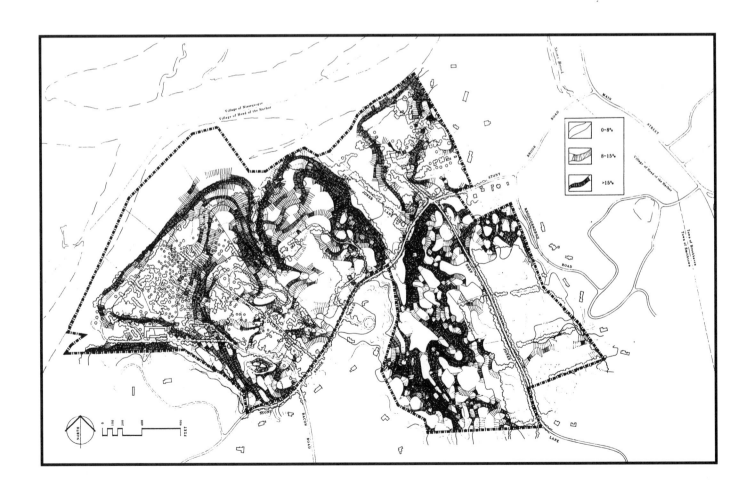

In cities, public parks provide recreation areas and an access to greenery. Ironically most small communities may have a village green or a playground, a baseball field, and a local lake or pond for swimming, but many have not anticipated the recreational needs of future growth—especially in rural areas where large farms provided abundant open space. Population growth and the suburbanizing effect of new residential subdivisions are swallowing up once rural and resort areas. Alarmed citizenry in many parts of the country have followed the lead of the Nature Conservancy and other environmental groups in the preservation of large tracts of scenic open space. The acquisition of scenic easements, large farms, and estate lands are an easier alternative to the assemblage of open land from small parcels with many individual owners.

Land Trusts

As our aging urban areas, smaller cities, and towns have become more crowded, there has been an increasing suburbanization of the countryside. The spread of residential housing development into traditional farming regions causes friction. The increasing public awareness of environmental pollution hazards has been an additional irritant. For the farmer it is a constant struggle against the vagaries of weather and natural predators who attack their crops. The new residential neighbors are not tolerant of crop-dusting or spraying that drifts onto their homes nor the pesticides and herbicides that leach into underground aquifers compromising drinking water quality.

Finding alternative farming methods to minimize pollution has magnified the increasingly dismal economic prospects for many families who have been farming for generations. Sometimes even if they wish to struggle on, their children are unwilling to make the commitment. The mechanization of agriculture has favored large commercial growers because the cost of equipment is beyond the reach of small family farms. The complex economics of modern farming are further compounded by the increasing value of the land and the escalation of tax assessments, added to which are the tempting offers of developers. The result is that many farm families are abandoning their way of life.

Actually the decline of the small farm has been going on for a long time. The land for most of the great estates of Long Island, the largest concentration of country estates of any area of the country, was assembled by buying up small family farms. Shelburne Farms, begun in Vermont in the 1890s, is an aggregate of 30 farms.

In Suffolk County on New York's Long Island, since 1983 the Peconic Land Trust has been assisting conservation-minded landowners as they grapple with the future use and management of their land. The Peconic Land Trust is a nonprofit, tax-exempt conservation organization that is dedicated to the preservation of farmland and open space on Long Island. The trust acquires and manages land as well as easements for conservation purposes. In addition, the trust assists farmers and other landowners in the identification and implementation of alternatives to outright development. Peconic Land Trust President John V. H. Halsey has supplied some examples of their activities.

As an example, the Peconic Land Trust is working with the Borkowski family of Watermill to preserve farmland and open space on Lake Nowedonah, also known as Mill Pond, situated north of Watermill hamlet. This area was formerly an inland farming community; it lies between Southampton and Bridgehampton resort towns, an area in which vacation homes are sprouting in the nearby fields. The family owns 50 acres, which they have farmed for many years. The trust has proposed conservation easements and a limited development approach that will enable the family to reduce future estate taxes, yet retain a portion of their equity in the land.

In the case of the Borkowski family, the trust has sought to identify a means to reduce inheritance taxes that could easily exceed 50 percent of the value of the land, so that the next generation will not be forced to sell the land for development. Upon the death of her husband in the mid-1980s, Mrs. Borkowski and her six children set about the task of cushioning the blow of the impending tax liability. They decided to

Overleaf Map of steep slopes, difficult to build on, which aided in determining areas to be included in the conservation easements. (Lawrence property, Head of the Harbor, Smithtown, New York)

sell a 25-acre parcel on the north side of the lake to provide the necessary cash for future tax payments. By the late 1980s the family was under contract to sell land that had a potential yield of 12 residential lots under the current zoning laws. With the downturn in the economy, however, the sale was never concluded, and the family retained both the property and the specter of financial disaster.

In late 1990, the Borkowski family retained the Peconic Land Trust to prepare a conservation plan for their land on Lake Nowedonah. Several concept plans were put forward by the trust and refined by family members, town officials, and others. Conservation easements were proposed that would perpetually protect the most environmentally sensitive and scenic portions of the property—farmland and land bordering on the pond. The easements would also dramatically reduce the zoning density of the property as well as the value of the land for inheritance tax purposes. Thus the density of the 25-acre parcel on the pond will be reduced from 12 to 4 units. With the advice of a local real estate firm, a final concept plan has been prepared with 4 well-sited lots within a preserve of over 17 acres. The reduced-density plan affords additional benefits to the family such as a reduction in improvement costs (such as roads and site utilities) as well as the relative ease of moving through the subdivision approval process quickly. In addition, the trust can play a significant role in the management of the farmland and open space, a matter often left to homeowners' associations with limited success.

Another instance arose in the village of Head of the Harbor, in western Suffolk County, in the town of Smithtown. Head of the Harbor, which was the home of architect Stanford White, still retains much of its rural character. Hundreds of acres of farmland and open space remain in this village on Stony Brook Harbor. The conservation easement was the culmination of several years of planning with Evelyn Lawrence, her daughter Louisa, and family advisors. The easement perpetually protects about 30 acres of woodland, pastures, and wetlands including a scenic vista over the harbor and

Map of adjoining properties showing areas of conservation easements. The study includes neighboring properties which would extend the area.

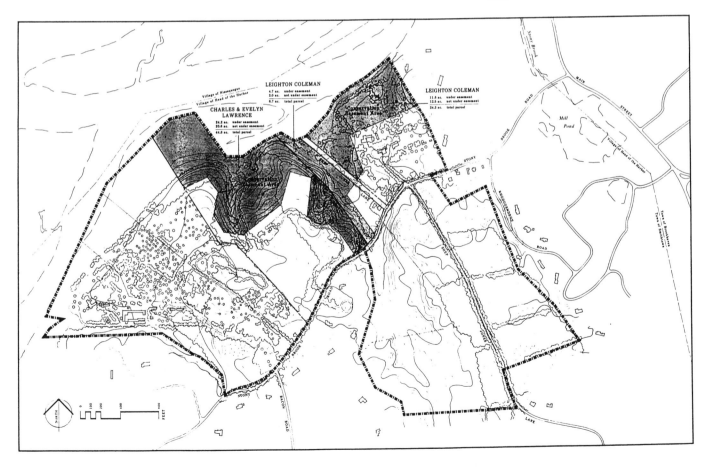

Long Island Sound, to the shores of Connecticut. The Peconic Land Trust is now advising the owners of adjacent parcels so that a comprehensive plan can be developed to preserve scenic features and vistas that run continuously through all the properties.

A *conservation easement* is a voluntary agreement between a landowner and the land trust that restricts the use of the land in perpetuity. The donor is entitled to a charitable gift equal to the difference between the value of the property before and after the conveyance of the easement as determined by a qualified appraiser. The easement also reduces the value of the land for inheritance purposes.

Another plan for limited development was prepared jointly by the Peconic Land Trust in conjunction with Conservation Advisors of Chadds Ford, Pennsylvania, on a grant from the town of Southold. The town leadership sought an alternative to a developer's proposal for maximum exploitation of a beach-front site in East Marion on Long Island Sound.

Andrew L. Johnson of Conservation Advisors puts forth his analysis of the concept of "limited development." He feels that while many landowners may want to do the right thing, they feel that their choices are limited and that they must sell out to a developer and leave town or leave it to their heirs to resolve.

As the environmental movement has gained in popularity, local governments have responded by increasing the regulations in the process of subdividing of large acreage. Insistence on town standard roads, water runoff, and sewage treatment can result in elaborate consulting studies.

Many landowners are tempted by a large sale price offered by a developer, which is usually based on the assumption of maximum exploitation of the site. Many owners fail to take into account the tax consequences and how long it will take to receive payment. Most developers' agreements contain numerous conditions that must be met before payment will be made. These may include subdivision approval, financing, and permits for sewer and water. Often the approval process drags on for years; then there are sales commissions, capital gains tax, and legal fees. Landowners are often surprised at the real return on their land after this lengthy and costly process.

Johnson feels that the technique of limited development offers promise since it involves the landowner in a process in which they can forecast their net returns and those of their heirs. Johnson assists owners in obtaining approvals themselves and garnering some of the profit. He believes that this, together with tax savings for donations such as conservation easements, permits the landowner to benefit from some of the profits normally reaped by the developer.

The first step in the limited-development process requires base-line mapping of the landowners' parcel to determine three categories:

1. Lands that must be preserved and are essentially unbuildable (e.g., wetlands and steep slopes)

2. Land we would like to preserve but may not be able to afford (e.g., farmlands and historic areas)

3. Lands that are too valuable to preserve (i.e., lands that are easily developed)

From the base-line mapping, concept plans are developed that begin to show the landowner the true preservation advantages of limited development and various options. Johnson outlines some features a limited-development concept plan may contain:

- Donation of a conservation easement, perpetually restricting or prohibiting development on a portion of the land

- Donation of an open-space parcel in fee simple to a land trust with land stewardship capabilities, affording the landowner a larger contribution than he or she might have received from the donation of a conservation easement

- Gifts of approved building lots to the landowner's children or grandchildren if the value is below the gift tax threshold

- Retention of a lot with the family homestead for landowners who choose to remain in their home and sell other lots adjacent to the open lands
- Creation of a homeowners' association to provide for perpetual upkeep of open space, perhaps in cooperation with a land trust, in order to spread the costs of maintenance among new buyers
- Bargain sale of lands (selling lands below appraised value as a way of providing endowment funds for a land trust to maintain the open space)
- Reservation of a life estate for the parcel that contains the residence, allowing the landowner or another designated individual to remain on the land for the rest of his or her life

Johnson suggests that since the property will be subdivided into approved parcels at the end of this process, the landowner does not have to sell the entire property as they would if sold to a developer. The concept plan may be implemented over many years to ensure the best result for the landowner's own tax status or personal satisfaction.

At this stage Johnson reviews the landowner's financial goals and needs for the funds that will be generated by the project. Usually Johnson discusses three types of needs:

1. Critical cash needs (1 to 3 years)

2. Chronic needs for annual funds (Often landowners sell their land simply to get out of management responsibilities or because the taxes and maintenance costs are beyond their income.)

3. Inheritance funds for their heirs

These factors are taken into account in refining the plan and the timing of implementing it.

Once the concept plans are reviewed by the landowners and their advisors, a final concept plan is then used as the basis for appraisals, marketing studies, capital gains tax calculations, inheritance tax estimates, discussions with local and state government officials, and final implementation.

The Manor House, Mashomack Preserve, Shelter Island, New York

SITE

Initially settled circa 1600 by the Manhanset Indians, the area was called Sachem's Neck, the word sachem referring to the tribe's leader. Mashomack, Native American for "where they go by water," referred only to the southeastern tip of the area. By the mid-seventeenth century, English settlers had appeared on the island, and by 1706, Englishman William Nicholl, whose descendants would own Sachem's Neck for nearly 200 years, had acquired the land.

Of the many Nicholl households, only the Manor House survives. The Shingle Style house was built circa 1890 by Dr. Samuel Nicholl and is thought to have been designed by architect John White, who designed several similar houses in East Hampton. By the turn of the century, ownership was divided among several family members who began selling off the property in the early decades of this century. In the 1920s, financier Otto Kahn, who only visited the island twice, had reunited the parcels, on speculation that a bridge would be built across Long Island Sound. Probably without Kahn's knowledge, Sachem's Neck served as a haven for illicit smuggling during prohibition, providing a modicum of prosperity for the then-sleepy island.

Upon Kahn's death in 1934, Mashomack was purchased by a real estate investment group headed by Sumner Gerard, in anticipation of the cross-sound bridge that never materialized. In 1969, Gerard leased Mashomack as a hunt club.

The restored manor house, Mashomack Preserve, on Shelter Island now serves as a meeting center for The Nature Conservancy.

PRESERVATION ISSUES

The state, county, and even National Park Service were among those interested in the property, and in 1980 The Nature Conservancy acquired the property for $6 million, raising much of the funding with local support. From then on, Sachem's Neck has been known as Mashomack, a 2039-acre nature preserve that occupies nearly one-third of Shelter Island.

Since 1980 Mashomack Preserve has been in the hands of The Nature Conservancy, a nationally based, nonprofit land conservation organization that maintains the property as a natural landscape for study and passive recreation. Before it was acquired as a conservancy, Mashomack was home to several families, and several historic buildings left by these earlier residents are preserved and used as part of Mashomack's conservation program.

In 1971, during the tenure of the Mashomack Fish and Game Club, a fire damaged the main surviving residential building, the Manor House. The front porch was lost, and repairs after the fire included a new roofline at the rear wing. Although the primary focus of the nature center is, obviously, the preservation of and education about the natural environment, it was decided that retention and preservation of the Manor House would assist in their programming goals. The Manor House has been restored in as near original condition as possible, and the building serves as a meeting place for preserve programs and members and activities. It also provides a gracious setting for fund-raising events.

The restoration, completed in 1986, included painting, reshingling, and stripping the exterior and restoring the rear roofline with documentation from historic

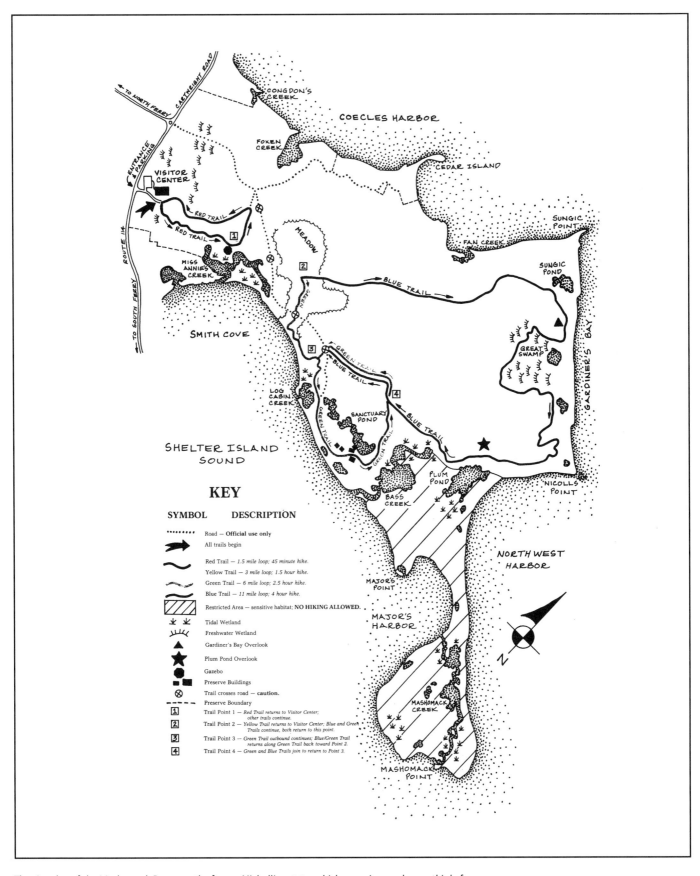

The site plan of the Mashomack Preserve, the former Nicholl's estate, which occupies nearly one-third of Shelter Island.

photos. The interior woodwork was refinished, and mechanical systems were upgraded. The porch was not replaced.

The building serves as a conference and meeting center that can accommodate 40 overnight guests. Many of the original outbuildings are used as staff houses, and the barn is used for maintenance. Each spring, in an attempt to encourage new visitors to Mashomack, the community is invited to a cocktail reception on the lawn, during which they can tour the Manor House. Two major fund-raising events, one at New Year's Eve and the other in August, are well attended by Shelter Islanders and raise funds for the Manor House and Mashomack's programs.

SIGNIFICANCE

Shelter Island, New York, located between the north and south forks of Long Island's east end, and linked to the mainland by a series of small ferries, has been a summer resort since the mid-nineteenth century with the arrival of the railway to nearby Greenport. The island has a thriving year-round population that quadruples with summer residents.

Mashomack occupies nearly one-third of the island. The $6 million purchase price was quickly subscribed with support from both year-round and summer residents, who realized that the loss of tax revenues would be offset by several other benefits. As the year-round and vacation homes proliferate, it remains the largest public open space in the community. It is large enough to maintain the diversity of plant and wildlife that once covered most of the island. In addition, designating the preserve as open space has relieved population pressure and protected the fresh-water supply and the delicate aquifer, which is vital to the life of a small island.

Kaolin Commons, New Garden Township, Pennsylvania

SITE

New Garden Township, in Chester County, Pennsylvania, on the border of Delaware only 10 miles from Wilmington and 30 miles from Philadelphia, is a rural community in which mushroom farming is a major activity. This community unfortunately faces development pressure from the surrounding metropolises.

In 1985, the family home of Charles A. Robinson and Josephine Raskob Robinson was placed on the market. The house, a rambling 10-bedroom Colonial Revival building remodeled in 1953 to 1954, by Colonial Williamsburg architect George Bennet, is sited on 460 acres. Initially, the family planned to sell the house with 30 acres and retain the rest, but prospective buyers were concerned with the potential development of the surrounding land, and many people expressed interest in the preservation of the landscape of rolling hills.

At about the same time Hewlett-Packard, the largest employer in the community, explored the area for a new corporate headquarters but rejected it in favor of a site in nearby Avondale.

The Robinson land is adjacent to two long-established mushroom farms owned by the Pia and Ciarrochia families, as well as several other smaller parcels totaling nearly 2000 acres. The land is bisected by Pennsylvania Route 41, a main artery connecting Philadelphia with Wilmington.

Understanding that development would come at its own pace, the Robinson's son, banker Charles Raskob Robinson, envisioned a master plan for his family property and the two mushroom farms that would preserve the open space of the area while providing housing, commercial, office, and recreational opportunities for new residents. His neighbors agreed, and they embarked on a planned development controlled by those with a long-time community interest.

New Garden Township retains a rural, pastoral quality quite remarkable for its proximity to Philadelphia and Wilmington. Like many rural communities near growing cities, the large expanses of open farmland or estate property are both a resource and potential liability. The very qualities of open space that make the area appealing for new residents also attract overdevelopment. The land could, if developed randomly—selling a parcel here, a parcel there—ultimately become a source of development so dense that the natural qualities of the community would be destroyed.

In New Garden Township, the threat of conventional, small-scale suburban subdivisions became more real to residents after Hewlett-Packard considered the site for their corporate headquarters. Large property owners and the community responded by creating a development plan for 2000 acres. The group commissioned Bernadon & Associates of Kennett Square to draft a master plan for the development, which they called Kaolin Commons. The plan calls for two housing communities, two corporate campuses, a retirement community, a hotel and conference center, a town center, and a golf course.

The land in the master plan represents 25 percent of the land in New Garden Township and a small part of Kennett Township. While the planning board and town board have approved the concept of the master plan, they cannot authorize development approval at the concept level. Therefore, each portion of the project will go through the conventional land development review process at both the local and county levels. The community is assured of ample open space without compromising its review control over the specific aspects of development. Accessibility to the open space is a key to this project: A network of "green" open space winds through the development, allowing residents, workers, and visitors to walk around nearly the entire 2000 acres and the golf course, which is open to the public. Project planners attribute the success that the housing developments and golf course have had in obtaining approvals to the fact that the pertinent boards have a full picture of the long-term effects on the community, as well as to the accessibility of the property to the community.

Since much of the land has been in family hands for years, the pressure to extract every possible penny of profit was not as great as if the property had been purchased by developers and encumbered with debt. The scheme calls for individual owners to retain ownership of their property while developing the land in accordance with the master plan. The Kaolin Commons Master Plan is an unusual demonstration that through private-sector-initiated planning, property owners can protect their property from overdevelopment while still realizing economic benefit.

Two luxury housing developments—Hartefeld at the north on the Robinson family land and Somerset Lake at the south owned by Bellevue Holding Company—are already under way, and numerous units are occupied.

The Hartefeld residential development revolves around the Robinson family house, an 11,500-square-foot mansion originally built as a seventeenth-century plantation house in Salisbury, Maryland, that was moved and remodeled in 1953 to 1954 for the Robinsons by George Bennet, a Colonial Williamsburg architect. The fieldstone-surfaced building has a significant Colonial Revival interior with carved paneling and wainscoting. The mansion will serve as the clubhouse for the golf course. It will be operated by the 1492 Hospitality Group, which owns a string of restaurants, the flagship of which is the Columbus Inn in Delaware. The Robinson House will also serve as the firm's corporate headquarters, and all of their catering will be out of this site. A "permanent" tent for 300 guests will increase the available function space. The National Golf Foundation did the market study that determined that a good golf course in this area would be successful as a golf destination. Consequently, the 18-hole course, designed by Tom Fazio, will be open to the public.

In Hartefeld, each of the houses will be individually designed and built by one of a group of architects and builders preselected by the developer. This should provide visual coherence and variety.

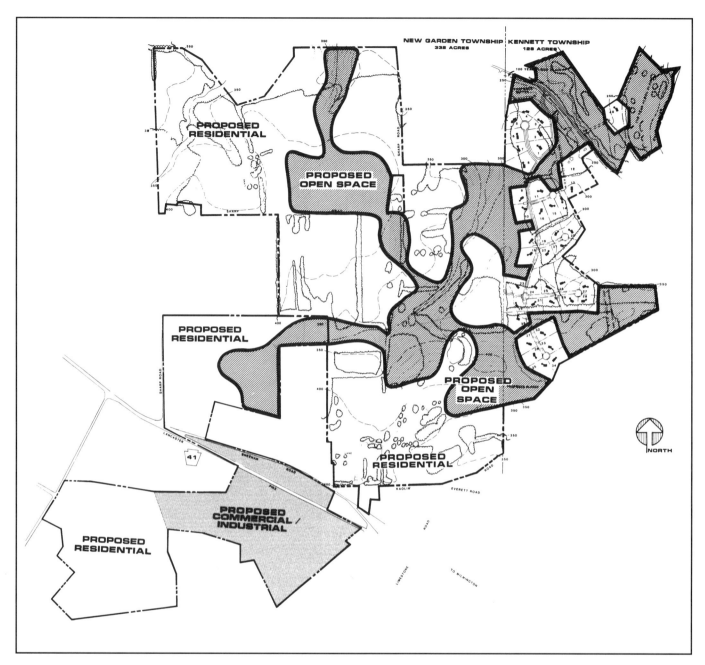

The Kaolin Commons Master Plan demonstrates the benefit to both the large property owners and the local community of their joint efforts. This conceptual plan illustrates that large contiguous open space is well distributed and provides a buffer to the new residential development. A preliminary scheme for the Hartefeld subdivision is shown in the Kennett Township portion of the site.

SIGNIFICANCE

The principal significance of Kaolin Commons is that it is a successful, working model of large-scale master planning used as a tool for open-space preservation and controlled development which no owner could ever effect as an individual. By working together and with local residents including a group of property owners who have a vested interest in the community, the preservationists were able to realize a development project from which everyone would benefit. Both the property owners and surrounding residents profit from planning and then controlling new development.

CHAPTER 4

Government Role: Coming to Terms with Zoning and Environmental Concerns

At present, tremendous landholdings and parks are maintained by the federal and state governments and many counties. Public efforts at open-space and land conservation have never been well coordinated, especially because of the traditional autonomy of local towns and villages. The lack of clear public policy and the paucity of "master plans" for open-space preservation and land acquisition has left the burden on the private sector. Individual owners of mansions and vast estates have had to struggle to transfer these properties to the public domain. In England, historic property may be donated to the government in lieu of inheritance or estate taxes, and the hereditary owners are encouraged to remain in residence. Current U.S. tax policy is so prohibitive that it forces private owners to divest themselves of large landholdings, discouraging them from transfering them to succeeding generations. This arrangement is very inefficient since it usually costs the public more for a government agency to provide the same quality of stewardship as a private owner. A vivid example is provided by Dumbarton Oaks, in Washington, D.C., where the landscaped portion of the property maintained by Harvard University is in superb condition, and the remainder donated to the National Park Service as a public park is in ruins and overgrown. What is needed is a public policy of rewarding rather than discouraging private preservation efforts.

Large Site Master Planning

The three estates cited as examples represent enormous landholdings which have remained in private ownership since the turn of the century, but they are currently seeking solutions for their own future. Both Shelburne Farms, in rural Vermont, and Biltmore, located in Asheville, North Carolina, are in relatively rural surroundings so that the integrity of the estates and the preservation of their original character are more at issue than open-space preservation. Kykuit, the Rockefeller family compound in Pocantico Hills in Westchester County, north of New York City, is surrounded by suburban communities. All of the families have sought very different approaches to opening portions of their estates to public visitation in order to cope with operating and maintenance costs, taxation, and Internal Revenue Service inheritance regulations.

Shelburne Farms, Shelburne, Vermont

SITE

Unlike many of their Vanderbilt siblings and their wealthy contemporaries, who clustered themselves in fashionable resort colonies, Lila Vanderbilt Webb and William Seward Webb set up their country estate in splendid isolation on the pristine shores of

Overleaf Corner turret and courtyard of the Shelburne farm barn.

The main house of Shelburne Farms as restored and converted to an elegant seasonal inn and restaurant.

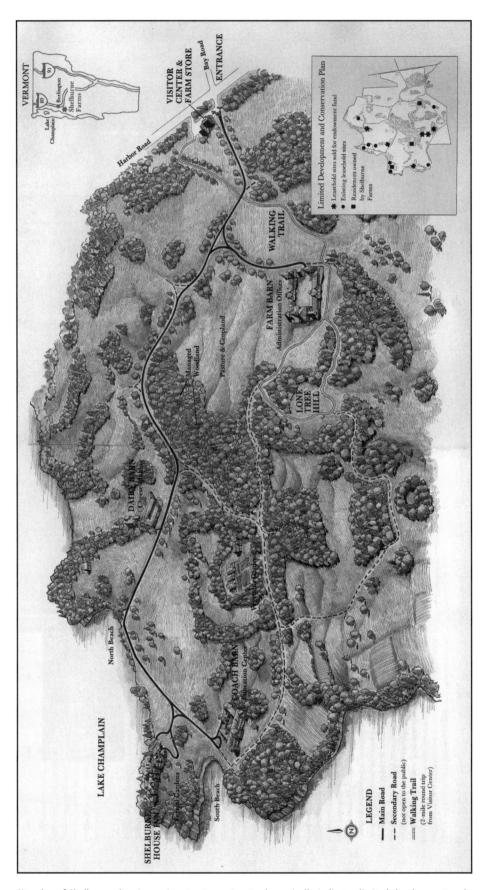

Site plan of Shelburne showing major structures. Inset schematically indicates limited-development and conservation plan.

At Shelburne Farms is one of the largest barn complexes ever constructed in the United States. This barn has been restored, and a portion of its vast interior contains the administrative offices.

Lake Champlain. Both Lila and her brother George, who created Biltmore House, a French Renaissance chateau in Asheville, North Carolina, were grandchildren of Commodore Vanderbilt. Both channeled their formidable inheritances to transform vast stretches of picturesque rural American countryside into private realms of elegance and cultivation. Typical of the gilded age, the Webbs maintained a townhouse on Fifth Avenue in New York City and Nehasane, a 40,000-acre family game park in the Adirondacks. The Webbs had traveled extensively. Mrs. Webb's niece Consuelo, the Duchess of Marlborough, resided at Blenheim Palace in Oxfordshire, England. The Vanderbilt-Webbs decided to create for themselves an estate in the grand manner, in which to pursue the English country lifestyle, including coaching, hunting, and outdoor sports. They created one the first private golf courses in America. "Back to nature" at Shelburne Farms meant building a 100-room "farmhouse" to accommodate family and guests on 4000 acres of rural Vermont farmland. "Model farming" required the largest barn complex in America.

The Webbs consulted Fredrick Law Olmstead on the estate plan and landscaping, which was to be "naturalistic." Miles of winding macadamed roads formed a network connecting all parts of the estate. Olmstead's vision enhanced the existing sensuous rolling hills, lake vistas, forests, and farmland into an English park.

Several major structures were constructed: the mansion, the coach barn, the dairy, the farm barn, and the breeding barn. All except the breeding barn remain a part of Shelburne Farms today.

PRESERVATION ISSUE

Dr. William Seward Webb's ideal of an experimental farm was short-lived. By the time of World War I the heyday of Shelburne Farms had passed, income taxes were instituted in 1913, and in 1914 the southern acres, containing the huge horse breeding barn, were deeded to son James Watson Webb and his wife Electra (nee Havemeyer) as a wedding present. The internal combustion engine had revolutionized farming and rendered much of the farm activities obsolete; Shelburne acquired its first tractor in 1917.

Dr. William Seward Webb died in 1926, and in the thirties the house began a long period of genteel neglect. Lila Webb died in 1936, and her children inherited Shelburne Farms. Throughout the next 50 years the Webb family continued to own the land. The basic land area was retained and actively farmed, although much maintenance was deferred. In 1946 the 3 acres of greenhouses were dismantled and sold. But by the early sixties, the financial pressures became too great: Something else would have to be done, or the farms would have to be broken up and sold off as acreage. In 1972 Shelburne Farms Resources, a nonprofit corporation was created.

Planning for the Future The current generation of the Webb family, committed to preserving Shelburne Farms intact, rejected any development of the land for commercial purposes. In planning for the future, Shelburne Farms has sought advice and assistance of professional land planners, attorneys, financial managers, land conservation organizations, natural resource specialists, and local and state government officials. In 1975, a 200-acre parcel on Shelburne Bay, including important wetlands, was sold to The Nature Conservancy. The property was subsequently transferred to the town of Shelburne, which manages it as a public park. Shelburne has worked with the Vermont Land Trust, a statewide land conservation organization, to protect the core of the farm through permanent, legally binding conservation restrictions.

Shelburne Farms has developed a long-term land-use plan based on the technique of "limited development." Less sensitive portions of the property have been identified for long-term lease for possible future development. Several sites have been sold, and the proceeds placed in an endowment fund.

The Webb family is committed to the concept of stewardship. In 1976 the main house and most of Shelburne Farms were transferred to the foundation. Once an overall plan was developed, the restoration and adaptive use of various estate buildings was begun. Shelburne House now functions as an elegant country inn and restaurant from late May till mid-October.

Shelburne House New York City architect Robert H. Robertson designed an ample Shingle Style cottage, constructed in 1887 to 1888, which was to serve as a temporary residence. In March 1895, Robertson prepared plans and specifications for the conversion of the cottage into a main residence roughly triple its size. The servants' wing was to be moved and turned into an annex. The roof of the cottage was raised, allowing for a full third story. A new large wing, called the Westerly Extension, included an attached service wing. The new plan configuration was a Y shape. Robertson continued in the Shingle Style with Queen Anne detailing, with stucco infilled half-timbering on the upper story. In 1903 the exterior was refaced in brick, and a black slate roof replaced the earlier wooden shingles. This is the appearance it retains today.

After the death of Lila Webb in 1936, Shelburne Farms was used by various family members as a summer residence. The mansion was maintained as a year-round residence until the 1940s during World War II, when the heating system was removed and the severe Vermont winters began to take their toll on the structure. The family continued to use the mansion as a summer residence until 1974. Starting with a Mozart festival in 1974, the Webb family hosted summer programs and events that drew the public to the mansion. In 1983 the decision was made to restore the mansion and turn it into an inn. A capital campaign was successful in raising the money for the restoration.

Under the guidance of architect Martin Tierney, Shelburne House has been successfully transformed into an elegant inn, with 24 guest rooms, which recaptures the ambiance of the Webb's home with much of the original furnishings. The architect confronted many challenges. The most serious difficulties were in accommodating the requirements of public safety. Vermont's building code did permit the inspectors some discretion because of its historic status. A compromise was reached with the Vermont Department of Historic Preservation regarding the seriously deteriorated service wing, which was reduced to a third of its size. Asbestos removal was another major hurdle to clear before new electrical and plumbing systems could be installed.

The other buildings on the estate are being authentically restored on the exterior, but their interiors are being designed to adapt to the numerous innovative activities and programs that Shelburne continues to generate. The gate lodge now serves as a visitor center and shop promoting Vermont products and produce. The dairy barn contains a cheddar cheese production operation, and the cheese is marketed in the Shelburne Farms mail-order catalog. The coach barn presently contains an educational center but will be renovated as a conference and special-events center. The enormous farm barn contains administrative offices and newly expanded facilities for school groups participating in agricultural and natural science educational programs. Some small local businesses lease space, for example, a bakery and a furniture-making shop.

SIGNIFICANCE

A century later Shelburne Farms remains in splendid, if reduced (now 1000 acres), isolation. The Webb's descendants are still living on the property, and true to his original vision, they have created a "model farm" experimenting with techiques for our own age.

The portion of Vermont's hilly landscape bordering on Lake Champlain remains largely a continuum of green farms and picturesque small villages that have escaped the commercialization of trendy vacation and ski resort communities elsewhere in the state. Shelburne Farms and the nearby Shelburne Museum of Americana, founded by Electra Havemeyer Webb, occupy and preserve huge existing assemblages of beautifully cultivated landscape accessible to visitors. The farm provides its rural neighbors and the local economy with a handsome noncommercial tourist attraction while protecting vast areas of open space against the pressures of resort development. Through an imaginative summer cultural and outdoors recreational program enjoyed by 50,000 people, as well as an off-season agricultural education and dairy operations, everyone benefits.

Biltmore House, Asheville, North Carolina

SITE

William Amherst Vanderbilt Cecil's family estate, Biltmore House, Asheville, North Carolina, presents some interesting parallels to the dilemmas facing the British aristocracy struggling to maintain their hereditary homes and great estates.

Cecil's grandfather George Vanderbilt, a son of the New York Central Railroad tycoon Commodore Cornelius Vanderbilt, set out in 1888 to establish his personal domain in Asheville, North Carolina, far from the exclusive salons of New York society. As a bachelor, he had visited Asheville, already a fashionable health resort in the 1880s. After the completion of the house, on one of his trips to Europe, he met his future wife Edith Stuyvesant Dresser, an American living in Paris, and was married in 1898. To tame his newly acquired Blue Ridge Mountain wilderness of 125,000 acres, he engaged the renowned landscape architect of New York's Central Park, Frederick Law Olmstead, and as chief forester Gifford Pinchot, who would later assist Teddy Roosevelt in establishing the national parks in the West. At Biltmore the first school of forestry in the United States was established in 1898.

For the central focus of his private realm, Vanderbilt commissioned the fashionable New York architect Richard Morris Hunt (Hunt had designed Marble House and the Breakers at Newport for his brothers) to design a French Renaissance castle suitable for a king. Hunt's grandiose result was an eclectic amalgam of several Loire Valley Chateaux completed in 1895 containing more than 250 rooms. Vanderbilt and Hunt toured Europe to find furnishings and inspiration for Biltmore. In the spirit of a royal European manor, the grounds contain a working deer park and a model dairy farm in addition to extensive formal gardens, parterres, rose gardens, reflecting pools, statuary, and a conservatory.

The construction of the vast estate required the creation in advance of a village to house the workers. In 1889 Vanderbilt acquired the local village of Best, which was

Main facade of George W. Vanderbilt's chateau, Biltmore House, reflected in the pool.

transformed into Biltmore Village, complete with a new parish church, to resemble a small hamlet on an English estate. Unlike the English stately home, the local population consisted of workers and service people, most of whom were Vanderbilt's employees and not hereditary tenants living in tied cottages on the estate. The major period of construction, undertaken by hundreds of workers, took place from 1890 to 1895.

After George Vanderbilt's untimely death in 1914, his widow deeded a large portion of the estate to the U.S. government, which later incorporated it as part of Pisgah National Forest. In the 1920s other portions of the acreage including Biltmore Village were sold. After Vanderbilt's widow remarried and moved to Washington, D.C., she spent less time at Biltmore. It was first opened to the public in 1936.

PRESERVATION ISSUE

Born at Biltmore in 1928, the son of George Vanderbilt's daughter and a father descended directly from Lord Burghley, Cecil's parents divorced in 1936 and he moved to Britain. In 1960 the Anglo-American Cecil abandoned a promising career in international banking to assume the full-time stewardship of Biltmore. Biltmore had already been open to the public for 30 years. But after three decades the revenues from 50,000 visitors were falling $250,000 short of maintenance costs. Over the years the vast grounds had been reduced to 8000 acres.

Just as other aristocratic English property owners who have created safari parks, tearooms, and other distractions on their hereditary domains, Cecil has applied his

The original Biltmore House greenhouse with trellised pergola and formal flower gardens.

Biltmore House dairy barns, now converted to a winery.

business acumen to developing innovative visitor programs, advertising, and promotional campaigns. He has raised annual visitorship to 700,000 at more than $20 per head. To attract visitors, he has added restaurants and a winery, as well as seasonal events such as candlelight tours and elaborate displays of Christmas decorations.

SIGNIFICANCE

It is a remarkable irony of that one of America's grandest mansions and a huge estate have survived to the present in family ownership. Cecil's enormously profitable Biltmore Company is now in jeopardy because of its success. When he dies, the IRS will lay claim to 55 percent of Biltmore's value in estate taxes. The challenge here, as well as in England, is to maintain such valuable properties in private ownership. Whereas the English attitude encourages family continuity in exchange for tax breaks, the American system does not tolerate the wealthy's receiving any tax benefit while simultaneously enjoying the usage of a donation, whether it be artwork or a large estate.

It is also unlikely that any government agency or not-for-profit group could manage the Biltmore Estate as imaginatively and successfully as the family has itself. The National Park Service and the National Trust for Historic Preservation are struggling to maintain their own landmark historic houses in various parts of the country. Although Biltmore is an exception because of its size, if other large mansions and estates are to survive, some accommodation must be made for family management.

Kykuit, Pocantico Hills, New York

SITE

With the increasing shifting of his business activities from Cleveland to New York City, John D. Rockefeller, Sr.'s choice of Pocantico Hills, Tarrytown, in Westchester County was a practical choice as a site for his country house. The steep hillsides and the picturesque landscapes of the winding Hudson River had been the favorite destination of New York City's prominent families, even prior to the construction of the railroad along its eastern shore early in the nineteenth century. Because of its convenient railroad commute 30 miles from Manhattan, most of Tarrytown's riverfront sites had already been ennobled by Victorian mansions. Kykuit's panoramic hilltop view 500 feet above the river was the outstanding feature of the inland site that Rockefeller assembled. Rockefeller originally occupied a mansarded house acquired with the property in 1893. It burned down in 1902, and the long process of transforming Kykuit was initiated.

John D. Rockefeller, Jr., was instrumental in orchestrating the rebuilding of his father's mansion as a more substantial and stately house more suitable to his wealth and prominence. He chose Delano and Aldrich as architects, and somewhat to their chagrin insisted on Ogden Codman for the interiors. To this ensemble he added Welles Bosworth for the design of the gardens. Each of these professionals sometimes held very independent views and the coordination efforts did not always produce satisfactory results. Despite considerable cost overruns, much of the work was done over until the family was satisfied.

Within the park John D. Rockefeller, Jr., and later his sons built their own homes. The estate grounds contained a substantial carriage house that was later enlarged to include an automobile garage, a large "playhouse" that incorporated many recreational facilities normally found in a country club, as well as a golf course whose manicured greens formed the rolling lawns surrounding the family's residences. An authentic teahouse was imported as the focus of a Japanese garden.

Over the years the family's extensive collection of fine art, antique furniture, and decorative arts have filled the mansion at Kykuit as well as the surrounding outdoor terraces and gardens where an extraordinary sculpture collection has been superbly sited.

Following the death of Nelson Rockefeller in 1979, a bequest of a substantial portion of the estate was made to the National Trust for Historic Preservation. Known as the Pocantico Historic Area, the 86-acre portion contains Kykuit, the estate's principal residence. In 1991 agreements were made with the Rockefeller family to open Kykuit and the Pocantico Historic Area in 1994 for public visitation as the National Trust's eighteenth museum property.

Over the years the Rockefeller family amassed properties surrounding the original estate until their holdings expanded to approximately 6 square miles. The late John D. Rockefeller III left 750 of these wooded acres to the state of New York as the Rockefeller Park Conservancy. Members of the Rockefeller family still live on the estate in homes adjacent to the conservancy.

PRESERVATION ISSUE

A century has passed since John D. Rockefeller's initial 1893 Pocantico Hills land purchase from which Kykuit evolved. The estate was developed as a family compound. Surrounded by walls, fences, and plantings, the enclosed estate provided a bastion of privacy and security to suit the needs and desires of the growing Rockefeller clan. As the various family residences, recreational, and service buildings were built, no consideration was ever given to its being eventually subdivided or transferred to public visitation or outside ownership. Thus the noble gesture of the family to donate the mansion and its art collections to the National Trust has necessitated complex studies to resolve the thorny legal and practical ramifications of introducing public visitation into the intensely private compound in which family members still reside.

SIGNIFICANCE

Wealthy Americans at the turn of the century sought out picturesque bucolic sites where they could create country houses as retreats from the crowded and industrialized cities. Many of these once-rural communities, in which these great estates were created, have evolved over time into suburban communities. Often because individual homeowners had their own front lawn and backyard garden, little thought was given to the conservation of the original landscape or the creation of public parks. Nowadays the popular practice of carving up of these great estates into small, albeit exclusive, homesites is a tragic waste of these superb landscapes, which have been so carefully cultivated and lavishly maintained throughout generations of family ownership. Seldom has the complex process of transition from private family usage to public benefit and enjoyment been so thoroughly and skillfully studied.

Suburban Historic Districts and Zoning in the Preservation of Mansions and Estates

Traditionally, the historic district authorized by preservation legislation has been used as a tool for a community to preserve and protect its historic resources. The underlying philosophy is that by regulating to ensure that alterations or new construction meets the setback, massing, scale, and materials of the historic components, the district will retain its essential characteristics and, hence, its appeal.

To a large extent this has been successful within the confines of suburban areas that designate historic districts that form neighborhoods in which buildings have obvious relationships. While the typical historic district format and regulation, which generally covers those elements that can be viewed from the street, works well for many nineteenth- and early-twentieth-century suburban residential neighborhoods, it does not work well for some resources, specifically estates, and widely spaced groupings of historic structures such as suburban or rural historic districts.

A large estate is not in itself a historic district according to the urban model, on which most preservation tools and design regulations have been based. Since, for a community, the essential and significant character of a historic estate may, in fact, be the amount of open space provided by relatively undeveloped acreage, the regulation of new construction according to conventional historic district guidelines, according to scale, compatible materials and setback, can, in fact, destroy the resource by overdevelopment.

Furthermore, urban and suburban, densely developed historic districts usually conform to the zoning density that regulates their neighborhoods, and often new development within the district boundary requires no zoning density variance, simply historic design review. Suburban estates, however, are generally located within zoning grids that allow a much higher as-of-right density than utilized by the estate. As a consequence, individuals desirous of subdividing and developing estates can challenge (whether they are successful or not) the community's authority to preserve the estate and its open space.

The roadscape is distinct from the streetscape. The free-standing estate structures ranging along winding lanes often require a very different approach, one in which the open-space characteristics of the resource are preserved for the passerby from the road. Design control of walls, fences, hedges, trees, open lawns, and planting can be highly intrusive and problematic for both owners and municipalities charged with their protection.

Since mansions and their estate settings often create a pride of place in a community that makes residents want to preserve them or at least control their development, communities can explore a variety of methods to preserve and protect these resources. Although the disposition of estates and open space can generate noisy debate about a community's desire for open space with an owner's need or desire to realize a profit on his or her property, the creation and adoption of well-planned special-use regulations for these properties can ensure that goals of the private owner can be balanced with those of the larger community.

In addition, regardless of the applicability of the urban preservation model, only a small percentage of communities have enacted preservation ordinances, and it is unlikely that an effort to enact such an ordinance can be marshaled in time to protect a major mansion or estate property that is endangered.

Even communities where strong local preservation zoning ordinances exist, private owners may oppose restrictions placed on their properties, crying economic hardship. Regardless of whether the preservation ordinance is legal and enforceable, private owners may be pitted against municipalities and preservation groups in long battles, both economically costly and potentially detrimental for the cause of preservation in the community and the condition of the landmark. In Rye, New York, for example, an 11-year battle to save the Jay mansion and prevent single-family homes from being built on the site resulted in a public-private partnership in which Westchester County and a nonprofit organization, the Jay Heritage Center, acquired the property that will ultimately be open to the public.

Consequently, different approaches to the preservation of large estates must be explored, and the solution may vary with each resource. Some may be best left as individual buildings in institutional use, for example, as nonprofit headquarters or a museum; others might be appropriate for multifamily housing; still others could be used as offices or commercial retail space. The different uses depend on the resource, its location, and local zoning. There seem to be two common denominators for success, however: Either the local community is strongly behind the landmark, with both energy and financial commitment, or the community has done a good job of planning and will encourage a creative approach to the adaptive use of the resource.

The preservation of open space has obvious benefits for a community. Recreation areas or even beautiful vistas are enjoyed by residents on a daily basis. In many cases, although the municipality may not earn tax revenue that might have been generated by development, the costs associated with development such as roads, police and fire service, and the burden on the school system may offset any tax revenue. Intensive development of an estate site may cause an undue traffic burden on the surrounding streets. The end result may be a higher tax bill, loss of the historic resource, and a more crowded community.

The suburban paranoia with keeping all property outside of the commercial district residential is in direct conflict with the preservation of the very estates that initially provided a draw for suburban development. Unless a municipality is willing to take a stand, it is unrealistic for most individuals or institutions to assume management of an estate. One possibility is to allow for transitional zoning, permitting the division of mansions into apartments to act as a buffer between the commercial or those located along heavily trafficked routes. Despite successful results in some areas such as Southampton, New York, Princeton, New Jersey, and Newport, Rhode Island, this is still an uphill battle in most prestigious suburban communities.

Open space need not be in public ownership for the community to benefit, but public entities can take a leadership role in establishing mechanisms that encourage private owners to maintain open spaces. In the last few years, several communities have explored techniques that would allow them to protect these resources. Some have adopted legislation that addresses types of historic resources particular to their communities. Many suburban communities are revising their local zoning ordinances to balance the desire to preserve the beneficial aspects of estates, such as open space and historic buildings and landscapes, without undertaking the ownership and management of these properties.

Preservation and zoning can be tailored to legitimately accomplish a community's goals. For example, East Fishkill, in Dutchess County, New York, has recently adopted legislation geared toward preserving the stone houses that are recognized as a significant building type in this area of the state. The legislation provides special zoning exemptions for stone buildings listed in their Cultural Resource Survey. Eligible properties located in areas zoned for single-family residences may use the accessory buildings on the property for commercial purposes such as antiques stores or even, square footage permitting, multiple-family residences. In this way, the community is able to effect the preservation of an important local building type without any danger of engaging in spot zoning or weakening the zoning regulations. It must be noted, however, that the stone houses are not mansions and are not situated on large acreage.

Country clubs provide an especially interesting suburban model. As American suburbs were developing between and after the world wars, many large estates were converted, without much ado, to country clubs. Often possessing rolling golf courses, these clubs provided both a draw for new residents to build in the community and visible open space that the community did not bear the cost of maintaining. These clubs are often in desirable neighborhoods and if developed into housing, would command great purchase prices, especially when the country clubs' tax appraisals are based on their potential value as smaller home sites. This has often pressured clubs into selling off strips of roadside frontage.

In a real sense, many estates were quasi-local businesses as well as residential retreats. In Long Island, for example, estates such as those owned by the Vanderbilt and Pratt families were active farms and gardens, employing hundreds of workers. Entertaining requirements at other more modest estates still provided jobs and consumers for local business. When these properties were converted to country clubs, they continued to be a source of jobs, including summer jobs for teenagers, while providing the benefit of open space to the surrounding community.

Many communities are now grappling with the issue of development of these large tracts of land, once thought beyond bounds of development. For example, in the town of Mamaroneck, a suburb of New York City, a townwide, 18-month moratorium on building development for waterfront sites and country clubs was adopted to evaluate the potential residential development of these last remaining large concentrations of land within the community. Specifically, one property, the Bonnie Briar Country Club, with 138 acres, is proposed for residential development in 1997. The town also includes another, even larger golf club, and part of a third. Each of these country clubs uses the mansion as its clubhouse and the grounds for recreational activities such as swimming and golf. Residential development of any would severely tax the community's resources and greatly reduce the amount of open space in the town. The community commissioned an environmental impact study (EIS) to determine the impact of development on the town's services as well as the effect on the water tables and other environmental issues. The EIS also addressed alternate development schemes that clustered development and saved significant elements in the landscape. Although the project is still pending, the community is well prepared to deal with the permit and approval process knowledgeably and fairly.

In Garden City, Long Island, legislation is now under consideration to allow a now-defunct parochial school, Saint Paul's, located in a residential area, to be developed as corporate offices. In return for this concession, however, the 38 acres of the estate are to be forever undeveloped. In this instance, breaking the taboo of introducing a commercial use in a residential neighborhood really serves to limit density in the neighborhood.

Rockledge, in Rowayton, Connecticut, addressed at length in another chapter, is significant as an example of a situation in which a commercial office use of a landmark mansion in an exclusive residential neighborhood preserved the grounds and setting to a much greater degree than any as-of-right residential development could.

In situations where increased taxes from development would not offset the cost of municipal services or where the municipality simply perceives a benefit to the retention of open space, communities can encourage the preservation of open space by offering tax incentives to private owners in return for a low density of use or development. These incentives can be structured to ensure that the private owner does not enjoy a low tax level for a period of years only to sell the land later at a higher price as property values rise. Open space and preservation easements can ensure the goals of the larger community while relieving the tax burden and ensuing development incentive of the owner. In addition, assessments can be made on a more equitable tax formula structured to encourage the preservation of historic resources and open space over intensive development.

Greentree, the Whitney Estate in North Hempstead, New York, although still in private, individual ownership, like many other Long Island estates, has been the subject of substantial local planning efforts. Its large size relative to its community could create a tremendous overload on municipal services were it to be developed quickly. After much consideration, many Long Island communities have created zoning overlays for large, still undeveloped estates that reduce potential density, and they require clustered development to preserve the open-space characteristics of the property as well as to preserve the groundwater tables. Enacted long before development is contemplated, these regulations and restrictions are a part of the planning process from the beginning, ensuring that the community's goals are considered and met.

All of this is not to say that no development should occur but, rather, that municipalities have the right to plan and manage the development of existing mansions and estates in ways that benefit the community. Recognizing these resources as architecturally, historically, or culturally significant is only one step toward their preservation. By utilizing creative planning tools in a comprehensive, objective, and timely manner, municipalities can balance the public good with the rights of individual property owners and preserve the quality and characteristic of the community that make it a unique and appealing place in which to reside.

One of the most daunting problems in the matter of suburban zoning and historic preservation is the increasing congestion on existing road systems. If we consider the period of 1880 to 1940 as the great age of mansion and estate building, we realize that this coincides with the development of the automobile. The old existing pattern of roads linked towns and villages. Early in the 1900s it was recognized that the transition from city to suburb required a road system that bypassed small towns. Most pre–World War II suburbs outside major cities were linked by commuter railroads. Since the wealthy builders of mansions and estates were seeking to escape from the congestion of cities, they sought out remote or farming communities or coastal areas. They had luxury automobiles, often chauffeur driven, and did not represent a significant traffic problem. In the 1920s and 1930s "garden" apartments were built in some exclusive communities, usually near the commuter railroad lines. Following the postwar explosion of suburban development for the middle class, the bucolic winding local roads were becoming overwhelmed. Many of these new homes were built without any provision for public transportation and necessitated an automobile for access, often two if the husband commuted. The new arrivals were soon drawn to suburban shopping centers that required vast parking lots and generated still more traffic. This trend siphoned off the commerce of many small independent merchants in the old core of suburban villages and towns. The new parkways and highways cut through or very close to many estates, exposing them to view and a subsequent loss of privacy and exclusiveness.

As discussed elsewhere in the book, the depression and the war had wrought many changes in American life at all economic levels. Other factors changed the character of suburban life. The lack of sound planning and zoning ordinances in former suburban hamlets led to patterns of speculative residential development that ruined estate areas and are hard to reverse. Attempts to protect large estates now surrounded by smaller homes can often be challenged as spot zoning. Following World War II many large mansions and estates, located in the midst of desirable estate areas, were donated or bought by charitable or institutional organizations. Most of these organizations were exempt from local taxation. Even without the obligation to pay taxes, many of these owners found the mansions too costly to maintain and later put them on the market with no preservation restrictions, reaping the benefits of years of appreciation in land value. If their communities had designated them as landmarks, there might have been some greater degree of control over typical speculative developers who buy these properties assuming that they can demolish the mansion and subdivide the acreage.

The village of Brookville, an exclusive enclave on Long Island's north shore, is an excellent example of several aspects of this problem. In the 1960s the trustees of the New York Institute of Technology acquired an estate of 101 acres adjacent to its Old Westbury campus as a potential expansion site. The 1920s Georgian Revival mansion was adapted as the deSeversky Conference Center for seminars and as a video center. It was occasionally used for weddings and catering when it wasn't being used by the school. In the nineties NIT was suffering a decline in enrollment, and in 1992 it decided to put the mansion on the market.

The school's excellent stewardship had preserved the mansion for 30 years, which has no historic designation and is not visible from the entry, when many others in the area were being demolished. Canon USA had occupied 600,000 square feet of leased space in nearby Lake Success. The company had been frustrated for many years in searching for a property on which to expand its headquarters on Long Island.

Nassau County officials and business leaders felt that Canon's proposal would be an ideal low-impact usage, compatible with its residential neighbors. They were also anxious to keep Canon in the community, which is suffering the effects of a prolonged recession and loss of jobs. Rejection they felt would scare off other large corporations they were seeking to attract. Many of the village's 3700 residents were anxious about an increase in traffic and commercialization in an area that already has New York Institute of Technology and the C. W. Post Campus of Long Island University (which is Hillwood, the former estate of Marjorie Merriweather Post). To assuage this concern, NIT agreed to drop its maximum enrollment to 6000 from 7500.

Sensing Brookville's reluctance to accept a commercial use, over the course of a year Canon met with residents of Brookville and the surrounding villages to listen to their concerns. Finally as a result, the plans filed by Canon proposed to use only 5 acres on Northern Boulevard, a heavily used route, to build campuslike research laboratories and offices employing between 1000 and 1800 people. The plan would have preserved the deSeversky Center and a 95-acre greenbelt. A two-level garage structure would be buried underground. The site is now zoned residential with a 5-acre minimum lot size.

Despite all this effort at reaching a consensus, the mayor and the Brookville village trustees rejected Canon's proposal, claiming to base their opposition on an opinion by their lawyer. The decision said that a special exception granted for exemption from residential zoning to the school for the deSeversky Center could not be legally extended to Canon. In contrast, a superb mansion and estate in the same Brookville village was granted permission to convert a mansion to the corporate headquarters of Villa Banfi, a wine producer. Completed in 1927, the Elizabethan Style Rynwood, designed by noted architect Roger H. Bullard, is a rambling asymmetrical limestone mansion. The estate complex includes the mansion with its service wings, an award-winning gate house, bridges and walls along the driveway, garage, greenhouse, and two garden buildings. The Rynwood garden, designed by landscape architect Ellen Shipman, was known as one of the finest on Long Island.

Villa Banfi, with a staff of approximately 40 employees, occupies the mansion. Brookville required very strict restrictive controls including a provision for no expansion on the site. An adjacent farm has been acquired and planted in vinyards.

Another possibly controversial issue regarding preserving mansions that are set on large parcels such as the deSeversky Center is that they are screened by landscaping. Because much of the estate cannot be seen from the road, the owners could contend that the community does not have the right to regulate it. That argument might apply in situations where individuals are retaining the properties for residential use but, not in cases like the Jay property, where the large-scale development would destroy the resource. Unfortunately, it can't be an either-or situation. If only what can be seen from a public right of way is regulatable, then the center (and rear) sections of designated estates could be developed, leaving an open space toward the road.

This leads to the matter of preservation of the suburban roadscape that defines the character of most estate areas. Many rural areas have accepted restrictions on "scenic routes" since often the local economy is dependent on tourism. Scenic routes are generally more concerned with preserving landscapes and vistas and less concerned with individual structures. In suburban areas this kind of regulation is more difficult to apply because of the extensive development of commercial strips along the roadside. Even the widening of major highways has diminished or virtually eliminated the buffer once provided by trees that for years shielded the residential areas along the route. The Boston Post Road Historic District in Rye, New York, is a good example of the complexities of protecting historic structures and scenic vistas along a major suburban transportation corridor.

BOSTON POST ROAD HISTORIC DISTRICT, RYE, NEW YORK

Whitby, Rye Golf Club, Rye, New York ❧ Lounsberry, Private Mansion (not in use), Rye, New York ❧ Alansten (being restored by the Jay Heritage Center), Rye, New York ❧ Rye Marshlands Conservancy (originally part of Alansten), Rye, New York

SITES

Lounsberry (1836) was donated in 1988 to the city of Rye, which has not yet decided on its future.

The properties that form the Boston Post Road Historic District in Rye have been designated as both National Register and Rye City landmarks. The district forms a collection of outstanding examples of nineteenth-century architecture not paralleled elsewhere in Westchester County. Lounsberry (1836) and Alansten (1838) are sophisticated versions of the Greek Revival Style. Lounsberry was built by New York businessman Edward Lamb Parsons, and, with the exception of the years 1850 through 1858, it was in the family's ownership until 1988. Alansten was built by Peter Augustus Jay, the son of John Jay, the first chief justice of the U.S. Supreme Court, and sits on the site of John Jay's boyhood home. Whitby was designed by Alexander Jackson Davis in 1852 in the Gothic Revival Style, which he helped to popularize in America.

Alansten (1838), the Jay property, has been the focus of an 11-year struggle to preserve the mansion and prevent its replacement by new residential development.

The district is situated in suburban Westchester County, New York, on the Boston Post Road, a major commercial thoroughfare. Rye is an affluent community, and the area surrounding the district is developed with single-family homes of considerably smaller scale than that of the mansions. It is also a critical environmental area and backs up to Milton Harbor, a protected and active recreational harbor on Long Island Sound.

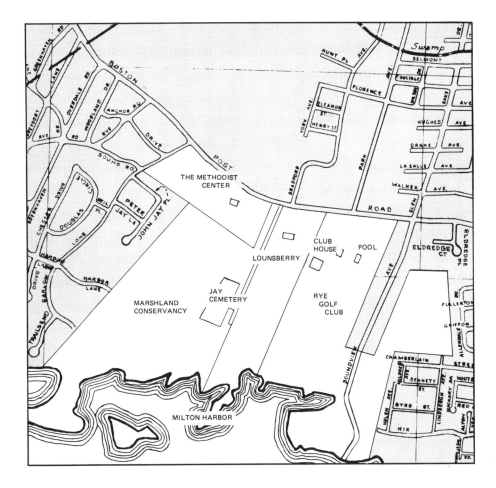

The Boston Post Road historic district.

Whitby, an 1852 Gothic Revival villa designed by architect Alexander Jackson Davis, is now the Rye Golf Club, a public golf course.

PRESERVATION ISSUE

Two of the properties, Whitby and the Marshlands, have been in their current uses since 1921 and 1966, respectively, but the disposition of the other estates has inspired Westchester's most controversial preservation debate in recent years. Alansten was a private residence until 1966 when it was donated to the United Methodist Church. At the same time, 180 acres of land historically associated with the house was given to Westchester County and is now operated by the county as the Rye Marshlands Conservancy. The gift of the house to the United Methodist Church was made without any restrictions, and in 1981 a local developer purchased it and proposed to demolish the house and outbuildings and build 36 single-family homes. Its National Register listing and designation as a local landmark helped to mobilize the community to fight an 11-year battle to convert the property to public ownership.

Preservationists, environmentalists, and community activists lobbied together to preserve the Jay property, Alansten. The county began condemnation proceedings, and in August 1992, it bought (at fair market price with a substantial grant from New York State) the 23 acres from the developer, DGM Partnerships owned by Diane Millstein, who donated the mansion and the carriage house to the Jay Heritage Center.

The Jay Heritage Center (JHC) is now restoring the carriage house for use as an environmental center for the Long Island Sound Bioregion, JHC offices, and a visitor and interpretative center for the Marshlands Conservancy. The programs for the main house are not finalized but are likely to include office and meeting space for nonprofit organizations, as well as conference or public gathering space.

During this period of debate, Fanny Parsons, owner of Lounsberry, decided to donate the property to the city of Rye, with preservation covenants, and upon her death in 1988, the city became the owner of the property. Various uses, including a restaurant, conference center, museum, and private residence, have been discussed for the property, but the city is undecided, and it is currently empty, save for a caretaker.

SIGNIFICANCE

The three estate properties, including the Marshlands Conservancy, form a contiguous grouping of open land either in public ownership or use.

Sited close to the road in a busy, suburban setting, the mansions are not likely to be desirable again for use as single-family residential retreats. They survive, however, with all their original land. The question of how to adapt these buildings and their settings to a contemporary use that preserves, as much as possible, the qualities of the historic estate settings has been answered by a combination of active and passive recreational uses, as well as low-intensity institutional use, achieved with a partnership of both public and private ownership.

The success of the Jay coalition in preserving Alansten has had a marked effect on the entire district. Their success was due to the combined efforts of environmentalists and preservationists who convinced the public and the county of the need to save the Jay property both for the stability of the Marshlands Conservancy as well as for the preservation of a significant surviving element of Westchester's history. It has spurred interest in the careful restoration of Whitby, and although the use for Lounsberry, the center of the three mansions, has not been determined, its public ownership and the stable situations of the flanking properties, will ensure that a use compatible with the estate setting will be found.

The properties are used as a city golf and swimming club, a nature center, and an environmental lab and environmental interpretive center with some of the smaller outbuildings used as residences for caretakers. Whitby, the Rye Golf Club, is partially self-sustaining due to user fees. Alansten will probably be used as offices for nonprofit organizations and as a conference center, but the grounds will be preserved, in their undeveloped state for passive recreational use. Rye's Boston Post Road Historic District will continue to provide an oasis of open space in the community because the buildings have successfully made the transition from private use to spaces redesigned to serve the communities needs.

Resort Zoning

A comparison of practices in three major resort areas with large concentrations of mansions provides some interesting insights. Both Palm Beach, Florida, and Newport, Rhode Island, have designated numerous historic districts and individual landmarks. East Hampton has been less successful in convincing the owners of the resort's summer colony, where most of the mansions are located, to accept historic district designation. The community has also been very resistant to any deviation from single-family residential occupancy. Palm Beach has been the most restrictive in the application of zoning, architectural review, and landmark preservation standards. Newport has developed the most innovative strategies, preserving some of the extravagant mansions as museums and allowing the creation of condominiums in many others.

PALM BEACH, FLORIDA

The *Landmark Architecture of Palm Beach,* by Barbara D. Hoffstot, was published by Ober Park Associates in 1974. Mrs. Hoffstot and her husband Henry were residents of Pittsburgh and Palm Beach. Having served as a trustee of the National Trust for Historic Preservation as well as on the boards of other historic preservation organizations, she was concerned about the fate of Palm Beach's distinctive architecture.

Palm Beach is not an old community: Its oldest extant building dates from 1885, and following the ups and downs of Florida's periodic booms and busts, the majority of its fabulous array of houses had been built by the late 1930s. This period coincided with the golden age of mansions and great estates in other parts of the country. The earliest houses were of modest size, built of wood in the Shingle Style, and bungalow types. 1900 saw the introduction of Colonial Revival and the Carrere and Hastings Beaux-Arts mansion for Henry Flagler.

But the dominant Spanish and Mediterranean flavor that is so distinctive to Palm Beach is the result of Addison Mizner's arrival in Palm Beach in 1918. Together with Paris Singer, heir to the Singer sewing machine fortune, they developed the Everglades Club in the Hispano-Moresque Style filled with Singer's personal collection of Spanish antiques, tapestries, old wood paneling from churches, and paintings. Mizner planned the landscaping and the yacht basin, lushly planted with tropical fauna, orange trees, and palms, and the club captivated the resort community. Over the years the club was expanded, and a golf course and villas were added. Numerous commissions for large houses followed. Mizner set up his own manufactures to produce the "antique" tiles, cast stone, ironwork, furniture, and even a stoneyard to provide native coquina stone elements for his clients' houses.

Architect Marion Syms Wyeth, who arrived in 1919, also produced houses in the Spanish and Italian Styles, and many other prominent northern architects designed houses for their clients who wintered in Palm Beach. In the early 1920s Mizner and Wyeth dominated the building of great villas, and in 1925 Maurice Fatio set up a practice and continued designing in the same Mediterranean Style.

Palm Beach is a compact narrow sandy strip of land fronting on one side on the Atlantic ocean and the other on Lake Worth. It is connected to West Palm Beach on the mainland by a series of causeways and bridges. Fortunately much of the expansion of recent years, including office buildings and commercial structures, has been absorbed by West Palm Beach, providing many of the community services and relieving the pressure on Palm Beach itself. Since most of the limited area of Palm Beach was already built up by the 1930s, there are virtually no available building sites.

In general, Palm Beach's architectural taste is quite conservative, and there never was any significant art deco or modern design. Because of the limited lot sizes, many houses are surrounded by walled enclosures or so heavily landscaped that they are concealed from the street. From the water one can observe much more than from the roads.

Following World War II, lifestyles changed, and many of the owners of the largest and most extravagant houses saw them as out of date, too large to air-condition, and too hard to staff. Consequently, many were demolished, and the land was subdivided for new construction. Addison Mizner's, Playa Riente, El Mirasol, Casa Bendita, The Towers, Casa Florencia, Casa Joseto, and La Fontana were destroyed, making way for new high-rise condominiums.

In 1977, when the owner of the William Gray Warden house—one of the last of Mizner's great houses on an ocean-front site occupying a whole block—requested permission to demolish it and replace it with townhouses, 2 years of litigation ensued. Finally another developer stepped forward, and permission was granted to divide the house into six condominium units. The controversy over the Warden house convinced the Palm Beach Town Council to adopt the Landmarks Ordinance in 1979.

Hoffstot's book was a personal survey that laid the basis for the formal two surveys, one in 1981 and the other in 1989. The original list included 450 possible landmark sites, but since Palm Beach has adopted the 50-year threshold of the National Register of Historic Places, it has been a gradual process. As of 1991, 158 sites had been designated.

One of the largest and most dramatic houses ever constructed in Palm Beach was begun in 1923 for Marjorie Post and her husband E. F. Hutton. They originally commissioned Marion Sims Wyeth but then turned it over to architect Joseph Urban to create a showplace designed for entertaining. Urban was a highly versatile and theatrical designer whose eclectic background from his native Vienna at the turn of the century gave him a versatility to design the whole gamut of traditional and modern styles. For the Huttons he produced a 115-room Hispano-Moresque fantasy with a tall

tower overlooking Mar-a-Lago's dramatic 17-acre site that stretches from the Atlantic Ocean to Lake Worth. Clustered about the main house were a service wing, a generous circular patio, a guest house, garages, a ballroom, and a nine-hole golf course. On the interior, superbly crafted and detailed entertaining spaces were glittering stage sets out of an Arabian Nights fantasy.

In 1972 prior to the Palm Beach Landmarks Ordinance, Mar-a-Lago had been fully documented by the Historic American Buildings Survey and listed in the National Register of Historic Places. Mrs. Post originally offered to donate Mar-a-Lago to the state of Florida, but the gift was not accepted because some of the Palm Beach residents feared greatly increased traffic on South Ocean Boulevard. Upon her death in 1973, the estate was willed to the U.S. government to be used as a retreat for visiting foreign dignitaries or the president. Because of its prominent location and closeness to roads and waterways, it was considered too difficult to provide adequate security, so Mar-a-Lago was returned to the Post Foundation. Palm Beach residents were greatly relieved when Donald Trump acquired the property in 1985 and set about refurbishing it. The house had been vacant and essentially unoccupied for 12 years. After this long hiatus, Mar-a-Lago's fate finally seemed secure. This hope was, however, short-lived; the recession of the early nineties brought financial difficulties for Trump.

In 1991 an application was filed to subdivide the approximately 17½-acre grounds of Mar-a-Lago to permit the construction of luxury residences of 5000 to 7000 square feet, on eight lots located on the north and south boundaries of the property. The Palm Beach Landmarks Commission engaged the firm of Clarion Associates to prepare an analysis of the proposed subdivision plan. The report thoroughly analyzed the house, its grounds, and landscaping. It was their conclusion that a preservation plan could be developed that would permit the development of the new houses. Their principal reservation regarded the need to add landfill and change the existing topography, adjusting the landscaping, and the preservation of view corridors within the site, as well as from the mansion itself. Ultimately this proposal was rejected by the town of Palm Beach, and the owner has prepared another study for Mar-a-Lago's conversion to a club. In June 1993 the town council of Palm Beach finally granted Trump permission to convert Mar-a-Lago to a beach club and spa.

Although this solution hopefully will prove successful in maintaining Mar-a-Lago's exterior architectural features, it will no doubt require some internal changes to suit its new use. Most of the preservation community and Trump's neighbors will be relieved that their efforts staved off subdivision. The negative side of all the publicity generated by the Mar-a-Lago controversy makes other property owners wary of the tough stand of the Palm Beach Landmarks Commission and may scare off potential purchasers of designated properties when they come on the market.

NEWPORT, RHODE ISLAND

A discussion with Ted Sanderson of the Rhode Island Preservation Commission shed some light on the workings of Newport zoning, which does not have a specific ordinance or category for mansions. Individual Rhode Island towns are allowed to devise their own zoning and preservation plans, but they must be reviewed at the state level.

Newport residents rejected an ordinance that would have allowed planned unit development or cluster development. One aspect of the Newport Zoning Code which would affect the division of large mansions into residential, inn, or commercial usage are its very detailed regulations for on-site parking, number of spaces based on the number of units, layout, aisles, appropriate screening, and lighting.

Owners of properties within the historic district areas must apply for a certificate of appropriateness for any exterior modifications. There are also very carefully defined conditions for granting a demolition permit. The historic district commission does not regulate paint colors, normal landscape features (unless specially noted in the designation), window air-conditioning units, or storm windows.

The most successful mansion conversion projects were properties listed in the National Register of Historic Places and were done in the 1980s during the period of tax act incentives that required thorough review by the Rhode Island Preservation Commission. The rigorous standards of the secretary of the interior were applied so that not only the exterior but significant interior spaces and features would be preserved.

Architect John Grosvenor of the Newport Collaborative has designed many mansion conversions in Newport and nearby Rhode Island coastal resorts. He has observed that zoning variances for multifamily occupancy were granted on sites that were located inland rather than on the most prestigious ocean-front sites. In his opinion they were architecturally interesting but not as spectacular as the highly desirable ocean-front houses, many of which still remain in single-family occupancy. The collaborative has found that coastal resort communities that can no longer find individual buyers for mansions have become more flexible in allowing zoning variances for condominiums in the main house or at least in accessory structures such as carriage houses.

There are a few notable exceptions, however, such as Harbor Court, a 1905 French Renaissance Style chateau, which was designed by the noted architectural firm of Cram, Goodhue, and Ferguson for John Nicholas Brown, who sold it to a private syndicate for use as the Newport headquarters of the New York Yacht Club. Easements were given, but a part of the property was retained for future development.

The Rhode Island Preservation Commission has accepted façade easements, as well as scenic easements on coastal properties. These resulted in tax benefits to the property owners and assured that the surrounding landscape and context of the mansion's settings would be maintained.

As in other resort areas, economics still seems to be the major determinant in the fate of mansions. The Preservation Society of Newport has acquired and operates as house museums many of the grandest mansions. Most of these mansions were first offered for sale as single-family residences. Rose Cliff (1898), a beautiful evocation of the Grand Trianon executed in white glazed terra cotta by Stanford White, was acquired by The Preservation Society of Newport and provides income, as many of their properties do, by functioning as a house museum as well as a catering facility.

The restoration of the Lansmere, Newport, a handsome nineteenth-century mansarded stone house is an important element in its historic district. There is no hint of its conversion to condominiums.

Others such as Bonniecrest (1912 to 1914), designed by architect John Russell Pope for Stuart Duncan, in an English Tudor manor, with tapestry brick, half timbering, and leaded casements, is one of the great Ocean Drive mansions that has been lost. Currently threatened is Castle Hill Inn, the 1875 mansion and chalet that had operated successfully since the 1940s when they were denied a zoning variance.

A few case studies of mansions divided into condominium apartments by the Newport Collaborative during the early 1980s, when the tax laws provided the incentives to do so, are included here to demonstrate how successfully and handsomely this has been accomplished. Newport has several firms who will contract for the management, operations, and maintenance of mansions divided into condominium units. Thus the burden is removed from the individual owners who may be full-time residents, second-home owners, or seasonal occupants. In several instances investors have bought several condominium units that they rent seasonally. This practice has been a source of irritation between the full-time occupants and the transient tenants, especially in the sharing of common rooms and outdoor facilities, trash collection, and other housekeeping matters.

An unusual Newport trend has been for wealthy purchasers to buy up the condominium units in a mansion and convert it back to a large luxurious single-family residence.

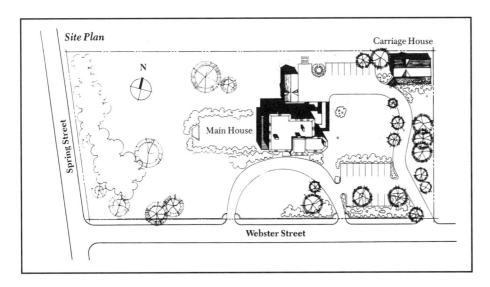

Lansmere's site plan indicates how discretely the Newport Collaborative has located the larger parking lot to meet the increased parking requirements, preserving as much as possible the original landscaping and character of the property.

The striking character and distinctive Italianate detailing of Bienvenue have been restored during its conversion to condominiums.

Bienvenue, Newport, Rhode Island

SITE

Bienvenue is an Italianate Style villa built in 1854 for Joseph M. Hart, an industrialist from Troy, New York. It is located on a 2½-acre site, with mature trees, in the Bellevue Avenue Historic District. Originally a single-family residence, with numerous additions, it was later converted to a college dormitory with 14 rooms. It contained 8600 gross square footage and was in a very derelict condition when it was acquired by builder Fred Dallinger's company Dallinger Associates. The property also contained an old carriage house.

PRESERVATION ISSUE

Builder Dallinger and architects John Grosvenor and Michele Foster of the Newport Collaborative, felt that Bienvenue could be restored and adapted to condominium use. The major incentives during this period were a strong real estate market and the

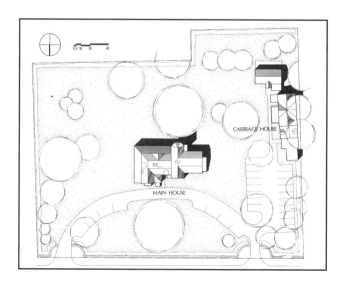

This site plan demonstrates the Newport Collaborative's skill in minimizing the impact of additional parking required on the site.

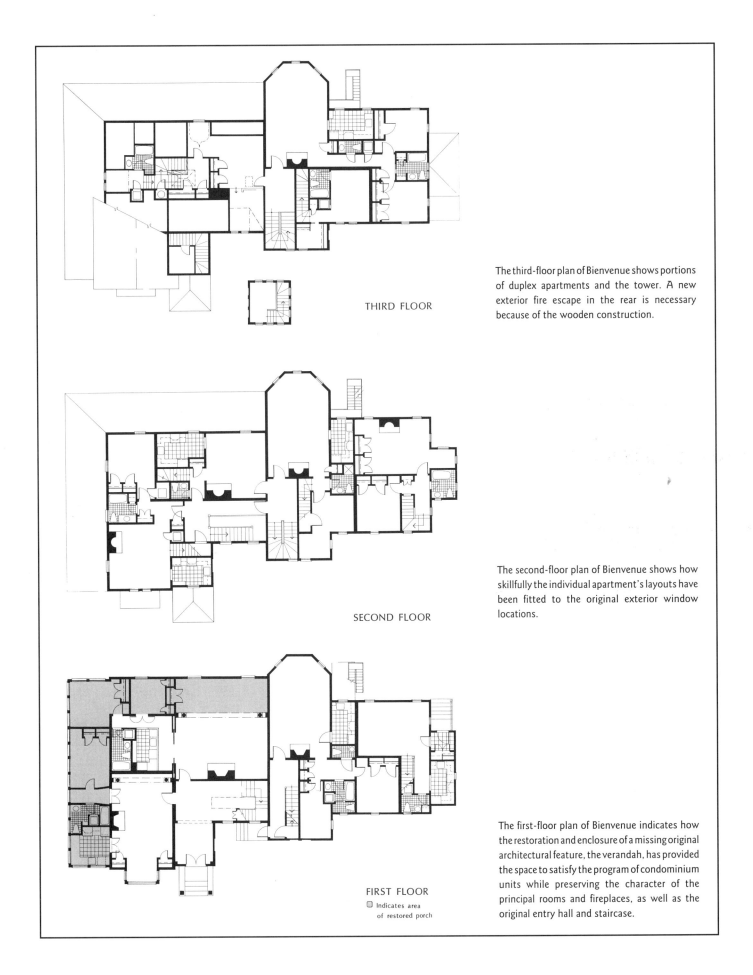

THIRD FLOOR

The third-floor plan of Bienvenue shows portions of duplex apartments and the tower. A new exterior fire escape in the rear is necessary because of the wooden construction.

SECOND FLOOR

The second-floor plan of Bienvenue shows how skillfully the individual apartment's layouts have been fitted to the original exterior window locations.

FIRST FLOOR
☐ Indicates area of restored porch

The first-floor plan of Bienvenue indicates how the restoration and enclosure of a missing original architectural feature, the verandah, has provided the space to satisfy the program of condominium units while preserving the character of the principal rooms and fireplaces, as well as the original entry hall and staircase.

benefits of the federal tax act. The client Betancourt/Carrington & Co. felt that for marketing, two-bedroom units would be the most desirable. The challenge was to provide as many units as possible and still adhere to the strict historic preservation guidelines. The imaginative solution to provide additional volume involved re-creating an original verandah that had long since disappeared. This made it possible to fit in an additional two units for a total of eight in the main house.

The restored verandah was enclosed to appear as though it were a glazed conservatory. By locating secondary spaces such as kitchen and bath and bedrooms within the verandah, it was possible to retain and restore the principal rooms as living-dining rooms. The original entrance and stair leading to the second floor were retained. The building has three stories, and many of the units are duplexes with their own internal stairs. Ranging from 800 to 1200 square feet, no two layouts are the same.

The carriage house, which the developers originally intended to restore, turned out to be in such poor condition it had to be almost rebuilt, salvaging only some original windows and dormers. With the addition of a unit in an old potting shed, the carriage house yielded four units of 800 to 1000 square feet.

Because the project required a zoning variance and was located in a historic district, the approval process was fairly rigorous. Finding a balance between the historic preservation guidelines and the building code, which often conflict, was not always easy. Since the reconstruction involved more than 50 percent of the main house, all state fire and building codes were complied with. To preserve old wooden elements in the structure required installing sprinklers in the building. All of the units in the main house that were more expensive sold quickly; those in the carriage house sold out in the year that the project was completed.

The restored exterior of Codman Place, Bristol, Rhode Island, gives no hint of its conversion to condominiums. It is a handsome example of a distinctive old house adapted during the heyday of the 1980's tax reform act, which stimulated private investment.

SIGNIFICANCE

Many communities contain mid-nineteenth-century mansions of the same character as Bienvenue, but Bienvenue was unusual in several ways that justified the large investment it took to restore it and adapt it to condominiums. There were two key elements that made the project feasible and profitable. Because Newport was a resort, the units could be sold at higher prices. In addition, sizeable tax credits were available. Architect John Grosvenor has observed that even in Newport and other Rhode Island resort communities, the conversion of mansions to condominiums has slowed because of the loss of significant tax act benefits after 1984.

EAST HAMPTON, NEW YORK

East Hampton has been called "America's most beautiful village." This is obviously a highly subjective opinion, but the village is indeed quaint and natural, and it has, in fact, been rigorously watched over by the Ladies' Village Improvement Society (LVIS) since its founding in 1895. The organization is an outgrowth of the city beautiful movement following the World's Columbian Exposition of 1893. The LVIS has been especially involved in preserving the landscape and picturesque character of the village. Early on, as electricity and telephone service was introduced, the society was instrumental in urging that it be buried underground; this practice continues to the present with all utilities concealed, preserving the antique charm of the village. East Hampton possesses a unique inventory of buildings from the seventeenth through twentieth centuries including an exceptional collection of early-nineteenth-century windmills.

In 1978 to 1979 an architectural survey of the village was conducted, resulting in the nomination of 13 historic districts and 22 individual properties within the village to the National Register of Historic Places. The LVIS supported and published the survey "East Hampton's Heritage," organized by architect Robert Stern, historian Clay Lancaster, and preservationist Robert Hefner.

The earliest summer visitors to discover East Hampton were clergy from Manhattan and Brooklyn, following the Civil War, who stayed at boarding houses or rented cottages. Early Victorian Gothic and Stick Style cottages were modest in scale and set on relatively large plots. East Hampton was next discovered in 1877 by artist members of the Tile Club. Winslow Homer visited, but Childe Hassam and Thomas Moran became life-long summer residents. The next 15 years have been referred to as the "boarding house era." The summer colony was not firmly established until around 1890. Then the size and elaborateness of the cottages began to grow.

East Hampton never attracted the conspicuous display of wealth and ostentation of Bar Harbor, Maine, Newport, Rhode Island, or Deal or Elberon on the New Jersey shore. There were mansions, but they were not as grand as the Berkshire cottages and there were no marble palaces or French chateaux. Many of the fashionable turn-of-the-century New Jersey resorts were built in such a way that the coastal road separated the houses from the beaches. This arrangement, however, proved troublesome later on as automobile traffic increased, which obstructed the vista of the ocean and resulted in a loss of privacy for the large mansions. Unlike the New Jersey resorts, in East Hampton the coastal road runs inland, and access to the ocean beaches and ponds is restricted by limited parking that requires permits favoring local residents.

The cottages sit on large ocean-front lots, sited high up on the dunes that extend directly down to the water. The beach itself cannot be fenced off, restricted from public access. The resort colony area of East Hampton began to develop in the late nineteenth century as an extension of the main street of the old village leading to the ocean beaches. Neither the natives nor the summer residents wanted either a railroad or a hotel, and this certainly slowed the development of East Hampton as a resort. As a result, the railroad did not reach East Hampton until 1896. This timing coincided with the popularity of the Shingle Style house, which was fortuitous because, from its seventeenth-century origins, the use of wooden shingles had been the local vernacular building tradition. Despite the increased size and porches, turrets, and verandahs of the resort cottages, there was generally a continuity of material, color, and texture.

The Shingle Style adopted the details of the Colonial Revival and Adamesque Styles, and from 1900 through the twenties it also extended to the half-timbered neo-Elizabethan, the English "freestyle," and the sand-colored stucco cottages. These houses evoked the spirit of Maidstone, England, the Kentish village of the original settlers.

After World War II, between the 1950s and the 1970s, the artistic community flourished in East Hampton and so did experiments in modern architecture. During the same period some exceptional icons of Modern and International Style architecture, designed by architects Gordon Bunschaft, Charles Gwathmey, Richard Meier, and others, were built and discretely screened by lush landscaping. Robert Stern was instrumental in reviving the Shingle Style in several new large villas. In the 1990s the

Large single-family residence, turn-of-the-century Shingle Style mansion on large acreage in the East Hampton Village "summer colony" near the beach. Strict local zoning rejects division apartments or conversion of accessory structures, such as carriage houses, to residential use.

A mansion typical of the East Hampton ocean-front cottages, which are the pride of this fashionable resort. Its privacy has been diminished by its proximity to a popular beach access parking lot. Strict zoning forbids conversion to condominiums or use as an inn. Increased coastal erosion also threatens the privacy and safety of the huge ocean-front houses, as the dunes that served as a buffer to the public beach have been eaten away.

mood has turned conservative, and there has been some strong negative reaction to large experimental modern houses, that have not blended successfully into the landscape.

PRESENT-DAY PRESSURES

Because of its proximity to New York City, the "Hamptons" have become increasingly popular as a second-home community. Unlike the pattern of the rest of the United States, most New Yorkers live in apartments, so the prospect of getting out to the countryside and the novelty of owning a house is very appealing.

There is limited ocean frontage, and almost all the land in the core of the historic village has been built on. Newcomers have been forced to build in the nearby wooded interior areas of East Hampton town. Because land is so scarce, sites are relatively small, some less than half an acre. Along the ocean front 5-acre minimum zoning has preserved much of the natural character of the sand dunes. However, since the turn of the century when the ocean-front mansions began to appear perched atop the dunes 200 or 300 feet from the water's edge, serious erosion has brought many houses to the brink of danger. Some in fact have had to be moved back on their lots. But still the ocean front is the most desirable and prestigious area of East Hampton. Thus far individual owners have exercised considerable restraint in the renovation of the older, architecturally distinctive ocean-front mansions.

THREAT TO DESIGN INTEGRITY

Recently there has been cause for alarm in the nearby resort of Southampton, where a large ocean-front 1920s Georgian Revival mansion built by the Du Pont family was acquired by a newly rich owner who decided to transform it into his dream castle. This Disney World turreted-style mansion became the center of a huge controversy and was abandoned in a hail of lawsuits. It became apparent that in the age of rock stars and media moguls, wealth no longer was a sufficient guarantee of good taste and restraint and that a more specific design review process was needed.

Since all of East Hampton's most distinctive landmarks and mansions lie within its proposed historic districts, the task of developing design guidelines is more easily focused. The *Design Manual for Landmark and Historic Districts for the Village of East Hampton* was prepared in 1991 under the direction of Robert Hefner, the village's historic preservation consultant, who had supervised the original 1979 survey.

Many of these guidelines follow a format similar to those of the secretary of the interior's standards; however, some aspects are particular to East Hampton's own special character.

BUILDING ORIENTATION

There is a long history in East Hampton of moving buildings, sometimes shifting them on their own site, often onto another property, which was easily accomplished because the terrain is so flat. In more recent times planners have concentrated the expansion of the commercial and shopping core of the village to avoid strip development along the approach roads. Old houses left isolated in the commercial area have been moved to vacant sites. In the past this practice has been condoned because it avoids demolition. The guidelines now discourage the practice of moving buildings but retain this option requiring first a determination of how significant an effect its removal will have on the historic district and the appropriateness of the new site.

FENCES AND MASONRY WALLS

From the earliest times individual plots were fenced from the common because, unlike rural New England where fieldstone was plentiful, East Hampton had only wood to work with. Early settlers had pales or horizontal rails and later on wood pickets, sometimes painted white. Although there were a few examples of stuccoed masonry garden walls in the early twentieth century, masonry walls on the property line are discouraged.

PLANTINGS

When the cottages of the summer visitors first appeared at the turn of the century, they stood out starkly in a treeless setting of undulating windswept sandy dunes covered with indigenous beach grass. After much experimentation with plantings tolerant of the salt atmosphere, formal cultivation and gardening began in earnest with clipped lawns, floral borders, specimen trees, and privet hedges. As more mansion-size cottages were built on relatively small sites, privacy became a more important factor, and privet hedge walls were allowed to grow to 12 feet, concealing many properties from the passersby. This formal landscape of hedge-walled compounds alternates with sweeping vistas of lawns, interspersed with an occasional farm field. The openness of the farm fields is deceptive since they are owned by wealthy residents who lease them to farmers to preserve their original character. In recent years some new large houses have begun to appear on the farm lots; some are quite large and styled to give the impression of large barns or stables.

      The guidelines define the landscaping patterns of the different historic districts. The mansion cottage owners in the proposed summer colony historic district vigorously objected to restrictions on planting and hedges. Seasonal storms and hurricanes have often played havoc with the mature trees and hedgerows. Owners also were concerned that they might be prevented from building on vacant sites. As result of their protests, no local designation was enacted in the proposed summer colony historic district, and property owners of some of the most architecturally distinctive mansions are bound only by the zoning and architectural review boards. The need to conceal a proliferation of swimming pools, pool houses, and tennis courts, none of which are permitted to be visible from the street, has led to more privet hedge walls and fences.

HOME LOTS

In 1648 the governors of the New Haven and Connecticut colonies purchased a vast tract at the end of Long Island from the Native American Montauk Tribe. They sold the tract to English emigrants already established in a settlement called Maidstone. In 1662 the name was changed to East Hampton. The settlers formed a proprietary dividing land, resources, and privileges alike. The proprietors laid out narrow deep "home lots" perpendicular to the broad main street, which, shaded by huge elm trees, served as a village green and common pasturage. They also dug out a bog to become the village pond. The special character of early East Hampton followed the New England tradition: The early settlers whose livelihoods revolved around fishing and farming clustered themselves on terra firma at a safe distance from the ocean rather than

The owners of the 1770 House, which contains a successful family-run restaurant, were not permitted to expand on the site. The purchase of the nearby Poor House subsequently enabled the owners to move out, thus increasing the available guest rooms. This is another example of rescuing two old buildings and preserving the original charm of the historic village.

building on the beaches or dunes. Unlike Newport or Bar Harbor with their hilly, rugged, rocky coastline, East Hampton's flat and fertile farm landscape runs down to the dunes and broad white sand beaches.

The last of 34 original home lots of 11 acres has remained in the ownership of one of the founding families, the Gardiners, since 1648. The present owner has been seeking permission to subdivide the lot for several years. Prominent on the front of the lot, which faces on the historic cemetery and town pond, is a windmill built in 1804 by Nathaniel Dominy V, a noted local artisan. The village had expressed interest in preserving some of the open farmed space, so in an effort to secure approval for the

The Poor House is a sprawling English Arts and Crafts Style mansion on the main street facing the village green. Set close to the road, increased traffic had discouraged well-to-do buyers from purchasing it as a single-family residence. The owners of the nearby 1770 House Inn bought the house and restored it, furnishing it with antiques. It is now used as the inn owner's residence, providing several elaborate guest suites.

A New York City restaurateur restored a formerly neglected old inn located on the main street at the edge of the commercial district. The refurbished Palm at the Huntting Inn was considered a nonconforming use in a residential zone. The successful operation could therefore not expand.

subdivision, the owner has offered the village a 5-year option to purchase the windmill, which requires a major restoration. Additionally the owner has offered to place an agricultural easement, preserving 3 acres in the middle of the site and restricting new development to the rear of the lot.

RESTORATION

The East Hampton *Design Manual for Landmarks and Historic Districts* follows the U.S. secretary of the interior's standards on the validity of preserving accretions over time. In one serious challenge to the ordinance, an owner, without first obtaining consent, removed a nineteenth-century front porch from an eighteenth-century house, revealing an elaborate wooden pediment over the entrance door. After much local debate, the owner was fined, but the porch was not restored.

CHANGING CHARACTER OF THE HISTORIC CORE

Several decades ago when undeveloped farmland and wooded acreage could have been acquired, East Hampton was unable to muster the support for a bypass route that would have diverted the principal highway route to Montauk from its main street. As a result the seasonal increase of traffic through the most historic core of the village is making the oldest and finest houses along its route less desirable, especially those in their original location close to the street. In the 1920s wealthy summer residents acquired some of the eighteenth-century houses, moved them back on their lots, and expanded them. East Hampton's single-family residential zoning is strictly enforced. Ironically, in order to preserve its original character, much of the streetscape is being turned into a stage set. Several properties are operated as museums by the village and the East Hampton Historical Society.

Hedges Inn, located on the village green in the historic district had passed through a succession of owners; it was acquired by The Palm for expansion. Thus two historic structures have been restored without disrupting the traditional character and scale of the old village core.

Among the few nonconforming uses on the main street are three old inns with restaurants that have not been allowed to expand. The 1770 House Inn has been permitted to acquire a large house facing the historic town pond in the village green to house the proprietor of the inn; the house also provides a few luxurious guest suites. The Palm at the Huntting Inn has acquired The Hedges, a former inn, as an annex. In all cases these annexes are not immediately adjacent to the existing inns.

The Gardiner Brown House is adjacent to the commercial center. The village board had sought to demolish the house to provide additional parking, but the house was rescued after a prolonged community effort, and it is now the headquarters of the LVIS, a local civic organization. This usage makes a convenient buffer to the adjacent residential area.

THE GARDINER BROWN HOUSE

A few years ago a dispute arose over a mansion at the edge of the business district. The eighteenth-century house had been moved back on its site and enlarged in 1925. The interior of the house was heavily damaged by fire, and the owner began restoring it. The village of East Hampton sought to purchase the site for the expansion of the adjacent public parking area serving the business district. A hue and cry from the neighbors and the local preservationists stopped the plan dead in its tracks, and the LVIS who campaigned for its rescue acquired the house for its own headquarters and thrift shop.

East Hampton Village is struggling to come to terms with preserving its past and the way of life of local residents, while at the same time trying to resist the pressures of gentrification by seasonal residents and visitors. In 1980, after considerable debate and controversy, the nearby town of Southampton did permit the conversion of McKim, Mead, and White's sprawling 52-room, Colonial Revival Style, Breese-Merrill mansion into condominium apartments with the construction of additional units on the site. Despite the success of the project, which is discretely concealed by tall hedgerows, there has not been another similar project attempted in the Hamptons. Only because these resorts have retained their fashionable status have the mansions been able to remain in single-family usage. As in well-to-do nonresort communities all over the country, there is tremendous resistance to permit multifamily conversions of mansions.

CHAPTER 5

Conservation of the Historic Landscape

In earlier chapters we have discussed the preservation of open space and large acreage. On the greatest estates with extensive landscape planting, the garden was a very specific element of the design. The garden was usually located immediately surrounding the house and provided pleasant vistas of the site as seen from the principal interior rooms. The approach drive to the main house was also a carefully orchestrated element of the landscaping. Sometimes the gardens incorporated existing site features and mature trees, but generally the garden was an artificial creation by the landscape architect, which required labor-intensive cultivation by a large specialized staff. In most cases neglected mansions have fared better than their gardens. This chapter provides some ideas on how traditional landscaping and gardens may be adapted to contemporary realities.

The Garden Story

In the mid-1970s when my book *Saving Large Estates* was published, the literature and documentation on American estate garden designs were very limited, and most period publications including Gertrude Jekyll's were out of print. That trend has now reversed, and there is a growing collection of illustrated books on the subject. One of the most comprehensive sources of information on the development of the landscape designs of American mansions and estates is the well-researched and lavishly illustrated book *The Golden Age of American Gardens: Proud Owners, Private Estates, 1890–1940,* by Mac Griswold, Eleanor Weller, Harry N. Abrams, in association with the Garden Club of America (1991).

The Garden Club of America was founded in 1913 in Germantown, Pennsylvania. By 1938 there were more than 2000 garden clubs with national affiliations across the country. This network became an important source of information on garden design and horticulture. The clubs organized garden tours and invited professional landscape designers to lecture. The garden clubs also photographed their gardens and amassed a collection of over a thousand hand color-tinted glass plate slides. These plus other photographic documentation are now a part of the Archives of American Gardens at the Office of Horticulture of the Smithsonian Institution.

In the twenties, in addition to gardening and horticultural journals, magazines such as *Country Life in America, House and Garden,* and *Town and Country* regularly featured country estates. These articles focused on architecture, interiors, gardens, and fashions. There was a great demand for illustrations, and women garden photographers such as Matty Hewitt became specialists.

When the professional education of both architects and landscape architecture were being formalized at the beginning of the century, both the faculties and the students were dominated by the male establishment, and women were refused admission. However, with the growth of the women's movement came the recognition that during the golden age, gardening was considered "lady's work." Horticulture was one of the first fields in which women's achievements were legitimately acknowledged. The most celebrated pioneering women garden designers were Beatrice Farrand (niece of Edith Wharton), Ellen Biddle Shipman, and Marian Cruger Coffin. These women became involved in landscape architecture before the formal schools would admit women, and consequently, they had to apprentice themselves with established male professionals in horticulture and landscape design to gain their education. Later they had to rely on their social connections to find clients.

Garden design reflected the changing modes of architectural style as well as variations in terrain and region. Transferring classic European garden design onto the American landscape was often problematic because of inhospitable climates such as existed in Santa Barbara, California. Dry desert climates required irrigation, and in Shelburne, Vermont, where extreme winter cold prevailed, all the bay trees had to be planted in tubs so that they could later be moved indoors under glass.

The landscapes of the Shingle Style cottages of the 1880s were a continuation of the gardenesque manner of the Victorian period. By 1890 the next generation of houses

Overleaf Garden facade of the John S. Phipps mansion, Old Westbury Gardens. It was originally only seasonal, but it is now planted for public visitation year-round. The continued involvement of the family has perpetuated its authentic and special character, and has been a major factor in its preservation.

became more elaborate and historically derived. They were built of masonry in the styles of Colonial Revival, French Renaissance, then Louis XVI, English Georgian, and Tudor. The garden design borrowed liberally from the European Renaissance tradition. In the next wave McKim, Mead, and White, Carrere and Hastings, and Charles Platt designed mansions based on the Beaux-Arts aesthetic. The formal axial plan of the house was extended out into the garden and the landscape. Leading out from the house, large terraces were paved in stone or brick, sometimes elaborated with a geometric pattern of flower parterres and stone balustrades. One usually descended gracious steps on a manicured lawn, or *tapis vert,* passing through a symmetrical *allée* of trees, which framed a monumental vista and which was decorated with ornamental urns and classical sculpture on pedestals. Reflecting pools and fountains were a usual component. Shaded loggias, gazebos, and teahouses created pleasant areas for strolling and enjoying the gardens. Over the years severe weather and neglect can play havoc with these ornamental features, and the cost of restoring the gardens may exceed that of the mansion.

At their grandest, estate landscapes, such as Deering's Vizcaya in Florida, Hearst's San Simeon in California, and George Vanderbilt's Biltmore in North Carolina emulated the tradition of European royalty. All three of these extraordinary mansions and their gardens have survived and are open to the public.

Snob appeal and the Anglophobia of the nouveau riche required importing "Kew-trained" English, Irish, or Scotish head gardeners or estate managers. Extravagant garden "fetes" and costume balls were a mark of social arrival. Before the turn of the century, poor transportation and remote locations required longer or seasonal stays. With fewer distractions—no radio, television, or cinema—the estate had to be self-sufficient providing varied entertainment and distractions for a multigenerational household, including guests and staff.

The post–Civil War period saw the introduction in America of English upper-class pastimes and sports: yachting, sailing, croquet, bowling, lawn tennis, badminton, golf, fishing, shooting, duck hunting, horse breeding and racing, polo, coach driving, fox hunting, and big game hunting. Trophies were to be won and displayed. Even though restricted membership clubs were being formed by the wealthy, the extremely rich set up their own private playgrounds requiring vast acreage.

In the 1920s there was a reaction to the formality and rigidity of the Beaux-Arts formula and return to a preference for a more picturesque and intimate relationship between house and garden. Derived from English Tudor manor houses and French Norman Style farm prototypes, constructed of stone and stucco, half-timbered and slate roofed, these houses were set in lushly planted gardens, enclosed with hedges and shrubs, mixing native species with imported trees for woodland settings. These sometimes walled gardens were well suited to suburban settings, where large mansions were sited on limited acreage.

Another important trend was the popularity of the Colonial Revival Style. Before World War I, architects Grovesnor Atterbury, John Russell Pope, and Delano and Aldrich had produced elegant sumptuous country houses in restrained Georgian and Adamesque modes set in the landscapes reminiscent of an English park. During the 1920s and 1930s, the restoration of Williamsburg by John D. Rockefeller, Jr., attracted a lot of attention. Perhaps even more than with Perry, Shaw, Hepburn, and Dean's architectural restorations, a great many of the gardens planned by landscape architect Arthur A. Shurcliff were based on scant historic documentation or archaeological evidence. More recent scholarship seems to indicate that Williamsburg's gardens were probably more sparse and less manicured.

Although many of the grand houses survive, very few of the gardens of the golden age survive, and those that have do so in considerably reduced splendor. Many were originally seasonal gardens, cultivated only for the brief period of the year when the owners were in residence during their annual perigrination following the climate and the fashionable resort calendar. In the days before year-round climate control and central air conditioning, travel was the only way to cope with bad weather, industrial pollution, and periodic epidemics.

Winter in Palm Beach, Pasadena, spring in Europe or at home in New York, Boston, or Philadelphia, summer in the Adirondacks, Mount Desert, Maine, New Hampshire, the Berkshires, or Asheville, fall at home again. Old Westbury Gardens, on New York's Long Island gold coast, was originally only seasonal but now is planted year-round for year-round visitors.

Even with proper maintenance gardens change over time due to natural causes such as plant disease (Dutch Elm disease), insect infestation (gypsy moths), or storm damage (heavy snow, hurricanes, high winds). Overgrowth is also a problem, often blocking original views (at Teddy Roosevelt's Sagamore Hill, Oyster Bay Harbor is no longer visible from the house). Many of the exotic and ornamental plants and flower varieties favored at the turn of the century are no longer available.

Cheap labor was a necessity since very little of the ancient gardening techniques had been mechanized or modernized at the turn of the century. Horses, teams, and hand-digging were the methods for clearing the land, draining marshes, creating canals and ponds, moving large stones, planting trees, and arranging sculpture and ornaments. The last hurrah for the golden age of American gardens was not so much the depression years as World War II when immigration was interrupted and the gardeners were drafted.

Despite the problems of maintaining historic gardens today, in various parts of the United States major estate gardens and landscapes are now open to the public.

The post-1960s interest in ecology and the out-of-doors has sparked an interest in gardening, and The Nature Conservancy movement has attracted broad public support as well as pressure for the preservation of open space. Since the great estate combines both the mansion and the cultivated landscape, there are instances in which the devotees of historic houses and the conservationists have joined forces.

A recently formed group, The Garden Conservancy, has a board of advisors drawn from all over the United States. They define their mission as a national organization working to preserve exceptional American gardens by facilitating their transition from private to nonprofit ownership and operation. In addition, the Conservancy assumes a role as advocate for the preservation or restoration of important American gardens, and it is a resource for community groups and public agencies seeking advice and support in such efforts, through its technical assistance program.

As an example of the kind of partnerships and cooperation that is possible, the conservancy has signed a 4-year management agreement with the New Hampshire Division of Parks, for the John Hay estate in Newbury, New Hampshire. The conservancy will develop and implement plans for the revitalization of the landscape at "The Fells," focusing on its period of peak development in the 1930s.

Using a pool of state and private funds, the conservancy will hire horticultural and administrative staff and begin a phased restoration of the gardens at the site, which include a hillside rock garden, a perennial border, and a romantic woodland ruin. The conservancy will coordinate its efforts with the John Hay Commission, which has oversight for the John Hay National Wildlife Refuge. The refuge includes a Colonial Revival Shingle Style house and designed landscape as well as the surrounding 165-acre natural area.

Lasdon Estate, Somers, New York

SITE

Lasdon, in Somers, New York, was one of many large suburban estates founded in northern Westchester County in the 1930s. It was built by Dr. A. P. Voislawsky in the 1930s and was designed by architects Taylor and Levi. It was owned by the Lasdon family from 1940 until 1985 when the county purchased the property. The rear facade of the rambling Colonial Revival building is distinguished by a five-bay, double-height portico reminiscent of Mount Vernon.

The rear garden facade of the Lasdon's Colonial Revival Style mansion. The public acquisition of a large scenic tract of open space, meadows, woods, trails, and ponds was of greater importance than the preservation of the mansion and its surrounding garden.

The mansion, which is a worthy Colonial Revival house but not of great architectural or historical significance, is only a part of what makes Lasdon special. Of greater significance are the 208 acres of open space. Lasdon encompasses a Vietnam memorial, 16 acres of lawn sloping toward the main road, a 3.5-acre house and garden compound, and 160 acres of meadows, wood trails, and ponds. The house and garden compound is situated at the rear of the property, not at all visible from the road.

PRESERVATION ISSUE

In private ownership until it came on the market in 1984, Lasdon was one of the largest undeveloped sites remaining in northern Westchester. Located near Muscoot Reservoir, a county-owned farm museum, and the Croton Reservoir, both of which are watershed areas for New York City's water system, the development of such a large site had the potential to jeopardize the stability of two environmentally sensitive sites. The estate is located on the community's main thoroughfare and was tempting for residential or corporate headquarters because two large corporations, Pepsi and IBM, had recently built large office complexes in the community.

Westchester County acquired the estate in 1985 with an eye to marketing the property as a development site for a conference center–inn in 1986 because of its proximity to these corporate facilities. Proposed development was limited to approximately 25 of the 208 acres, with the mansion to be preserved and used as a guest inn and dining and administrative facilities while a conference center and additional rooms designed in an architectural style compatible with the Colonial Revival mansion could be built on a portion of the property. The proposed development site was located at the rear property line and focused around the house and its ancillary structures. The conference center would not have been visible from the main road, and a development proviso was inserted that the views of the property be maintained. The sculpture garden was to be restored and maintained by the developer, and the trees and plantings of the estate were to be respected as much as possible in the development. The remaining property was to be left as undeveloped open space.

No adequate proposals were received, and Westchester County decided that the property, which had a mature and varied landscape, would be best used as an arboretum, gardens, and forest preserve for use by Westchester County residents.

Lasdon Arboretum preserved the existing established landscape while building on the site's aesthetic value. The arboretum, with plant specimens, theme gardens, and course instruction, was designed to be a place where anyone interested in plant materials, trees, shrubs, and perennials could obtain an informal education in a recreational activity. The extensive collection of mature trees and shrubs, the formal gardens, and the azalea and rhododendron garden of the original estate were preserved, while collections of woodland, wetland, shade-loving, and ornamental plantings, specimen trees, and many other plant species were added or enhanced. In addition, a walking trail system will ultimately connect with the Muscoot Reservoir to the south.

The main house serves as the office for the arboretum as well as office for the Federated Garden Clubs of New York State and the county horticultural library.

The county expects to have the park in operation in the near future. The 16 acres of lawn near the main road will be available for revenue-producing events such as arts and crafts shows and antique shows. Access to the house and garden compound is limited to pedestrians (with the exception of disabled access), and the house itself, the occupancy of which is limited by code to 50 people, is available only for use by government departments and nonprofit organizations for conference and meeting space.

SIGNIFICANCE

Westchester County, in preserving the 208-acre Lasdon estate, took advantage of the availability of an unusually large and scenic parcel of land to preserve both the character of northern Westchester, which was experiencing dramatic growth, and to protect two reservoirs that impact the drinking water of New York City and Westchester residents. The county is providing a recreational center that will be enjoyed by residents and school groups and that will eventually serve as a tourist attraction for the county, while essentially keeping the site in an undeveloped state. In creating an arboretum on the site when a modest-scale development was rejected by the private sector, the county has balanced public group cultural and recreational access to an environmentally sensitive property with the generation of limited revenue to help maintain the site.

Wethersfield, Amenia, New York

SITE

In the *Golden Age of American Gardens; Proud Owners, Private Estates, 1890–1940*, Chauncey Stillman's estate, Wethersfield, begun in 1937 at Amenia, New York, has the distinction of being one of the last of the great formal gardens created. Its 10 acres of garden are divided into three parts: the Inner and Outer Gardens, and the Wilderness Plantings. When Stillman acquired the initial acreage, it was a hillside cow farm on the highest point overlooking the Berkshires and the Catskills. By the time of his death in 1989, his country estate had grown to 1200 acres.

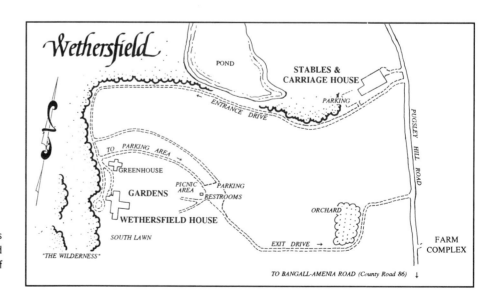

Small-scale overall site plan of Wethersfield as arranged for visitors. Thus far modest-sized parking lots are adequate for the number of visitors.

Wethersfield's main house in the Georgian Revival Style is compact and understated, providing views across the south terrace to the distant hills and valleys on one side and opening onto a loggia projecting into the intimate walled Inner Garden.

The gardens were Stillman's real love, and the 1939 Georgian Style, brick and brownstone house by architect Bancel La Farge is modest in scale, not really a "mansion" in the grand manner. The landscape architect Evelyn N. Poehler worked with the owner from 1947 through the mid-sixties. Sculptures, including a fountain group by Carl Milles, are an important focus of the gardens, which are arranged as a terraced series of outdoor rooms with distant vistas to the surrounding farm valleys.

Plantings frame the vista from the Hilltop Belvedere toward distant farm valleys.

The stable complex located on the flat terrain beneath the house on the hilltop, which contains a skylit, roofed-over former courtyard and an elegant collection of superbly maintained sporting and formal carriages, leather harnesses, prize ribbons, and polished silver trophies.

PRESERVATION ISSUE

Wethersfield garden plan as arranged for visitors. The primary focus of the property are the gardens and stable complex rather than the interior of the house.

Stillman planned for the future transition of his house and his beloved gardens to public visitation. He established the Homeland Foundation that now operates Wethersfield. Open seasonally, visitor parking, guided tours, picnic areas, and handicapped-accessible restrooms have been created. The carriage house and stable complex, with

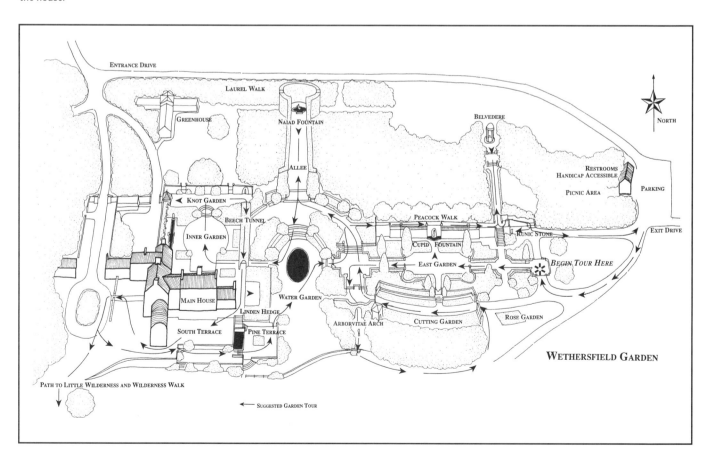

its elaborate collection of carriages and trophies, is maintained in immaculate condition and may also visited. Local equestrian events are held on the fenced fields and grounds.

SIGNIFICANCE

Like Chauncey Stillman, many owners who have devoted so much of their energy and resources in planning, developing, and cultivating their estate landscapes are moved to perpetuate and share the beauty of their formerly private domains. Because of the smooth transition planned by Stillman, many of those employed at Wethersfield represent the continuity of staff who personally served him and appreciated his high standards. Perhaps because of this, visitors can still sense the force of his personality, which pervades the estate. Whether this quality can be sustained in the future is a challenge to the Homeland Foundation. Thus far the newness of the arrangements for the public and its rural location have attracted neighbors and a modest stream of visitors.

Naumkeag, Stockbridge, Massachusetts

SITE

Joseph Hodges Choate was a noted attorney and ambassador to England at the turn of the century. When Choate and his wife Catherine Sterling Choate decided to build a summer home on their Stockbridge hill, they chose Charles McKim, who assigned it to Stanford White. To help site the house, they sought the advice of the Olmstead brothers. When they rejected the Olmsteads' suggestions, they gave the commission

The celebrated Perugino vista toward the Berkshires, inspired by the similarity to the landscapes in the background of the Italian masters' paintings, extends far beyond the boundaries of the Choates' property.

McKim, Mead, and White's Shingle Style cottage with its turrets adds a picturesque touch of variety to an otherwise bulky yet compact mansion.

to Nathan Barrett of Boston. The great unpainted Shingle Style "cottage" which Stanford White designed in 1885, one of the last he designed in that mode, was relatively comfortable and rustic compared to the extravagant mansions and showplaces that proliferated in the nearby resort communities of the Berkshire Hills at the turn of the century.

One of the afternoon gardens created by Mabel Choate and Fletcher Steele. A carpet of flower beds, a shallow reflecting pool, and imitation painted venetian gondola posts, as well as Frederick Macmonnies' sculpture of Boy with Heron, are the fanciful elements of this intimate garden terrace.

The Choates' daughter Mabel inherited Naumkeag from her parents in 1929 and maintained it until her death in 1958. She kept all the house furnishings and contents arranged as they had been in her childhood, while adding a few modern conveniences, American furniture, and her fabled collection of Chinese Lowestoft china.

She was a passionate gardener, and, together with Fletcher Steele, a pioneering modern landscape architect, between 1926 and 1955 transformed Barrett's original Victorian gardens into a unique and eclectic showplace. The "blue steps," the "floral carpet," and the ribbon pattern of the rose garden are some of its most distinctive features. Naumkeag possesses one of the four finest gardens ever created in the Berkshires.

PRESERVATION ISSUE

In 1958 Mabel Choate bequeathed Naumkeag to the Massachusetts Trustees of Reservations, and they have since operated Naumkeag as a house museum. The trustees are scrupulously faithful to the maintenance of the mansion, its interiors, and the formal gardens and landscape. Naumkeag represents the quintessential "Berkshire cottage," as exemplified by the Choate family's period furnishings and their own historic significance in the development of the Stockbridge summer colony. Naumkeag does justify its maintenance as a museum. Located on a steep narrow hillside road, its popularity does cause congestion, and parking is a problem. Because of the wealth of musical and cultural events available in Stockbridge and the nearby Berkshire resort town, there are always many visitors, and no special programs are offered on the site. There are fees for seasonal tours, and portions of the site are available for rental for private functions.

Naumkeag garden plan as arranged for visitors. The landscape and planting maintains the mature appearance Mabel Choate and Fletcher Steele nurtured over many decades.

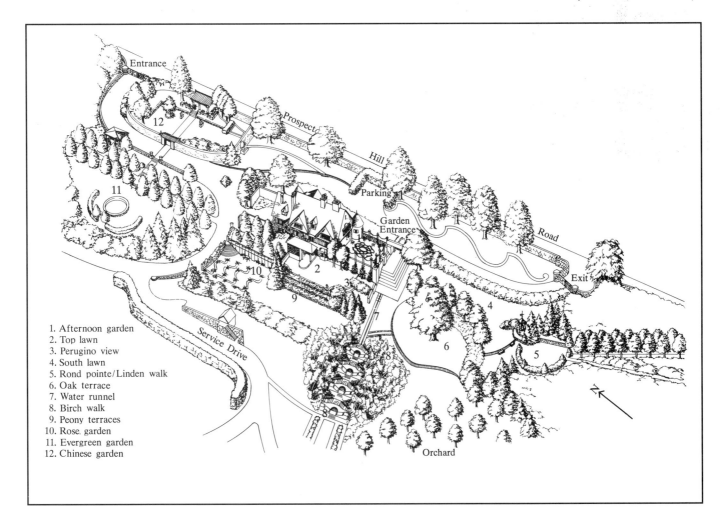

1. Afternoon garden
2. Top lawn
3. Perugino view
4. South lawn
5. Rond pointe/Linden walk
6. Oak terrace
7. Water runnel
8. Birch walk
9. Peony terraces
10. Rose garden
11. Evergreen garden
12. Chinese garden

SIGNIFICANCE

Because so many of the once-numerous great Berkshire estates have been demolished, altered, or adapted to other uses, it is important that Naumkeag remain open to the public. The Trustees of Reservations (TTOR) were founded in 1891 by Boston landscape architect Charles Eliot and served as the model for the British National Trust established in 1895. The Trustees of Reservations are dedicated to preserving for public use and enjoyment properties of exceptional scenic, historic, and ecological value throughout the Commonwealth of Massachusetts. From the beginning it has combined historic preservation with land conservation.

At Cherry-Hill Farm in Canton, the Georgian Style house and formal gardens were designed by architect Charles A. Platt in 1902. The Eleanor Cabot Bradley Reservation, as it is now known, is an 84-acre natural area open for hiking, picnicking, and cross-country skiing, but the house is open only by appointment. What is significant is that the house, as the focal point of the ensemble of house and grounds, is maintained.

As of 1992 this unique organization owns and manages 73 properties, totaling more than 18,000 acres, all open to the public. Over the years The Trustees of Reservations have been supported by donors, and they have built up a sizable endowment. Their membership is over 10,000, many of whom contribute volunteer services to assist the permanent staff in the operations and maintenance of their huge inventory of sites.

Through their recently founded Land Conservation Center, TTOR reaches out to landowners and cooperating land trusts, communities, and state agencies, with a program of technical assistance, strategic partnerships, encouragement, and public education.

In many ways The Trustees of Reservations serve a function much the same as the state parks systems, but their private nonprofit status gives them much greater flexibility than government agencies have.

CHAPTER 6

Modern House Museums

77

Many of the early "modern" houses from the beginning of the twentieth century through the early fifties have been recognized as classic examples of architectural design. Houses of this period seldom reached the enormous size of the more "traditional" houses of the same period. Many of them remain quite suitable for continued use as single-family residences. Ironically modern buildings have proved more difficult to sensitively adapt to new uses or enlarge. Some are complete with their original architect-designed furnishings and thus represent such an artistically unified ensemble inside and out that they must be preserved as a whole. The new and sometimes experimental materials and construction techniques employed in these houses now require major structural repairs in addition to the more usual cosmetic restoration.

Public recognition of the significance of modern architecture and American-born geniuses such as Frank Lloyd Wright and the Greene brothers has complicated their survival. There is now such a demand by collectors and museums that architectural elements and furniture are more valuable than preserving the houses intact. The Metropolitan Museum in New York displays the living room with its original furnishings of Frank Lloyd Wright's 1913 Little House, "Northome," Wayzata, Minnesota, which was demolished by its owners. The Victoria and Albert Museum in London has on display Edgar J. Kaufmann's 1937 Frank Lloyd Wright–designed office interior from Pittsburgh, Pennsylvania. "Modern" is now displayed along with other furnished "period" rooms.

Restoring Early Frank Lloyd Wright Houses

In the early 1980s, the Chicago architectural firm of Hasbrouck, Peterson, now HPZS (Hasbrouck, Peterson, Zimoch, and Sirirattumrong), was commissioned to guide the restoration of three of Frank Lloyd Wright's major residential commissions of his "Prairie Style" period, the Dana house in Springfield, Illinois, the Martin house in Buffalo, New York, and the Robie house in Chicago.

Wilburt R. Hasbrouck, FAIA, a principal in the HPZS firm, feels that he has gained an interesting professional perspective from being so intensively involved with three major Wright masterpieces of the pre–World War I era. All three had been transferred to institutional or governmental ownership when the restoration planning began, so that the approach to dealing with these bureaucracies was similar, requiring a great deal of patience and perseverance.

In each case the task had to be divided into several phases. The general pattern involved: first the preparation of the Historic Structure Report, then an analysis of alternative uses, followed by the preparation of detailed plans for the restoration of the exterior and interior, as well as coordinating a team of specialist consultants. These consultants were charged with revising the old mechanical systems to meet modern standards of efficiency, providing creative solutions to the unobtrusive concealment of climate control, fire protection, and security systems, and providing for barrier-free access. Additionally, experts on art glass restoration and museum consultants were sought out for advice. Detailed and accurate cost projections for all phases of the work were also required.

Dana-Thomas House, Springfield, Illinois

SITE

Susan Lawrence Dana commissioned Frank Lloyd Wright in 1902 to design an expansion of her father's nineteenth-century Italianate villa. Wright was somewhat restricted in developing the plan because of the necessity of building around the earlier house. The 12,600-square-foot extraordinary house was completed in 1904 and

Overleaf This interior view of the living room of the Meyer May house reveals its dazzling geometric stained glass windows, continuing above, forming skylights. The remarkable quality of this restoration, with its painstaking attention to architectural detail as well as furnishings and interior finishes, is exceptional.

contained several rooms that for the first time rose two stories. The design provided intimate private living quarters on the upper floor and generous entertaining spaces on the main-level floor as well as a billiard room and a bowling alley in the basement.

Located a few blocks from the state capitol, the house functioned as a gathering place for Springfield's progressive politicians and then as a center of the city's cultural life. Forty years later as Dana's fortunes and health declined, the house was allowed to deteriorate.

In 1943 Dana sold the house and the furnishings to Charles and Nanette Thomas, who used the structure for the next 35 years as offices for their small publishing company. The Thomases respected Wright's work and maintained the house as well as they could with their limited means.

PRESERVATION ISSUES

Few of Wright's early houses have had the good fortune to have remained with original furnishings intact and also to have had sympathetic later owners who did not significantly alter or damage the original interiors. But perhaps the most significant factor in the restoration was to have as a governor a man who also was an antiques collector and who was attracted to the preservation effort. Governor James Thomson convinced the state to acquire the house in 1983. Thompson personally oversaw the fund-raising for the $5 million restoration and for reacquisition of several missing objects. The value of Wright-designed artifacts and furnishings had already become astronomical. The house is now open, free to the public as a house museum, unique among Wright's surviving houses for the completeness of its original furnishings and decor.

Architects Hasbrouck Peterson Associates, now HPZS, oversaw various teams of skilled artisans in several phases from 1984 through 1990. Exterior work included reproducing the missing decorative plaster frieze under the eaves from the original molds and matching its green and bronze patina. The art windows were covered and protected with new theft-resistant storm windows. They repointed Wright's horizontally recessed brick joints and patched spalled colored concrete. On the interior they duplicated Wright's original textured tinted and glazed plaster finishes.

In order to accommodate the transition to a house museum, several modifications had to be made in the mechanical systems. The old electrical systems were abandoned, and the house was completely rewired, permitting Wright's innovative

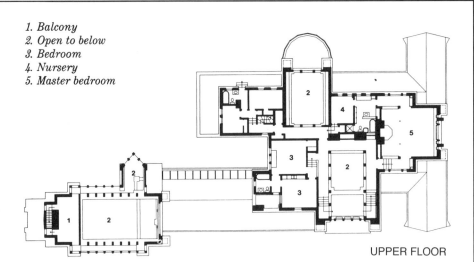

1. Balcony
2. Open to below
3. Bedroom
4. Nursery
5. Master bedroom

UPPER FLOOR

Upper-floor plan of the Dana house. A great deal of the upper floor is occupied by balconied upper spaces overlooking the major spaces below.

6. Gallery
7. Conservatory
8. Servants
9. Breakfast nook
10. Dining
11. Reception hall
12. Parlor
13. Living room
14. Porch

MAIN FLOOR

Main-floor plan of the Dana house. Remarkably almost all the original furnishings, light fixtures, and stained glass remain intact, making the Dana house one of the largest of Wright's residential commissions and the most exceptional of the Prairie houses open to the public.

15. Library
16. Bowling alley
17. Office
18. Coat room
19. Billiard room
20. Entry
21. Archival storage

N

BASEMENT

Basement floor plan of the Dana house. Because an on-site carriage house has been converted to a visitors' center, all the principal spaces have been restored to their original appearance. A few secondary spaces have been adapted to offices and archival usage.

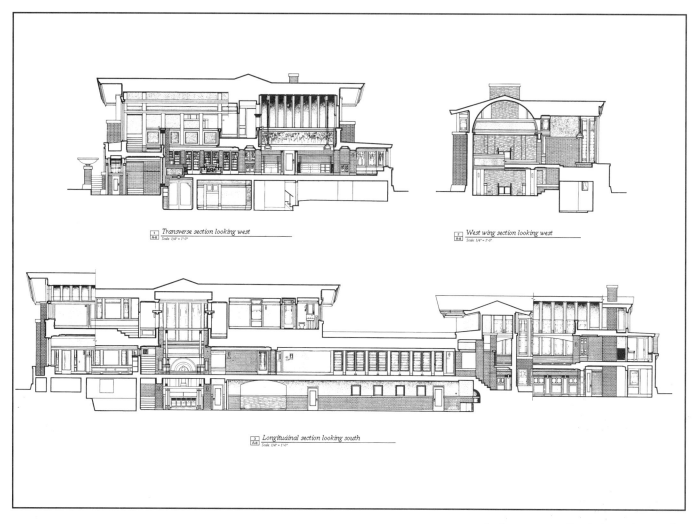

1
A-8
Transverse section looking west
Scale 1/4" = 1'-0"

2
A-8
West wing section looking west
Scale 1/4" = 1'-0"

3
A-8
Longitudinal section looking south
Scale 1/4" = 1'-0"

In these cross-sectional views, the complex spatial organization of the Dana house is revealed.

concealed lighting systems to be restored. A new forced-air hvac system was installed to provide year-round visitor comfort and also to provide better conservation conditions for the museum-quality artifacts and furnishings.

As is the case with much of Wright's residential work of this period, it was always in stark contrast to its more conventional neighbors and remains so today. The design of the house is bold enough to stand on its own despite the blandness of the adjacent buildings that abut the property.

SIGNIFICANCE

The rescue of the Dana-Thomas house demonstrates how a public official with an appreciation of historic buildings can really make a difference. Similarly Governor Nelson Rockefeller engineered the acquisition and restoration by New York State of Olana, the exotic creation of Frederick Edwin Church, the renowned painter of the Hudson River school.

This exceptional Wright house would have been difficult to adapt to another use even if its original furnishings had not remained intact. The escalating market of collectors and museums competing for Wright's furnishings, artifacts, and architectural elements means that even though more of his surviving houses may eventually be restored, there is scant possibility that any others will be able to reacquire their dispersed original furnishings. This certainly justifies the state of Illinois restoration of the Dana-Thomas residence and its operation as a house museum.

The main entrance of the Martin house facade as it appeared in 1989. In the background on the right can be seen the roofs of a modern apartment block built on the site of Martin's original garages, and a stained glass windowed corridor leading to the greenhouses. Otherwise, the general character of the surroundings maintains the original context in a neighborhood of substantial and well-maintained residences.

Darwin D. Martin House, Buffalo, New York

SITE

The Darwin D. Martin house, a National Historic Landmark, designed by Frank Lloyd Wright, was built in 1904 to 1906. The house is located on a large corner lot in a prestigious residential neighborhood of large homes of the well-to-do of Buffalo. It was commissioned by Darwin D. Martin, a high-ranking executive of the Larkin Company for whom Wright designed a unique headquarters in 1904 through 1906 that featured a large skylit central atrium. The headquarters building was demolished in 1950.

The original Martin complex was reportedly built on an unlimited budget and distinguished from most of Wright's Prairie Style houses by its large size and open plan. The site originally included the main residence, a long glazed pergola leading to a conservatory linked to a garage, and also another smaller house built for George W. Barton, Martin's brother-in-law. Barton was also involved in the Larkin Company management, and the house built for him in 1903 to 1904 still survives today on a separate lot.

By the 1950s the main house had experienced periods of neglect and vandalism; and in 1954 the Martin house was subdivided into two apartments and an owner's apartment. The conservatory, pergola, and garage were demolished and replaced by a group of undistinguished garden apartments.

In 1966 the Martin house was purchased by the State University of New York (SUNY), at the urging of Martin Meyerson as the university president's residence. In 1967 it was partially restored by architect Edgar Tafel, a former Wright apprentice at Taliesin in the late 1930s. After a few years Meyerson moved on and the next university president refused to live in the Martin house. It subsequently served as headquarters for the alumni association and the repository for the university archives. By the late 1980s the house was seriously in need of major repairs and restoration. Poorly or inappropriately maintained for two decades, much of its original decorative elements, including some of its "tree of life" pattern art glass panels were removed and sold to collectors and museums.

PRESERVATION ISSUE

The Chicago architectural firm of Hasbrouck, Peterson, Zimroch, and Sirirattumrong (HPZS) was engaged in 1989 to prepare a comprehensive conservation plan to restore

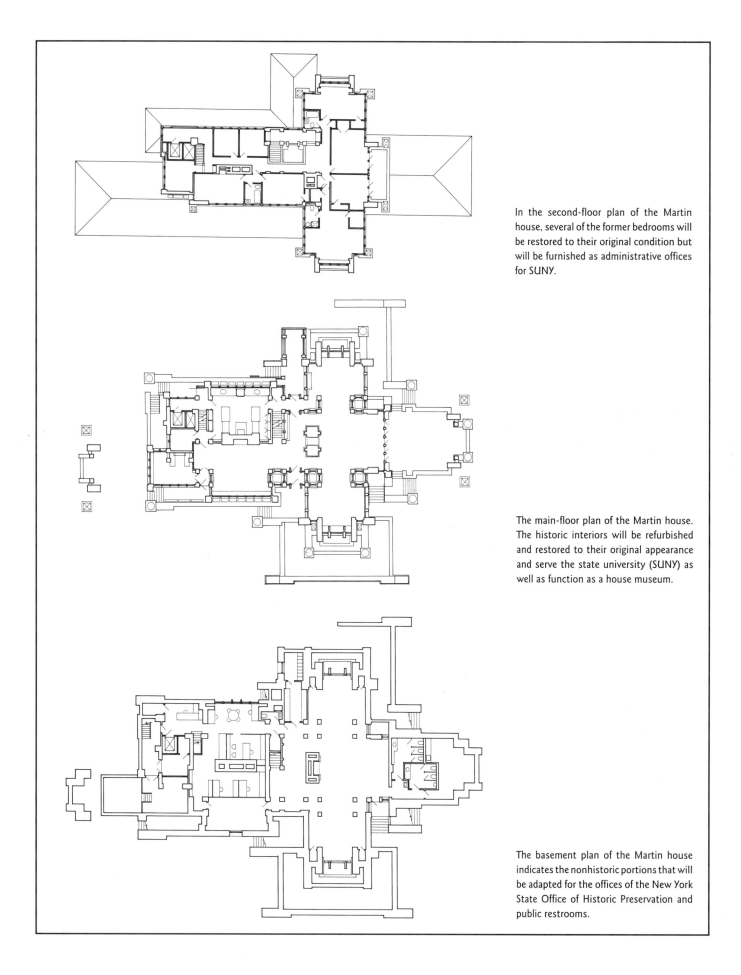

In the second-floor plan of the Martin house, several of the former bedrooms will be restored to their original condition but will be furnished as administrative offices for SUNY.

The main-floor plan of the Martin house. The historic interiors will be refurbished and restored to their original appearance and serve the state university (SUNY) as well as function as a house museum.

The basement plan of the Martin house indicates the nonhistoric portions that will be adapted for the offices of the New York State Office of Historic Preservation and public restrooms.

the building to its appearance circa 1915 to 1919 and to adapt various nonhistoric portions of the building as administrative spaces.

The program for the conservation plan is complex. The Martin house will be used as a museum example of Wright's Prairie Style architecture. The museum function is to be administered by SUNY, and several second-floor bedrooms will be restored to their original condition but will be furnished as administrative spaces. The actual ownership of the house is being transferred to the New York State Office of Historic Preservation (NYHPA), who will have offices in the nonhistoric basement area of the house. Certain facilities in the building will be used jointly by SUNY and NYHPA. All of these programmatic requirements must be accomplished while maintaining the basic architectural integrity of the Martin house.

HPZS, as in its Dana and Robie House restoration projects, included mechanical and electrical consultants, a museum advisor, historic landscape consultant, and several other specialists. Cost estimates were especially critical in view of the fact that funds would be available on a one-time-only appropriation from the state legislature.

SIGNIFICANCE

It is amazing that even though the significance of the Martin house has been long recognized locally and nationally, it has had to survive nearly four decades of neglect. As in the case of the Robie house in Chicago, which is still owned by the University of Chicago, it is clear that the institutional owners have many other demands and priorities that make it a burden to devote sufficient resources to the special needs of historic properties.

The New York Office of Historic Preservation was reluctant to take on the stewardship of the Martin house in addition to its existing responsibilities for a far-flung network of historic house museums, battlefields, and historic sites scattered all over New York State. Unlike SUNY it does have the experience of managing and maintaining historic structures. With its staff of preservation specialists and artisans, central conservation workshop facilities including the laboratories of the state archaeologist, it is better equipped than SUNY to cope with the problems of the Martin house. The NYHPA also depends on the shifting funding priorities of the state legislature to respond to the increased demands for technical assistance from local historic societies and groups owning historic structures.

The joint operation of a historic site by NYHPA and SUNY parallels a pattern of the National Trust for Historic Preservation, which has developed partnerships with local groups restoring and operating historic properties such as the Frank Lloyd Wright home and studio in Oak Park, Illinois.

Robie House, Chicago, Illinois

SITE

The Frederick C. Robie house, a National Historic Landmark, was completed in 1910 from plans prepared by Frank Lloyd Wright. It is located near the University of Chicago's South Side Campus and has been owned by the university for several decades. The Robie house had been previously refurbished by the Chicago office of Skidmore, Owings and Merrill, for use as a conference center.

PRESERVATION ISSUE

Architects Hasbrouck, Peterson, Zimroch, and Sirirattumrong (HPZS) were engaged in 1992 to prepare a comprehensive plan to restore the building to its appearance circa 1915 and to adapt various nonhistoric portions of the house as administrative spaces.

This exterior view of the Robie house emphasizes the exaggerated horizontality characteristic of Wright's Prairie houses of the early 1900s. Many of these cantilevered roof overhangs have proved a source of structural problems after 80 to 90 years of exposure to severe winter weather.

The program for the restoration was prepared by HPZS in conjunction with the university planner and a public advisory committee assembled for that purpose. The work began with an in-depth historic structure report. Various alternative uses were considered, and the ultimate plan calls for a meticulous restoration of the exterior and interior public spaces. Service areas, never conceived of as the visible part of the house, are being adapted as administrative offices and public restrooms. Complete new mechanical and security systems are to be integrated in the building in an unobtrusive manner. While the primary use of the Robie house will be as a house museum, provision has been made for its use for various university functions such as small seminars, meetings, and entertaining visiting dignitaries.

HPZS assembled a special team to perform the services required on this complex planning effort. Included were mechanical and electric consultants, an art glass specialist, security consultant, and several other specialists. The last stages of the planning process were completed in 1993, and the restoration will proceed. Cost estimates were extremely critical in view of the fact that funds were available only from private donors.

SIGNIFICANCE

Architect Hasbrouck has observed that the Robie house has not been well maintained over the past 30 years. Numerous interior decorative elements were missing, and all original interior surfaces had been painted or otherwise defaced. These circumstances are not unique to the Robie house. Typically university facilities management staffs have neither the expertise nor the funding available to monitor historic buildings and provide for their special needs. This is equally true for more traditional landmark structures as well as early "modern" masterpieces. The application of conventional university maintenance standards and methods can jeopardize these outstanding historic architectural artifacts.

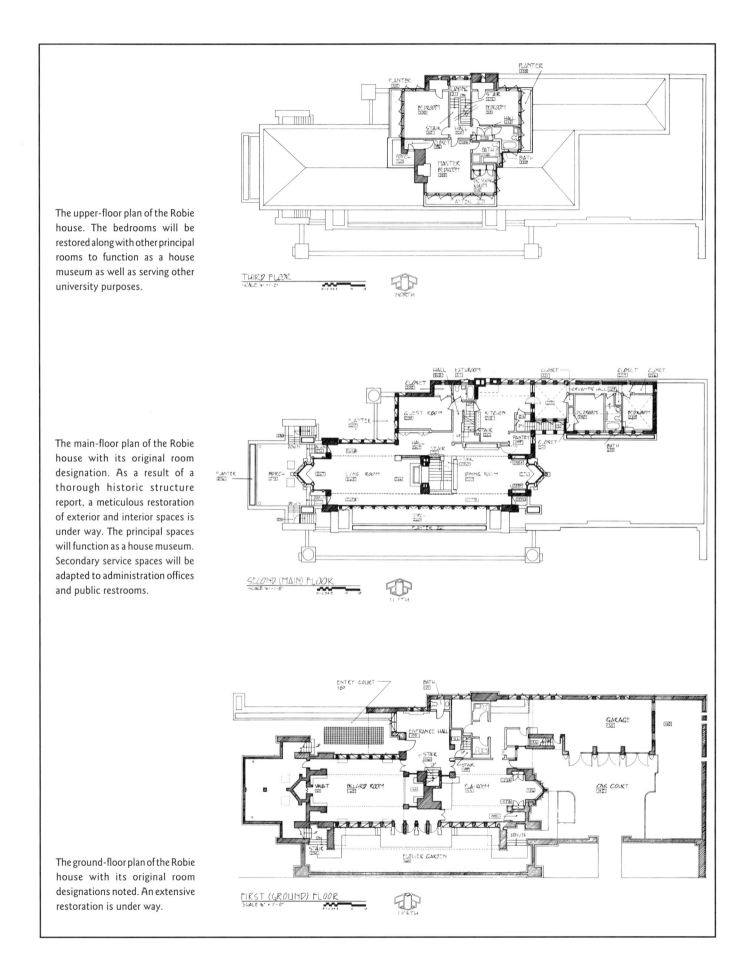

THIRD FLOOR
SCALE ⅛" = 1'-0"

NORTH

The upper-floor plan of the Robie house. The bedrooms will be restored along with other principal rooms to function as a house museum as well as serving other university purposes.

SECOND (MAIN) FLOOR
SCALE ⅛" = 1'-0"

NORTH

The main-floor plan of the Robie house with its original room designation. As a result of a thorough historic structure report, a meticulous restoration of exterior and interior spaces is under way. The principal spaces will function as a house museum. Secondary service spaces will be adapted to administration offices and public restrooms.

FIRST (GROUND) FLOOR
SCALE ⅛" = 1'-0"

NORTH

The ground-floor plan of the Robie house with its original room designations noted. An extensive restoration is under way.

Meyer May House, Grand Rapids, Michigan

SITE

The Meyer May house is located in Heritage Hill Historic District of Grand Rapids. The house was designed and built for Meyer S. May, a local clothier. The house was designed by Frank Lloyd Wright in 1909, during the prolific period of the development of his Prairie Style in Illinois and Wisconsin. It was designed and built at the same time as the Robie house in Chicago. Though not as large as some of his commissions at the time, it displays the same design characteristics of horizontality. Set back from the street, it has substantial stone-capped roman brick base walls and planters extending from the house and its projecting verandahs and low terraces. The large shallow pitched roofs hover over the masonry masses with broad overhangs. The house has the geometric patterned art glass strip windows on the upper story, and some unique copper sheathed mullions and faciae on the living room windows.

Over the years numerous additions had substantially altered the exterior appearance, and the interior had been damaged by many remodelings and conversion into apartments.

PRESERVATION ISSUE

To the rescue in 1985 came Steelcase, Inc., a Grand Rapids office furniture manufacturer, who acquired the house for educational purposes as well as public and corporate functions. Wright had collaborated with Steelcase in the 1930s designing innovative workstations for Johnson's Wax Company in Racine, Wisconsin.

Architect John Tilton of the Chicago firm of Tilton and Lewis and preservation coordinator Carla Lind assembled a team of art historians and decorative arts consultants to research the house's original design and furnishings. After considerable detective work, they were able to gather from various sources enough documentation

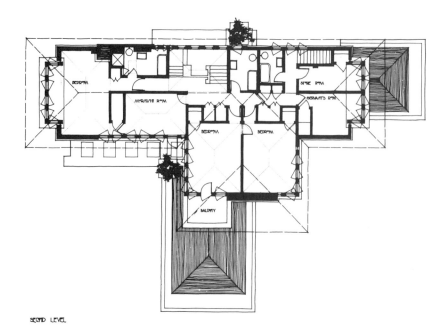

SECOND LEVEL

The second-level plan of the Meyer May
house reveals the compact arrangement of
the bedrooms, each having a windowed
corner or bay.

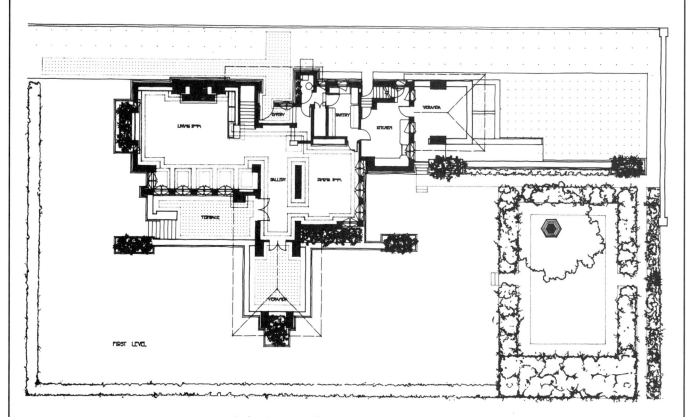

FIRST LEVEL

The first-level plan of the Meyer May house indicates the intricacies of Wright's spatial organization,
with principal spaces flowing into each other. There is a surprise around every corner.

to decide to return the house to its 1909 appearance. This would require the demolition of a 2000-square-foot addition and the removal of the masonry enclosure of the south verandah. Materials from the demolished wing were salvaged and reused in the restoration.

These were aesthetic preservation decisions, but the architects were to be far more challenged by the physical rehabilitation of the structure itself. As has occurred with other of Wright's houses, some of his experimental detailing has seriously deteriorated with the passage of time and severe weather. The 18-month restoration included almost complete dismantling and reconstruction of sections of the house. The broad cantilevered roofs required extensive replacement of rotted wooden framing and supporting posts. Steel was introduced, and the roof was reframed, sheathed and insulated, and covered with new red clay roof tiles produced by the same company that had made the originals.

Wright designed and selected all the interior furnishings, lighting, and decorative built-in elements that were custom-made for his houses and totally integrated into the architectural scheme. None of the original furnishings remained in the Meyer May house, which meant that the refurbishing of the interior was a major undertaking. The refurnishing has been accomplished with a mixture of originals, reproductions, and compatible arts and crafts pieces from the period. The result is a dazzling and homelike recreation of the original ambiance of the May house.

SIGNIFICANCE

Many Wright houses of the same vintage as the Meyer May house are still privately owned in areas like Chicago's Oak Park. The Meyer May residence is a "modern" house, yet its restoration has cost more than many older or larger houses of traditional design and construction. There are not enough corporate angels to rescue and restore Wright's prolific legacy. Because of the complex spatial organization and interior detailing of these houses, they are not easily adapted to other uses. Now that museums and private collectors covet Wright's furniture, it is virtually prohibitive to reacquire original furniture. Even though most states have landmarks preservation ordinances, there is no authority to require the retention of the furnishings and contents. Acknowledged Wright masterpieces such as the Darwin Martin house in Buffalo, which belongs to the state university, and the Robie house in Chicago, which is owned by the University of Chicago have become tremendous liabilities to their institutional owners. Both have served as conference centers, both are the same vintage as the Meyer May house and are similarly constructed. The escalating costs of restoration have taxed the abilities of these institutions to provide the needed maintenance and operating expenses.

Wingspread, Racine, Wisconsin

SITE

Herbert Fisk Johnson inherited the successful S. C. Johnson and Son, Inc. (Johnson's Wax) company following his father's death in 1928, just before the great crash of 1929. Johnson was of the pre–World War II generation of paternalistic heads of family businesses who felt a sense of responsibility for his employees and an obligation to his community. Johnson's Wax was a major employer in Racine. Through his optimism and determination, the company weathered the depression. In a bold move he chose Frank Lloyd Wright to design the "futuristic" new headquarters building, which was begun in 1936 and completed in 1939. This association with Wright was to influence Johnson's selection to design his new residence.

Johnson already owned a large tract of prairie, which contained a small lake, on the shore of Lake Michigan that he kept as a wild-fowl preserve. Johnson had just remarried in 1936, and he wanted a large house to provide room for their children.

A contemporary aerial view of Wingspread relates its organic relationship to its site.

Wright proposed a zoned plan concept, novel at the time, projecting itself out into the landscape.

The resulting 14,000-square-foot structure gives the impression of a "modern" country house; yet it contains all the elements of a traditional mansion. The 40- by 60-foot octagonal great hall "wigwamlike" central pavilion with its stepped skylit roof is dominated by a 30-foot-high massive chimney, containing five hearths projecting above the roof. The rounded-end forms of this masonry recall the headquarters building that is built of the same red Cherokee brick. Radiating out in pinwheel fashion from the central pavilion are the master bedroom wing, the children's wing, the guestrooms and carport wing, and the service wing. A large swimming pool is set in the quadrant framed by the children's wing and the service wing.

PRESERVATION ISSUE

The Johnson family lived in Wingspread from 1939 to 1959, when H. F. Johnson established the Johnson Foundation. Wingspread has been preserved by the Johnson Foundation as a center, devoted primarily to cosponsoring conferences. It does not contain guest accommodations. It has been sensitively adapted to its new conference center role with no sacrifice of its original character. The former guest quarters and garages were transformed into office space, and a storage space beneath the master wing was remodeled to provide lavatory and cloakroom space. Several small bathrooms were removed, and some rooms were expanded by the elimination of interior walls.

An additional adjacent building, The House, which was the residence of H. F. Johnson and his wife from 1959 to 1978, is now used as additional meeting space. The

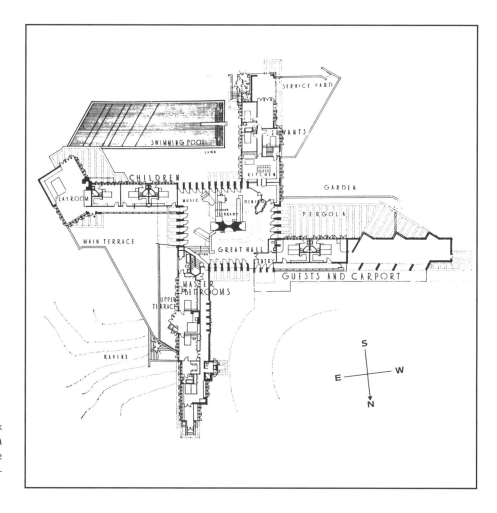

Wingspread's original plan as designed by Frank Lloyd Wright for the Johnson family in 1939. A striking example of the "zoned" plan that became a popular feature of modern houses in the post–World War II era.

A recent view looking toward the former children's wing of Wingspread, which is contemporary with Fallingwater, demonstrates a totally different form and expression than Wright's Prairie houses designed three decades earlier. Passing directly from the family to a foundation, the house has always been superbly maintained.

House allows seating for more conference participants than any single room in Wingspread can accommodate; it also has an audio recording studio.

The foundation's conference support offices are located in Wingspread; its administrative offices are housed in a two-story structure built in 1959 as a garage for The House.

SIGNIFICANCE

Wingspread was considered by Wright the last of his Prairie houses, and its unique setting nestles amid 30 acres on Wind Point, a peninsula that juts into Lake Michigan. "We called it Wingspread because spread its wings it did," Wright said in his autobiography. "The site was not at all stimulating before the house went up, but…when you view the environment framed by the architecture of the house from within, somehow, like magic, charm appears in the landscape….The site seems to come alive."

Over the years naturalistic landscape plantings have matured as have the vines trailing over the pergolas. It is indeed skillfully anchored to its site, taking advantage of the shallow ravines, the wings of the house projecting out over the surrounding expanses of manicured lawns, seemingly floating over the grassy slopes.

Though not as celebrated as its contemporary Fallingwater, the Kaufmann house in Pennsylvania, it is indeed an outstanding example of modern American architecture. What is significant is that not only have these modern country houses been meticulously maintained but also they have enough of their original sites intact. Unfortunately, many of the original sites upon which large traditional mansions were built were later compromised by encroaching development. In some of these situations, however, elaborate landscaping and formal gardens have provided enough camouflage to screen out the surrounding development and lost vistas.

Perhaps most important is that Wingspread continues to serve a useful function as an international conference center, and the public is also permitted to visit on a limited basis.

Pasadena, California

SITE

Pasadena, California, is perhaps best known to Americans as the home of the Rose Bowl, site of the annual pageant and football championship. However, it also contains a landmark cluster of some of the finest arts and crafts and modern houses of the early twentieth century.

PRESERVATION ISSUE

Pasadena was once an exclusive enclave of wealthy winter vacationers from the Midwest; it is now another community within the sprawling megalopolis of Greater Los Angeles. The challenge has been not only to preserve the unique cluster of surviving Greene and Greene residences but also the context of distinctive isolated modern houses by Frank Lloyd Wright, Richard Neutra, and Irving Gill. Urban sprawl and pollution have threatened the survival of these architectural masterpieces, and the repeated threat of earthquake damage has required special techniques to preserve their integrity. The Greene brothers' masterpiece Gamble house and the Wrigley mansion are open for visitors.

This Pasadena preservation community was shocked by the Blacker House scandal. The house was bought by an antiques dealer who emptied out all the original Greene and Greene lighting fixtures and furnishings and sold them at auction. This is an example of the growing problem of protecting the integrity of architect-designed residences containing original custom furniture and decorative objects. After a community protest, some originals from the Blacker House were replaced with reproductions.

SIGNIFICANCE

Preserving the community, not just the house: Pasadena has managed to survive urban blight, and its core eclectic "Old Town" has emerged as a gentrified National Register historic district. The lavish landscape of fashionable Millionaires' Row (now primarily luxury condominiums) has retained its desirability, and its low scale preserves the context of its exceptional architectural landmarks. The recent refurbishing by a local partnership of the venerable (86-year-old) Huntington Hotel, now rechristened as the Ritz-Carlton, Huntington has revived the traditional resort ambiance of the dowager favorite of this community.

The Cole house, 1906, is one of the Greene brothers' unique residences in the Craftsman Style. Its monumental stone chimney rises from a base of boulders. It is a neighbor of the celebrated Gamble house, 1908.

Gropius House, Lincoln, Massachusetts

With the construction of the Gropius house, the International Style appeared in America, given a new expression in wood.

SITE

The historic community of Lincoln, Massachusetts, with its roots dating from prerevolutionary times, was somewhat shocked when Walter Gropius began constructing his International Style villa in their midst. It was modest in size and set upon upon a hilltop on rolling farmland. Walter Gropius had directed the Bauhaus School in Germany from 1919 to 1928. Like many prominent intellectuals, liberals, and members of the avant-garde, Gropius was forced to leave Germany during the 1930s when the growth of national socialism became less tolerant of diversity. Gropius came to head Harvard University's Graduate School of Design. During his tenure from 1937 to 1952, he introduced the modernist ideal to architectural education, which heretofore, like most American architectural schools, had been dominated by the Beaux-Arts tradition. Nearby architect Marcel Breuer, who followed Gropius from the Bauhaus, built a similarly modern house.

PRESERVATION ISSUE

Gropius founded the Architects' Collaborative in 1945, and he influenced the development of modern architecture in the United States. Gropius died in 1969, and his widow Ilse lived on in the house. The Gropius house was reluctantly accepted by the venerable Society for the Preservation of New England Antiquities (SPNEA) as its first "modern" house museum. Founded in 1910, the SPNEA owns more than 40 historic properties located in Maine, New Hampshire, Massachusetts, Rhode Island, and Connecticut, of which 24 are open to the public. Prior to the acquisition of the Gropius house, their properties represented a span from the seventeenth to the early twentieth centuries. The society maintains the Conservation Services Center that provides

As much as the front narrow slotted strip windows and glass block ensure privacy, the rear facades open up to provide Gropius's family a sunny and expansive view of the hilltop site.

services for the buildings and furniture in its collection; the center also offers technical assistance to other owners of historic properties.

The Gropius house is a curious hybrid since the crisp European modern houses of this era were constructed of masonry and stuccoed. In his own house in Lincoln, he chose to use the American method of wood framing and vertical siding.

There is always a difficulty deciding which period to choose in restoring and furnishing historic houses, especially those occupied by the same family for many generations. In the case of the Gropius house which was completed only in 1938, it was decided to interpret the house up to the 1960s. In this case it seemed straightforward enough: SPNEA consulted with Ati Gropius Johansen, Gropius's daughter, who had grown up in the house and could therefore advise on many details. But the physical restoration of the house was another matter because the house was showing its age, and it looked worn and dirty. Modern houses do not achieve the patina of age gracefully. Gropius had chosen mass manufactured materials, and some, such as the distinctive thin profile steel strip window elements, were no longer in production. It was also desired to return the house's original luster as the Gropiuses knew it without making it appear too slick and new.

SIGNIFICANCE

It is clear that as time passes, the houses once considered "modern" will be deemed worthy of preservation. Generally these houses are not as large as the mansions of the golden age and are not easily adapted or added to. They are still more manageable for continued use as single-family residences. The smaller houses of Richard Neutra and Frank Lloyd Wright continue as residences in various parts of the country. The Pope-Leighy, one of Wright's smaller Usonian homes, was moved onto the grounds of the National Trust's Woodlawn Plantation in Mount Vernon, Virginia. Unfortunately its new foundation was sinking, and it will have to be transferred to firmer ground. In 1986 the National Trust accepted Philip Johnson's famous 1949 "glass" house set on 40 acres in New Canaan, Connecticut. Several other experimental buildings dot the grounds. Johnson has a life-long interest in the estate and has designed a visitor center. Johnson's neighbors have not been enthusiastic about the prospect of numerous visitors and have rejected the design for the visitor center. The early "modern" houses present a new series of restoration challenges.

CHAPTER 7

Adapting Mansions to Commercial
and Residential Uses

All over the country there are architecturally exceptional historic mansions, complete with furnishings and collections that do merit preservation as museums. Though it varies from year to year, there is a practical limit to the number of properties that public funds, grants, and private contributions can struggle to sustain. Beyond this select group, there is a vast inventory of architecturally distinctive mansions that are significant to their surroundings and function as contributing elements to historic districts. If we wish to preserve these mansions as part of the American landscape, we must seek realistic strategies to adapt them to new uses.

Over the years various adaptive uses have been successful in transforming mansions and large estates to new economically viable uses. From the background descriptions of these projects, it is evident that some mansions have passed through a number of adaptations since their original construction as single-family residences, and many have survived cycles of use and neglect. Though each property presents its own unique challenges, the adaptations illustrated in this chapter, which have been grouped by category, only begin to suggest the possibilities.

Historic Inns: Changing Patterns of American Tourism

Perhaps as a result of their experiences during the post–World War II European travel boom, sophisticated Americans have increasingly sought out alternatives to the major hotel chains' standard "hospitality" formulas. There is now an expanding network of mansions, old farms adapted as exclusive country inns, bed-and-breakfasts, and elegant small resorts that cater to weekend and seasonal visitors. These travelers are often couples without children who are seeking a leisurely weekend in the country in a region with charm, scenery, outdoor activities, antiquing, and/or cultural activities, in a picturesque or elegant setting. They are usually enticed by lavish homemade country breakfasts and afternoon tea. Sometimes the inn is incidental to vacation travel, but often the inn is the destination.

Attracting the Selective Guest

Indeed, a whole new genre of guidebooks has evolved to serve this audience. To offset the cost of advertising and registering guests in many resort communities and urban historic districts, proprietors of small inns and bed-and-breakfasts have combined forces to staff central reservation and booking services.

Expanding historic inns and hotel operations with large established clientele have begun another trend: acquiring mansions and historic houses to provide more exclusive and deluxe accommodations. Historic inns are often located on limited sites within picturesque old towns and landmark districts. Unable to expand on available land or provide sufficient parking, the newer trend is to acquire nearby elaborate, oversized, underutilized mansions to create additional luxurious guestrooms and suites in landscaped surroundings.

Community Cooperation

Nowadays, except in the most rural or isolated places, there is some mechanism of zoning ordinance or land-use control. The conversion of a large single-family mansion or estate to another usage will require some zoning and design review process. Community ordinances vary, and ultimately transforming a mansion or an estate into accommodations or a resort is an individual owner's business decision. In many established communities, there will be a resistance to the "commercialization" of a residential area by the introduction of guest accommodations. In order to develop a successful strategy for tourism, the local attitudes have to be supportive.

Overleaf The owners of the extremely popular Red Lion Inn, which operates year-round in Stockbridge, the historic village, felt from their years of experience that there was a niche for guests desiring the luxurious atmosphere of a mansion, with a first-class restaurant. Consequently they acquired Blantyre in Lee, Massachusetts, which was a somewhat isolated estate with a main house resembling an English country house. Operated seasonally as an annex to the Red Lion Inn's existing management, reservations, and bookkeeping staffs, it has proven very successful and has established its own fine reputation.

Delamater House is a charming 1844 Gothic Revival cottage. This architectural landmark has been restored to function as an elegant country inn, as an annex to the nearby Beekman Arms Hotel, which is a popular inn with a long-standing reputation and following.

Delamater House, Rhinebeck, New York

SITE

Delamater House is an 1844 Gothic Revival Style house, designed by Alexander Jackson Davis for Henry Delamater, the founder of Rhinebeck's First National Bank. The wooden framed building with its lacy barge boards, diamond paned wooden windows, board and batten siding, and front porch with elaborate pierced piers, railings and Gothic arches, is the quintessential example of an American Gothic Revival Cottage.

Its versatile architect, Alexander Jackson Davis, designed Lyndhurst, a Gothic Revival stone castle in Tarrytown, New York, which is now owned and operated as a house museum by the National Trust for Historic Preservation. Davis also designed several other Hudson River mansions in the Gothic Revival, Italianate, and Greek Revival modes and was one of the nineteenth century's most influential architects. Together with Andrew Jackson Davis, a nineteenth-century tastemaker, they promoted the romantic and picturesque movement that marked American architecture during the 1840s, 1850s, and 1860s.

Delamater House is located near the Beekman Arms Hotel, which has been operated as a hotel since 1766. The Beekman Arms began as single-story stone structure operating as a tavern. In 1769 it was raised to two stories and covered with a gambrel roof. The northern wood-framed wing was added in 1810, the third story in 1865, and the southern brick section in this century. Over the years its Greenhouse Restaurant and Tap Room remained popular, but the inn still required more guest accommodations.

Both the Beekman Arms and Delamater House are sited in Rhinebeck on Route 9, historically the main route linking the Hudson River towns and villages. Delamater House is set quite close to the road.

In the early 1970s Delamater House was in poor condition, and some restoration work was undertaken. It remained a private residence until 1981 when it was acquired by the Delamater Associates. The house and carriage barn were also in deteriorated condition when they were acquired by Delamater Associates. Delamater House is listed in the National Register of Historic Places, and the partners were able to benefit from a federal tax act that encouraged many adaptive-use projects during the 1980s. The new owners restored the property and adapted it to an inn, in compliance with the Secretary of the Interior's Guidelines.

One of the Delamater Associates partners, Charles LaForge, is the owner of the Beekman Arms Hotel. The other partners, Doris Masten and Timothy Toronto, were owners of a restoration firm. Despite its charm, its proximity to the road and the commercial crossroads of the village made the house undesirable for a single-family residence, but these same characteristics made it an ideal extension of the Beekman Arms Hotel complex. The enlargement of the complex to add the residences required a zoning change to commercial.

With only minor interior modifications, Delamater House was converted into seven guest bedrooms, each with a private bath and a sitting room. The carriage house was also restored to contain guest rooms. The project was so successful that another historic house, the Germand house—a Greek Revival Style building scheduled for demolition by its owners, the National Bank of Rhinebeck—was acquired and moved to the site. It was flanked by two new buildings containing additional guest rooms designed in a Gothic Revival mode by local architect Alfonse Cornacchini, who also designed another building containing guest rooms and an office. The Gables, adjacent to Delamater House, was also acquired and converted to guest rooms. The complex, now consisting of 40 rooms and a conference center, is rented out through a reservation system managed by the Beekman Arms Hotel.

SIGNIFICANCE

Many historic communities have their finest mansions and old houses located on the village green or main street, which through the passage of time has become heavily trafficked. The preservation of the architecturally significant residences is important to maintaining the architectural character of the village. The adaptive use of Delamater House is significant because it demonstrates that a structure too small to operate profitably as an independent bed-and-breakfast, when combined with other nearby houses and linked to a larger nearby historic inn, can function as a successful network. In East Hampton the opposite is true: A large mansion has been combined with a smaller historic inn to provide more guest accommodations.

Thus the number of guest accommodations is increased without disrupting the traditional scale and diversity of the village's street scape. In the Delamater House situation, the owners avoided the enlargement of the old Beekman Arms structure that would have thrown it out of scale to the rest of the village's buildings. In its new role the Delamater has a high visibility for tourists and is convenient to local shops and restaurants. All over the country, as more communities designate historic districts and limit new growth, the need to provide economically viable adaptive uses is essential to achieving the goal of historic preservation.

Colonnade House at The Greenbrier, White Sulphur Springs, West Virginia

SITE

Colonnade House, built in 1838 by Colonel Richard Singleton and Colonel Wade Hampton II, was the middle (and only surviving) of a group of three cottages on the grounds of The Greenbrier. Each house boasted a double portico supported by six

Colonnade house, the historic 1838 Greek Revival guest house on the grounds of The Greenbrier, has been handsomely restored on the exterior.

columns, and the ensemble of the three were known as "the Colonnades" because of their distinctive columns. Colonnade House was flanked by smaller private residences which were intended for their owner's guests. Part of a long history of private cottages maintained at the resort, the Colonnades were to that date the most ambitious cottages constructed at The Greenbrier.

The Greenbrier's history as a healing spa began in 1778, when a local settler was carried to the rural spring at which Native American lore said her rheumatism could be cured. Her recovery was such that the spring became a popular destination for rheumatics in the area.

Located at White Sulphur Springs in West Virginia's Allegheny Mountains, the area had been surveyed in the eighteenth century by Andrew Lewis of The Greenbrier Land Company, a group of speculators who had been given title to 1000 acres provided that they survey and eventually settle the land. Controversy with Native Americans, however, made the area difficult to safely inhabit, and the land was sparsely settled until 1774 when General Lewis defeated the Shawnee Chief Cornstalk.

It was a descendent of one of the area's first settlers, Nicholas Carpenter, who first developed and marketed the restorative powers of the spring. Carpenter was killed in a Native American attack in the 1750s, but his wife, Kate, and daughter, Frances, survived and moved to Staunton. Frances married Captain Michael Bowyer, Jr., a lawyer and merchant in Fincastle, Virginia, in 1766. In 1783, Bowyer obtained a deed to his wife's family's land and was granted title to 950 acres by the Virginia Court of Appeals the following year. Frances soon died, and in 1787 he hired Mr. and Mrs. Leven Gibson to manage the resort. By 1790 he was in full-time residence.

The resort grew, but slowly due largely to its isolated location. At the time of Bowyer's death in 1808, the resort included a tavern with a dining room and some guest rooms as well as a few cottages to accommodate lodgers.

One of his patrons, James Calwell, a Baltimore merchant, had married Bowyer's daughter Mary (Polly) in 1797. After Bowyer's death they took over the management of the property, transforming it into a grand resort.

From Calwell's early management, he encouraged "private" cottages. Retaining architectural and other control over all of Greenbrier's development, during the off-season, he would construct these cottages at his guests' expense. The owner-guests would then stay in their own cottage, paying the usual rate, but Calwell could let them to others when the owners were not in residence. In this manner, Calwell developed The Greenbrier with groupings of cottages such as Baltimore, Paradise, Alabama, and Hesitancy Rows, a convention still used today. The Colonnade House is among the grandest of these privately built cottages. Colonel Wade Hampton II and Colonel Richard Singleton, both successful cotton plantation owners, were friends. Singleton had owned a smaller cottage at The Greenbrier since 1825 and was a substantial investor in Calwell's resort. In 1838, the year the Colonnades cottages were completed, President Martin Van Buren spent much of August, probably staying in the Colonnades guest house. Colonel Singleton's daughter Angelica was married to Abraham Van Buren, the president's son, in November of that year.

In 1857 a new consortium built a new wooden hotel affectionately dubbed "Old White," which remained in use until its demolition in 1922 when it no longer met the fire-code standards.

The Colonnades cottages were the most elegant of the Greenbrier accommodations and were owned by many notables including Virginia state senator Allen Caperton, and W. W. Corcoran of Washington, D.C., and founder of the Corcoran Gallery of Art. In 1910, the Chesapeake and Ohio Railway purchased White Sulphur Springs, and the upper two Colonnades cottages were demolished and replaced with a new cottage used by a railroad executive. The railroad invested heavily in the refurbishing and adding of new guest rooms and facilities from 1913 through 1930. Colonnade House, however, was still a fine accommodation, and William Gibbs McAdoo, the secretary of the treasury under Woodrow Wilson, used the cottage frequently.

The faithful clientele returned annually even during the great depression. The Greenbrier was seized by the government from 1941 to 1946 and closed to the public during World War II. It served first as an internment camp for the foreign diplomatic core, and then as an army hospital. Most of its original furnishings were dispersed during this period.

PRESERVATION ISSUE

After World War II, the railroad reacquired The Greenbrier and set about its refurbishing. Colonnade House served as the home of Dr. James P. Baker, the founder of The Greenbrier's diagnostic clinic, and subsequently served as the home of The Greenbrier Clinic's medical director.

During this same period the legendary Dorothy Draper, the New York decorator of "cabbage rose" fame, was engaged to furnish and redecorate the entire resort. Designer Carleton Varney took over the task from his mentor in 1965. In 1980 the resort was transferred from the Chesapeake and Ohio Railway to the CSX Corporation who continues to operate it. They have continued to invest in upgrading and adding new guest accommodations and amenities as well as developing corporate conference and convention facilities. Today 70 percent of the hotel guest bookings are business related, and only 30 percent are individual vacationers.

In 1989 Carleton Varney and architect Paul Hansen undertook a major transformation of Colonnade House, officially listed as Room 6216, and it is once again the showpiece of The Greenbrier. The exterior of the property was simply restored, its verandahs still providing sheltered outdoor seating, but the interior was much modified to accommodate large-scale entertaining. The house, which now contains three bedrooms and can accommodate 24 at a private sit-down dinner, is in demand for corporate guests and visiting foreign dignitaries.

The house is furnished in the manner of a nineteenth-century plantation owner. A mixture of eighteenth- and nineteenth-century American and European furniture

The interior public spaces on the main floor of Colonnade House have been opened up and provide an expanded and elegant setting for private receptions. The traditional character and period furnishings are appropriate to the house.

fills the house. The Greenbrier's kitchen prepares meals that are brought over and served on the Colonnade House china, which is a replica of the pattern used by President Martin Van Buren at the White House.

SIGNIFICANCE

The establishment of large resort hotels at mineral springs was not unique to The Greenbrier. For example, the Bedford Springs (a magnesia spring) in Pennsylvania's Allegheny Mountains was founded in 1800. The main building grew through a series of additions to a frontage of 557 feet. It also was in reasonable proximity to Washington, D.C., and it had President Buchanan and other notables of the period as guests. In the nineteenth century further north in New York, Saratoga Springs and Sharon Springs became fashionable resorts.

The newly refurbished dining room of Colonnade House provides a formal and distinguished ambiance for elaborate dinners and diplomatic receptions. It, too, has been expanded to accommodate 24 guests.

The pattern of creating individual guest cottages on the hotel grounds also developed in the New England resorts. Nowadays we continue to think of spas as healthful and restorative, but these effects do not necessarily involve drinking the local water. Few of these resort hotels have carried their prestige into the twentieth century. Part of the continuing success of Greenbrier has been its ability to renew itself and adjust to changing demands of its clientele. The elaborate restoration of Colonnade House is an indication that there still is a market for these "exclusive" accommodations. Colonnade House serves as a link with The Greenbrier's past as social center and resort.

Historic Inns of Annapolis, Maryland

SITE

The entry facade of the restored Governor Calvert House on State Circle. The newer additions, including indoor parking, are concealed behind the inn.

Annapolis, which has a rich history dating back to 1659 as a seaport town, now serves as the capital of Maryland and is considered by some to be the Sailing Capital of the East. The U.S Naval Academy was founded here in 1845 on a 300-acre site. The entire midcity area of Annapolis is a national historic district, with more than 1500 restored and preserved buildings. The center of Annapolis is the Maryland Statehouse, the oldest U.S. state capitol in continuous legislative use (built 1772 to 1779). Because of its closeness to Baltimore, Washington, D.C., and the Chesapeake Bay and its link to the eastern shore ocean resorts, Annapolis attracts many visitors.

PRESERVATION ISSUE

With the demands of visitors on legislative business, the Naval Academy, and tourism, it was desirable to have a hotel close to the statehouse. Given the low-scale, narrow streets and the density of landmark buildings, it was difficult and unacceptable to construct a major hotel in the historic district. Thanks to the dedication of the local preservationist and developer Paul Pearson, five of Annapolis's most historic buildings were saved from destruction in the early 1970s. With the guidance and encouragement of the nonprofit group Historic Annapolis, Pearson imaginatively turned the disparate structures into four elegant inns. They are all located on two of Annapolis's major focal points, State Circle and Church Circle. The group of inns is now operated as the Historic Inns of Annapolis. Altogether the four inns contain 125 rooms and 12 suites.

The Governor Calvert House is an assemblage of a mansion dating from the eighteenth century with nineteenth-century accretions. Its facade on State Circle has

A map of the historic center of Annapolis showing the scattered sites, of the Historic Inns, all in close proximity to the Maryland Statehouse.

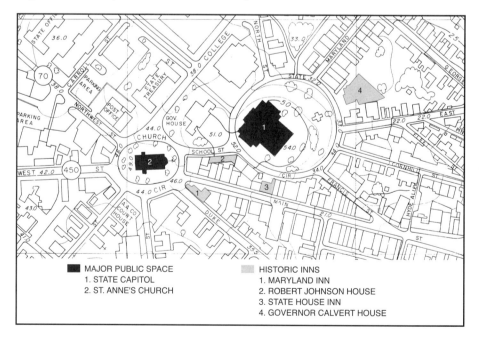

MAJOR PUBLIC SPACE	HISTORIC INNS
1. STATE CAPITOL	1. MARYLAND INN
2. ST. ANNE'S CHURCH	2. ROBERT JOHNSON HOUSE
	3. STATE HOUSE INN
	4. GOVERNOR CALVERT HOUSE

The Robert Johnson House, which combines three adjoining eighteenth-century Georgian houses, has preserved another section of State Circle, which provides the historic context for the Maryland state capitol.

been restored. In collaboration with Historic Annapolis, an archaeological dig revealed the remains of an eighteenth-century hypocaust heating system. Through clever design this feature is visible through glass panels set in the floor of one of the public spaces in the basement. In order to accommodate conference facilities, a restaurant, an elevator, additional guest rooms, and parking, a brick addition was constructed at the rear, which cannot be seen from the street.

The Robert Johnson House on State Circle combined three adjoining Georgian houses dating from 1773 and operates as a bed-and-breakfast inn. Each of the buildings has had a history of prior adaptations that included law offices, a cabinetmaker, a tailor shop, and finally apartments. It has retained its original restored street facades but has been reconfigured on the interior.

The State House Inn also fronts on Main Street, but an addition runs through to State Circle. Its core is a restored 1820 house that was enlarged several times. It now serves as a bed-and-breakfast. It also contains a restaurant on the main floor, which is operated by a separate management.

The Maryland Inn, a wedge-shaped structure on Church Circle, has been functioning as an inn since the 1770s. Its restored facade represents later-nineteenth-century modifications and additions, including a mansard roof. In 1868 it was acquired by the Maryland Hotel Company and remained the most prominent Annapolis hotel until the turn of the century. Somewhat faded by the time of World War I, it languished through several ownerships until 1953 when a restoration and internal modernization began. Since the 1970s the restoration has been completed. It now contains meeting facilities and an elegant restaurant.

SIGNIFICANCE

In addition to the obvious benefit of finding adaptive uses for several distinctive landmark structures that are key architectural historic houses, there are considerable economic advantages to operating the inns as a group. The Historic Inns of Annapolis were acquired by Grand Heritage in 1989, which has specialized in operating a network of refurbished historic and architecturally distinctive hotels and inns in the South. This arrangement provides a broader management, marketing, and reservation network than any individual inn or independent hotel could afford.

The restored Maryland Inn, which functions as part of the Historic Inns of Annapolis, preserves a significant architectural element on a wedge-shaped site formed by streets radiating from Church Circle, another of Annapolis's historic districts.

The neighboring Chesapeake Bay Maritime Museum with its historic watercraft, picturesque old structures, and distinctive lighthouse permanently frames the vista from the lawns of The Inn at Perry Cabin.

The Inn at Perry Cabin, Saint Michael's, Maryland

SITE

Saint Michael's, on the historic eastern shore of Maryland, on the Miles River adjacent to the Chesapeake Bay Maritime Museum, provides a picturesque and romantic setting for The Inn at Perry Cabin. Saint Michael's dates from the mid-seventeenth century. After its involvement in the Revolution and the War of 1812, it lost its importance as a harbor. Boat building remained important as well as harvesting and processing crabs and shellfish. In the 1970s it was "rediscovered," and gentrification is quite evident in the antique shops, art galleries, and boutiques that have replaced most of the town's original main street commerce. Easily reached from Washington, D.C., Baltimore, Philadelphia, and Wilmington, and nearby Annapolis, it is a convenient port for the Chesapeake Bay boating enthusiasts. The Chesapeake Bay Maritime Museum, whose collections also include an old lighthouse, preserves the inn's unobstructed vista of the harbor.

PRESERVATION ISSUE

Perry Cabin began as an early-nineteenth-century manor house, built just after the War of 1812 and named after Commodore Oliver Hazard Perry, a friend of the original owner. Over the years it has served as a private residence and a riding academy before first opening its doors as an inn in 1980. The Colonial Revival Style inn was acquired by Sir Bernard Ashley, cofounder of the Laura Ashley Company. The inn was expanded, extensively renovated, and redecorated. It opened in 1990 as The Inn at Perry Cabin, offering luxurious accommodations and an excellent restaurant. A sister hotel in Great Britain, Llangoed Hall near Brecon, Wales, was opened at the same time. Both were considered pilot projects for a series of picturesque English Style country inns, promoting Laura Ashley products.

Although the mansion was not architecturally extraordinary, the rear of the manor house retains much of the original character as viewed from the water. However, on the front facing the entrance drive, the new reception area, the expansion of accommodations, dining and lounge spaces, as well as the additions to provide kitchen and service areas, have been less sensitive. The original manor house facade seems to have gotten lost in the renovations.

SIGNIFICANCE

Laura Ashley is an English firm that has opened an extensive network of shops in the United States. The Inn at Perry Cabin has been designed as a showcase for the firm's furniture, fabrics, wall coverings, lamps, and bed linens and towels. The company has photographed the inn as a background for one of its Christmas catalogs, which also includes a line of women's fashions. Models posed in these settings promote the complete "Laura Ashley look." It is interesting that no American firm has chosen to open such an elaborate showcase for its merchandise. *The New York Times* home fashions section commented on Sir Bernard Ashley's opening of The Inn at Perry Cabin, "Can Ralph Lauren be far behind?" More typically American home furnishings manufacturers and fashion designers seek out and lease mansions only as photographic backgrounds to provide a "mood" or setting for their collections.

The entrance front of The Inn at Perry Cabin, showing a new pavilion added for guest registration as well as a sheltered entrance.

The view of the rear of The Inn at Perry Cabin facing the harbor. The central core of the original house and its colonnade have been greatly extended.

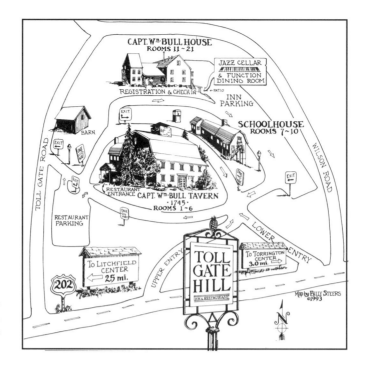

A view of the Tollgate Hill Inn, showing various elements, which make up the complex. Shrouded by mature trees and shrubbery, it is difficult to photograph.

Tollgate Hill Inn, Litchfield, Connecticut

SITE

The Tollgate Hill Inn was built in 1745 as a manor house for a farm in Litchfield, Connecticut. It was purchased after the Revolutionary War by Captain William Bull, a revolutionary soldier. Then located on the main route between Hartford and Litchfield, the building was run by Bull as a tavern and served as a way station on the Old East Litchfield Road.

In 1923, at the height of America's infatuation with the Colonial Revival, a local industrialist and noted American antiquarian Frederick Feussenich purchased the manor house, then in terrible disrepair. He had it moved 2½ miles west to Litchfield's historic district. Feussenich converted the inn into his home in the Colonial Revival Style, adding a wing with a 20- by 40-foot second-story ballroom with a vaulted ceiling and a musicians' balcony (fiddler's loft).

After the depression and before World War II, the Feusseniches operated their home as a tearoom and restaurant without overnight accommodations.

PRESERVATION ISSUE

The building was in deteriorated condition when the current owner Frederick J. Zivic acquired it with plans to convert it into the Tollgate Hill Inn. An experienced restaurateur who has previously restored several historic structures, he worked to have it listed in the National Register of Historic Places as the Captain William Bull Tavern. This was accomplished in 1983, and the inn conversion involved a careful process of restoration. The tax benefits of adaptive-use projects of designated historic structures provided the incentive for many imaginative restorations and considerable investment during the 1980s.

With a commitment to maintain its historic integrity, paint analysis was conducted, and it revealed the original colors that were replicated. In addition, interior details—including the curved corner cupboard, original to the house, in the main dining room—have been preserved.

The main building contains dining facilities on the first floor, three guest rooms on the second floor, and three additional guest rooms that were created in the story-

and-a-half-high gambrel roof. The main building is linked by an underground tunnel to an eighteenth-century schoolhouse that was moved to the property in 1924. The schoolhouse now contains four guest rooms, and the lower level with a fireplace will be used as a private dining room. In order to provide additional accommodations, a new building in a compatible Colonial Revival Style was constructed in 1990, behind the inn. This new building contains a reception and check-in center, the "Jazz Cellar," a dining room, and 10 guest rooms. The addition of this new structure permits a central guest-receiving area separate from the restaurant entrance in the Bull Tavern. The owner has been able to preserve the Bull Tavern as the key element in a profitable inn complex by expanding into additional structures on the site.

SIGNIFICANCE

The formula for the rescue of many old mansions and historic houses may be to adapt them to use as restaurants and inns. Several of the examples illustrated in this book indicate that it is often necessary to expand the existing buildings to provide additional guest accommodations. In the case of the Tollgate Hill Inn, this was accomplished by a combination of reuse of existing structures on the site plus some new construction. From the preservation point of view, because the manor house had already been moved from its original site, then renovated and enlarged in the Colonial Revival mode as a residence in the 1920s, the house was not really a worthy candidate for a house museum, but it was perfect for adaptation.

John Rutledge House Inn, Charleston, South Carolina

SITE

The John Rutledge House Inn, a National Historic Landmark, was built in 1763 by John Rutledge upon his wedding to Elizabeth Grimke, in Charleston, South Carolina. Rutledge was a prominent South Carolina statesman and served as a delegate to the First and Second Continental Congresses. He also served as commander in chief of the South

John Rutledge's 1763 mansion was enlarged by Thomas Gadsden in 1853. The Italianate detailing and the imposing two-story lacy cast iron porch were added at this period.

Carolina Militia during the Revolution and, later, as governor of the state. Rutledge also served as chief justice of the South Carolina Supreme Court as well as chief justice of the U.S. Supreme Court. Rutledge drafted South Carolina's constitution, which served as a foundation for a draft of the U.S. Constitution at the Constitutional Convention. A number of the U.S. Constitution's components can be traced to Rutledge's authorship, and it is said that he drafted the Constitution in the library of the house. Significantly, the house is one of only 15 extant homes that belonged to signers of the Constitution. President George Washington was among the guests Rutledge entertained at the residence before his death in 1800.

The home was purchased by Thomas Gadsden, a real estate broker and slave trader, in 1853, to whose ownership many of the decorative interior details, including marble fireplaces and parquet floors, can be attributed. The imposing two-story cast-iron porch was also added during Gadsden's ownership under the direction of architect P. H. Hammarskold. The porch's motifs of palmetto trees, the symbol of South Carolina, and eagles were chosen by Gadsden to symbolize Rutledge's service and dedication to state and country. It is to the Italianate Style appearance of this period that the house has been restored.

Charleston Mayor Goodwyn Rhett owned the house during his term and notable Americans including George Vanderbilt and President Taft visited then. It is said that the Charleston delicacy "She Crab Soup" was created by Rhett's butler, William Deas.

PRESERVATION ISSUE

Like many buildings located in downtown areas that have evolved from residential to commercial neighborhoods, the Charleston house had fallen on hard times. It was divided into apartments in the 1950s and was subsequently used as a school and law offices. By 1988, when it was purchased by a partnership including Richard Widman, president of Lowcountry Hospitality, it was vacant and in deteriorated condition.

Broad Street is in the heart of Charleston's historic district, and is the demarcation between the antebellum residential area known as "Sough of Broad" and the historic commercial neighborhood. It is an ideal site for an inn for tourists in town to see the historic district. A painstaking restoration was executed by Evans and Schmidt, a Charleston architecture firm. Marble fireplaces, original plaster moldings and inlaid floors, and the cast-iron porch were all carefully refurbished. The opening of the house as the John Rutledge House Inn was in 1989 with a gala reception that benefited the National Trust Historic Preservation Center for Historic Houses.

By using the 11 rooms of the main house and 8 in the two adjoining carriage houses, the proprietors created 19 guest accommodations. A combination of antiques and historically accurate reproductions were used to recreate the historic ambiance, yet provide serviceable and comfortable guest rooms with modern amenities. Some of the ground floor's formal rooms serve as guest suites, and the second floor contained a library and a drawing room which could be combined to form a ballroom, where the Constitution was drafted. The library is now a suite sitting room, and the drawing room now serves as the inn's guest parlor.

SIGNIFICANCE

The changing fortunes of the John Rutledge house represent a cycle that is a common pattern with in-town mansions. Even the most superb individual restoration project alone could not transform the neighborhood. Charleston has long prided itself on its history, architectural heritage, and picturesque charm. In recent decades through a dedicated group of preservation-minded citizens, it has planned for its preservation. The creation of the annual Spoleto Festival each spring has brought a new stimulus to Charleston that attracts cultivated and affluent visitors. The increase in tourism and visitation has given a boost to all the economic strata of Charleston as well as the enjoyment of the events by the local citizenry.

Success has brought other problems including a shortage of parking and a hotly debated new convention center as well as a since-defeated proposal for a bridge that would have ruined the integrity of the historic district. Citizen efforts have forced stricter application of preservation regulations and the prevention of demolition as as a solution to growth. This provides a supportive climate in which investors are willing to take on a project such as the vacant and deteriorated John Rutledge house.

Charleston's rapid recovery in the wake of a major hurricane is a testament to its own faith and commitment to the restoration of its historic structures.

Naulakha, Dummerston, Vermont

SITE

Reflecting the eclectic background of its original owner and builder, the celebrated British author Rudyard Kipling, Naulakha reflects an unusual example of the American Shingle Style. The author was born in India in 1865 to English parents in Bombay. Naulakha was built in 1892 to 1893 by Rudyard Kipling, shortly after his marriage to the sister of an American friend, Carie Balestier. The site of 55 acres is a portion of her family's larger acreage in Vermont. Kipling envisioned the long narrow house as a Kashmiri houseboat which "sails" from its hilltop perch commanding spectacular views of the surrounding countryside and mountains. His study was located in the "prow." It was designed by architect Henry Rutgers Marshall.

Kipling's daughter Josephine was born in the house, and Kipling began the *Just So Stories* there. He also wrote *The Jungle Book, Captains Courageous, The Seven Seas,* and *A Day's Work* at the house. Kipling and his family used it as their summer house through 1896, when an unpleasant personal feud took place with his brother-in-law, who lived across the road. To avoid an impending lawsuit that threatened to violate the couple's cherished privacy, Kipling and his wife took their family to England, hoping to return some day. They kept their coachman as a caretaker and attempted to return in 1899, but tragically his favorite daughter Josephine died of pneumonia after a rough sea

An old view of Naulakha as it appeared when Rudyard Kipling and his family resided there. The English-based Landmark Trust has undertaken a restoration that will remove later modifications.

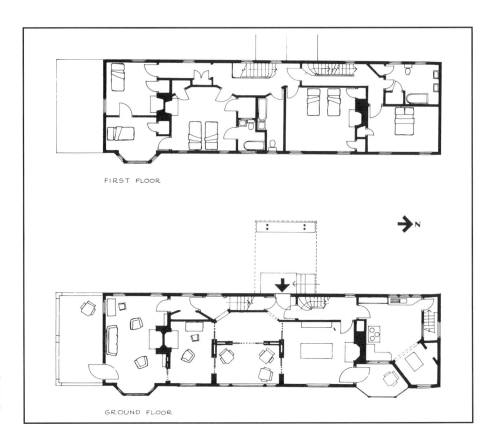

FIRST FLOOR

→N

GROUND FLOOR

Plans of Naulakha, indicating the layout of the house in its new function as a weekly vacation rental. Several of the rooms contain Kipling's original furniture.

voyage. Kipling never returned to Naulakha again. It was finally sold in 1903 to friends of the family, the Holbrooks. Members of the Holbrook family made some modifications and additions and used it until 1942. It remained in their ownership until the sale to the Landmark Trust.

PRESERVATION ISSUE

Naulakha was empty from 1942 when the Landmark Trust acquired the property a century after its construction. This is their first property in the United States, and it is certainly a fitting gesture considering Kipling's American connections. The Landmark Trust is a British organization founded in 1965 to give new life to historically significant buildings suffering from neglect and abuse. In England, the trust has saved over 200 buildings with much the same philosophy: Acquire and restore the building and let it out weekly as a vacation rental. The rental fees maintain the house, and the public can experience history. This formula also encourages a less invasive restoration philosophy. People are willing to put up with less modern accommodations on their vacations than in their own residences. The Landmark Trust has found that because guests are staying only for a week, they appreciate the historical accuracy of restorations and require fewer amenities than they might in a hotel or even at home. In England rental properties range from a water tower in Norfolk to an out-of-use railroad station in Staffordshire to a cotton mill in Derbyshire to a castle near Edinburgh.

Brattleboro Design Associates has been commissioned to undertake the restoration based on the archival sources including the original plans and surviving old photographs. Later accretions will be removed, and mechanical systems will be upgraded. When the Kiplings returned to England, they took only their books, carpets, and certain framed pictures. Despite Naulakha's 50-year abandonment, virtually all of the original Kipling furniture survives in the study, loggia, dining room, master bedroom, guest room, and the attic. Thus the original ambiance of the house can be re-created. Some additional structures remain from the Kiplings' occupancy including a barn, an icehouse, and a carriage house, and these will be restored to their original appearance. Other miscellaneous structures from the Holbrook family's occupancy will be removed, including a greenhouse and a garage.

Since local and regional interest in the house and property is substantial, the Landmark Trust intends to vary the vacation rental format somewhat for Naulakha. The house will be open several days each year for the public, and local school groups will also be able to visit the site. The Landmark Trust intends to limit occupancy to eight guests at a time, and no weddings or receptions will be permitted. Because Naulakha is a veritable house museum containing original period furnishings, it is not clear how the Landmark Trust can prevent excessive wear and possible theft of these valuable artifacts.

SIGNIFICANCE

The success of the Landmark Trust in England offers an interesting experiment with Naulakha in Dummerston, Vermont, their first acquisition in the United States. A network of historic houses available for vacation rental would be a novelty. If it were possible, perhaps a historic mansion's accessory structures such as barns or carriage houses could be adapted to this purpose. The National Trust in the United States already has promoted a program of historic hotels and inns. The Landmark Trust has been established as a nonprofit organization in Vermont. There are substantial differences between Great Britain and the United States with regard to maintaining tax-exempt status, which may affect the ability of nonprofit owners in the United States to offer seasonal rentals and vacation houses.

A Luxurious Spa

Bellefontaine, Lenox, Massachusetts

SITE

Bellefontaine was built in 1896 to 1898 by New York financier Giraud Foster and his wife Jane Van Nest Foster. Interestingly two of Giraud Foster's brothers assisted Pierre Lorillard in the establishment of the exclusive Tuxedo Park, north of New York City. The Fosters had traveled on the Continent and were familiar with Europe's historic

Main facade of Bellefontaine as it appears today, its portico restored, commanding a vista of lawns and mature landscaping.

Architect firm Jung/Brannen's rendering of an aerial view of Bellefontaine showing the new additions in the background, which were set at a distance to preserve the free-standing quality of the restored mansion.

landmarks and the French Beaux Arts Style in fashion at the turn of the century. This may have influenced their choice of Carrere and Hastings as architects, probably best known for their design of the New York Public Library and Henry Clay Frick's New York Mansion. Bellefontaine was a formal symmetrical mass in a style distantly reminiscent of the Petit Trianon at Versailles, plus an extra story. When built, it was not the largest of the Berkshire cottages, but it was one of the most conspicuous. The architects laid out the elaborate gardens as extensions of the axial plan of the house, with allées of trees and clipped hedges creating the vistas, defining the landscape replete with statuary, fountains, and a reflecting pool. Most Berkshire cottages were seasonal, but after its completion in 1898, Bellefontaine became the Fosters' permanent residence.

In 1946, soon after Mr. Foster's death, his son Giraud Van Nest Foster auctioned the contents and sold the house. It was sold again to the Jesuit order, and a 1949 fire destroyed all but the paneled library and the rotunda on the interior. Its subsequent use as a private boy's school further compromised the building's character. After the fire the Jesuits converted the building to the Immaculate Heart of Mary Seminary, replacing the original corinthian columned portico of the entry facade with a brick enclosure. The reflecting pool in the garden was filled with broken statuary and building remnants and then filled in.

PRESERVATION ISSUE

Bellefontaine is protected by the Lenox Great Estate Law, which allows an owner to change the use of a mansion with the proviso that the building and grounds be preserved. Wetlands on the property further complicated new development.

Mel and Enid Zuckerman, proprietors of the elegant Canyon Ranch Spa in Tuscon, Arizona, were seeking an East Coast site. They purchased the 120-acre estate

Architect firm Jung/Brannen's rendered site plan of Bellefontaine, indicating the distinct zoning of the reception and flanking guest room wings, the spa building complex, and the mansion linked by glazed covered walkways.

in 1987, and they commissioned Boston architects Jung and Brannen to restore the mansion and to add the required spa amenities. A previous owner had spent more than 5 years securing permission for the mansion's conversion to a hotel. Other developers proposed dividing it into condominiums.

Although it originally contained 35 rooms, Bellefontaine was not large enough to incorporate all the requirements of the spa. Local planning restrictions required a 200-foot buffer for new construction around the mansion and a 100-foot setback between the mansion and the street. The architects wanted to make the new additions "respectful of the estate."

Sited upon a hill, the mansion dominates the view from the sweeping entrance drive. It was decided to organize the resort into three sections, an inn, a spa building, and the mansion, all to be linked by glass-enclosed walkways, permitting year-round sheltered circulation. All of the new construction was set behind the mansion. The inn is divided into two wings containing 120 rooms and luxury suites. The wings are

The restored library of Bellefontaine, which now functions as a guest lounge, is one of the few interior spaces that survived a major fire during its ownership by a Jesuit order.

A view on the axis from the mansion of the restored reflecting pool, and the replica of the original semicircular pergola. The new guest entrance and registration pavilion are seen in the background.

connected to a central pavilion in which the reception area and offices are located. The architects have nestled the three-level, 100,000-square-foot spa into the sloping grade to reduce its bulk so that it does not overpower the mansion.

In deliberate contrast to the relaxed contemporary mood of the inn and spa, the mansion has been restored to approximate its former elegance. The architects began with a virtual shell as only two of the original rooms remained intact on the first floor. The library has since been refurbished as a book-lined dark wood paneled lounge, and the adjacent intimate rotunda with its domed ceiling serves as a waiting area for the dining rooms. Kitchens and service areas make up the rest of the main floor. The second and third floors contain medical and diagnostic assessment rooms and equipment as well as the executive offices.

Some of the later exterior additions and modifications were removed. The corinthian columned portico has been re-created, and the significant missing architectural detail has been reproduced. Most of Carrere and Hasting's extensive formal landscaping and statuary has been lost over the years. One important feature that has been recreated is the reflecting pool extending on an axis from the garden courtyard of the mansion and terminating in a semicircular wooden pergola.

SIGNIFICANCE

The Lenox Great Estate Law represents the kind of preservation planning that encourages the restoration and adaptive reuse of mansions. Bellefontaine was particularly adaptable because it retained its large acreage and could accommodate additional expansion on the site; in addition, it was an ideal site for a luxurious health spa. Bellefontaine's formality and beauty is an appropriate setting for the elegance of the Canyon Ranch experience.

Interestingly, when built nearly almost a century ago, Bellefontaine was a home in which to entertain and pursue the elite ideals of the time, culture, gardening, art, and manners. It is important to realize that Bellefontaine has survived a pattern typical of many other mansions and large estates all over the country; it has experienced cyclical adaptations to institutional use, extensive fire damage, and subsequent modifications, and eventually virtual abandonment. Often the next step is demolition. Today, after a dedicated and imaginative owner has devoted considerable time and investment to its rebirth as a health spa, Bellefontaine reflects a contemporary trend away from formal social obligations, toward a widespread American interest in health and wellness as an ideal recreation pastime.

Restaurants and Catering Facilities

The concept of using a mansion or old house as a restaurant is not a particularly novel concept; what is new, however, is the increase in the number of institutional and commercial owners of mansions and estates designated as landmark properties that now must negotiate with community groups. In the three cases selected none of the mansions were of such architectural or historic distinction that they warranted the restoration as house museums. None of the three contained any original furnishings which might have given cause for concern.

Almost all local preservation ordinances are limited in scope to the preservation of the exterior of structures. Many communities are genuinely concerned about historic preservation; others have begun to use historic ordinances as means to discourage demolition, zoning changes, and increased commercialization. Many property owners, both public and private, now realize that they can restore mansions and successfully adapt them to restaurants or catering establishments to generate some form of revenue. In prestigious residential neighborhoods there will be considerable opposition, but when the properties are located on major routes, it is a realistic option.

Exterior of Tarrywile, as restored. The semicircular conservatory now functions as an area for receptions.

Tarrywile, Danbury, Connecticut

SITE

Tarrywile, a 1897 gracious Shingle Style house, was built for Dr. William C. While, on a site of 110 acres. The building was used as a private residence until 1985 when the heirs of its second owner, Charles Darling Parks, sold it to the city of Danbury, which opened it as a community center in 1990.

The property is associated with Hearthstone Castle, which was built by photographer E. Sanford Starr at the turn of the century and which was purchased by Parks in 1921 as a wedding present for his daughter. Parks expanded his holdings by acquiring dairy farms and long-abandoned woodlots. At the time of Parks's death in 1929, the assemblage formed 1000 acres of open space in the middle of the city of Danbury, which has a densely developed urban downtown. When Tarrywile and the Hearthstone Castle came on the market, Danbury residents, in a public referendum, voted to acquire the property for use as a community facility. Today Tarrywile is part of the 535-acre Tarrywile Park.

PRESERVATION ISSUE

As noted on the National Register form, Tarrywile is perhaps of greater local historical importance than architectural distinction. It is unique in the sense that not many Shingle Style cottages were built in inland industrial centers. Of the two major buildings on the site, Tarrywile was the larger and more intact, and it was slated as the first restoration project. The Women's Club of Danbury and New Fairfield, realizing

Interior view of Tarrywile's reception areas, looking toward the conservatory.

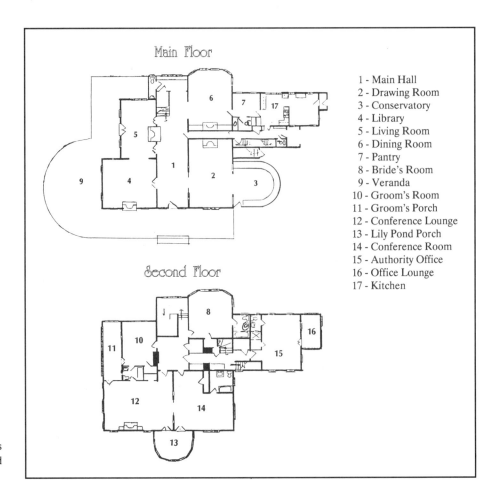

Main Floor

1 - Main Hall
2 - Drawing Room
3 - Conservatory
4 - Library
5 - Living Room
6 - Dining Room
7 - Pantry
8 - Bride's Room
9 - Veranda
10 - Groom's Room
11 - Groom's Porch
12 - Conference Lounge
13 - Lily Pond Porch
14 - Conference Room
15 - Authority Office
16 - Office Lounge
17 - Kitchen

Second Floor

The key to the plan of Tarrywile indicates its adaptation to its new function as a catering and conference center.

that it was unlikely that the city could soon afford to restore the building and upgrade it for use as a public facility, in 1987 organized a designer show house in conjunction with the Ives Arts Center in Danbury. Architect Roger Whitcomb supervised the restoration which, in this case, involved reviewing all proposed decorating schemes to ensure that all showroom designs maintained the architectural character of the house. Modest alterations including the mechanical systems upgrading, the kitchen modernization that retains the original glass-fronted cabinets, and the installation of an access ramp for disabled visitors left the house architecturally intact. Proceeds from the show house were spent on furnishing the building for use as a community center. The Tarrywile Park Authority was established in 1989 to manage the property and the roughly 20 other structures within its bounds. It has future plans to restore Hearthstone Castle to operate as a restaurant and bed-and-breakfast inn. In order to operate permanently, other improvements, such as roof repairs, installation of sprinklers, construction of additional exits, and handicapped-access ramps, were necessary.

By 1990, Tarrywile was opened as a catering facility. The Tarrywile Authority has developed a very clear guide to the appropriate usage of the mansion and its grounds for private parties.

SIGNIFICANCE

Conversion of Tarrywile to a community center available for functions such as weddings and parties has maintained a large open space in the middle of downtown Danbury while offsetting the cost of preserving and maintaining a significant local landmark. Willingness on the part of Danbury residents to purchase the property, combined with significant and creative volunteer efforts, resulted in a community facility that is partially self-supporting and that provides much needed parkland in Danbury which, previously, had no significant downtown park.

Tarrywile engaged architect Whitcomb to coordinate the initial designers' show house as well as the later modifications for permanent public use. It should be noted that the popularity of creating "designer showcases" to raise funds for charitable organizations sometimes leads to permanent damage to the house and its original architectural detailing. In their enthusiasm to demonstrate their own imagination, many decorators remove, cover up, or apply new paint or finishes directly on the original interior surfaces. This can become a serious handicap and lead to additional expense when a serious restoration is later undertaken.

Bragg-Mitchell Mansion, Mobile, Alabama

SITE

Bragg-Mitchell Mansion was built in 1855 by John Bragg, a judge, and later a congressman. It was designed by the judge's brother Alexander Bragg, a prominent Alabama architect. The oaks surrounding the house were leveled during the Civil War to permit the Confederate artillery a clear range in order to shell the approaching Union troops. The mature trees on the site today were planted from acorns saved by the judge and planted after the war. The house survived intact, but ironically most of the original furnishings that were sent upriver to a family plantation for safekeeping were destroyed.

The house and 12 acres were purchased in 1931 by Mr. and Mrs. A. S. Mitchell, who restored and maintained the house and garden for many years. After remaining vacant for 10 years, the Mitchell Foundation gave the house to the Junior League of Mobile to be turned into a hands-on science museum for children. The Junior League turned the property over to a community board to establish the science museum. The original plans were to use the mansion itself as the science museum. When that called for too much altering of the house at too great an expense, a separate structure was built on the property to house the science museum, now called The Exploreum.

PRESERVATION ISSUE

Mobile began preservation efforts in the 1930s, which spared much of the historic core during World War II. The Historic Development Commission was founded in 1962. The Bragg-Mitchell Mansion was listed on the National Register in 1972.

The Bragg-Mitchell Mansion, restored to its antebellum elegance, now functions as a catering facility.

While the fund-raising and construction of the science museum was under way, the board was faced with finding a way to turn the Bragg-Mitchell Mansion into a self-sufficient, multiuse facility. The house is not huge and contains 20 rooms. Following Mobile tradition, it has a T plan, which suits the climate by maximizing air circulation. The colonnade that wraps around three sides of the house is supported by 16 slender fluted columns. Stylistically the house is a hybrid of Greek Revival and Italianate detailing. The center hall, which extends the length of the house, terminates in a gracious curving stair. The ceiling heights are 15 feet on the ground floor and 13.5 feet on the upper floor.

The Mobile architectural firm Holmes and Holmes has been a major force in Alabama historic preservation projects. Both Nick Holmes, Jr., the architect, and Mrs. Baur, who has spearheaded the ongoing restoration efforts begun in 1986, agree emphatically that the Bragg-Mitchell Mansion is not a house museum. The principal rooms in the house are open for weekdays for public visitation, but evenings and weekends it may be rented for catered parties and receptions.

Architect Nick Holmes, Jr., has been meticulous in restoring original architectural interior details and finishes. Once the restoration efforts were under way, a stenciled cornice molding was uncovered, and a consultant performed a historic paint analysis to provide documentary evidence of the original color scheme. The architect also felt that it was necessary to make certain compromises to allow the mansion to function for its new use as a catering facility. To accomplish this, a former rear porch has been glazed to permit its use as a tearoom. He has added at the rear an elevator and chair lift for the handicapped, and also an exterior stair as a second means of egress.

Except for a few mirrors, none of the original contents survive, which in many ways has simplified the refurnishing. The house is now decorated with antiques and lavish window treatments to evoke the antebellum elegance of the house. The arrangement and choice of the furniture and decorative objects are designed to allow flexibility for its catering functions.

SIGNIFICANCE

Mobile and other southern communities already have many restored historic mansions and plantations that are complete with family furnishings and memorabilia. These are not only a source of local pride but also an important element in promoting annual historic house and garden tours. The visitor revenue is essential to meeting the costs of maintaining the historic houses but also in supporting the local economy. Preserving the Bragg-Mitchell Mansion was significant to maintaining its highly visible place in the landscape. The decision to adapt the mansion as a combined showplace and catering facility was met with local support, and the restoration has progressed entirely with private funds and volunteer labor and materials.

McDonald's, Denton House, New Hyde Park, New York

SITE

The Denton House is located on Jericho Turnpike, a busy commercial strip, in New Hyde Park, Long Island, New York. The wood clapboard farmhouse, with its Italianate bracketed cornices, was built for the locally prominent Denton family, circa 1870. The elaborate wooden front verandah terminating with an octagonal and a circular porch at each end can be seen in a period photograph. This photograph was an important source of reference for the later reproduction of missing architectural elements.

The property on which it is sited originally included thousands of acres that had gradually been diminished over time. In the 1920s the last large parcel of land consisting of 300 acres was sold and divided into some 900 individual lots, upon which was built much of the present-day residential development of the community of New Hyde Park.

Period photograph of the Denton House, New Hyde Park, which served as a guide to the restoration and from which missing elements could be replicated by McDonald's.

Shorn of its farmland, the Denton House was sold for commercial use as a restaurant known for many years as the Charred Oak Manor; it later became the Dallas Ribs and was subsequently sold to the McDonald's Corporation.

PRESERVATION ISSUE

After its purchase by the McDonald's Corporation, local residents grew concerned about the future of the run-down Denton House. They brought the matter to the attention of the North Hempstead Historic Landmarks Preservation Commission who designated it in November 1988. In the commission's opinion the Denton House was not unusual for late-nineteenth-century Long Island Farmhouses but was considered a fine example of its type, a Georgian-derived, five-bay central hall prototype with Italianate detailing on the exterior.

The Denton House, transformed as the 12,000th McDonald's, photographed without any automobiles. The new landscaping will fill out with time and perhaps temper the asphalt parking lots.

Interior view of the renovated Denton House showing the dramatic central courtyard dining area that rises three stories to the new wooden trusses that now frame the sloped ceiling of the former attic.

A local architectural firm, Raymond F. Fellman, AIA, of Amityville, was commissioned to restore the exterior, and the New York City firm Haverson Rockwell Architects, P.C., was commissioned to design the restaurant interior. While the exterior shell of the house was in relatively good condition, the interior was not deemed architecturally significant, having lost most of its original detailing and becoming quite dilapidated. Its existing layout was chopped up into spaces unsuitable to McDonald's restaurant operations.

McDonald's wanted to create a more appealing atmosphere and provide a more open feeling that would attract patrons to the second-story mezzanine dining areas, which also included a separate dining room available for rental for children's birthday parties. The central portion of the house was gutted and now opens up through a rectangular well to a dramatic three-story-high space rising to the former attic, now framed with new stout wooden trusses. A broad double stairway at one side of the well leads diners to the second-floor (mezzanine) dining areas. Even though the remodeled interior incorporated some traditional detailing such as wood-paneled wainscoting, decorative moldings, and a wood handrail supported by tapered wood spindle balusters, the overall effect is postmodern, light, and airy.

To accommodate the behind-the-scenes standard elements of McDonald's serving—preparation, walk-in refrigerated storage, storerooms, trash room, and public restrooms—a one-story addition with a full cellar equal in size to the Denton House was constructed behind the old building. To maximize the main- (first) floor dining areas, the octagonal and circular porches were enclosed by full-height glazed panels.

The restoration of the exterior required the demolition of some later accretions including a clumsy porte-cochere which had been constructed in front of the main entrance by the former restaurant tenants as well as modern windows enclosing the porch. To satisfy the local building code and public safety requirements, the house was stripped to its structural skeleton, salvaging original windows, trim, balustrades, cornices, and so on, which were later reinstalled, and missing portions were replicated from the original fragments.

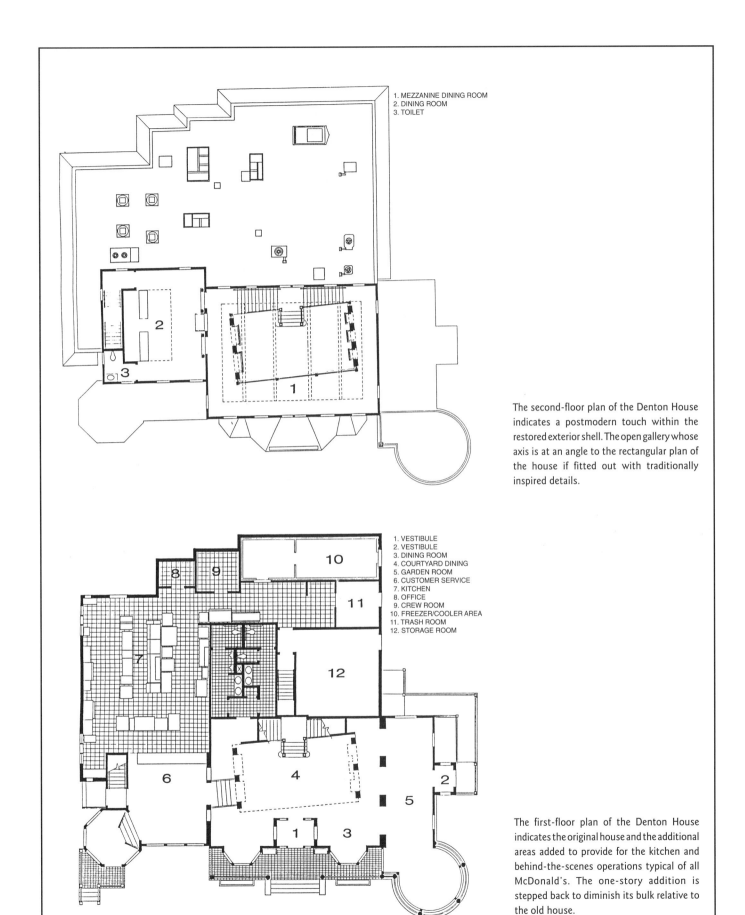

1. MEZZANINE DINING ROOM
2. DINING ROOM
3. TOILET

The second-floor plan of the Denton House indicates a postmodern touch within the restored exterior shell. The open gallery whose axis is at an angle to the rectangular plan of the house if fitted out with traditionally inspired details.

1. VESTIBULE
2. VESTIBULE
3. DINING ROOM
4. COURTYARD DINING
5. GARDEN ROOM
6. CUSTOMER SERVICE
7. KITCHEN
8. OFFICE
9. CREW ROOM
10. FREEZER/COOLER AREA
11. TRASH ROOM
12. STORAGE ROOM

The first-floor plan of the Denton House indicates the original house and the additional areas added to provide for the kitchen and behind-the-scenes operations typical of all McDonald's. The one-story addition is stepped back to diminish its bulk relative to the old house.

Side view of McDonald's with new access ramp and special vestibule. Floor-to-ceiling frameless glass panels have been deftly detailed to provide expanded dining areas in the former circular porch while preserving its original character.

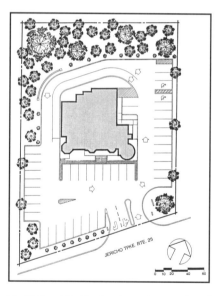

The McDonald's site plan shows the retention of tall trees at the rear of the property to provide a background for the house. Unfortunately, in order to provide access to parking areas, service, and a drive-in window lane, most of the site has been paved over.

Although not required for functional purposes, the four original chimneys were replicated in brick above the roof line. A ramp for the disabled leading to a special new vestibule was constructed at the side of the house, designed to blend in with the original architectural character of the Denton House. Deviating from McDonald's standard specifications, Belgian block curbing stones, brick and slate paved paths, and reproductions of traditional light poles were installed in the parking areas. Existing mature trees at the rear of the site were retained as a backdrop against which the house is seen from the road. New plantings and flower beds were placed around the house and along the side lot lines.

SIGNIFICANCE

Perhaps the most significant aspect of the New Hyde Park McDonald's Restoration of the Denton House is that it demonstrates the increased flexibility of nationwide corporate food chains. For several decades McDonald's and their competitors required the application of uniform layouts, exterior materials, and graphics, which were originally conceived for instant consumer recognition from a passing automobile, in all locations including urban areas. With the increase of center-city historic districts as well as suburban ordinances, community pressure has brought about a greater adaptability in the corporate merchandising attitudes. The 12,000th McDonald's at the Denton House in New Hyde Park can only be identified by a modest sign of black letters on a white background mounted above the white lacy gingerbread decorations of the wooden entrance porch, a far cry from the "Golden Arches," later "mansards" and brightly colored molded plastic giant logos typical of thousands of their locations across the country.

Many older large houses and mansions are located on roads that have become heavily trafficked and are no longer attractive for residential occupancy. Typical of many communities, the Denton House had already been seriously compromised by its previous commercial restaurant occupants and had long since lost its pastoral context. Most local civic groups and small historic societies do not have the resources to acquire, restore, and maintain this kind of structure. Nor is it always practical or desirable to relocate it to another more secluded site. Even in the midst of a bustling commercial strip, at least some vestige of the community's past can be restored to a dignified and self-supporting function.

Apartments and Residential Developments

In selecting examples of mansions adapted to apartment use, a variety have been chosen that represent a broad spectrum of types that exist in many parts of the country. Constitution Hill is a magnificent mansion in Princeton, New Jersey, that provides luxurious apartments within the main house and stables and additional clustered condominium housing on the site. It is also significant that Princeton has permitted this multifamily usage contrary to the strict single-family-residence zoning typical of most wealthy and prestigious communities.

Squire House is a representative Victorian Hudson River Valley villa that has lost its original setting and remains somewhat isolated in a transitional neighborhood. The house was rescued by a local preservation group whose offices are now located in part of its elegant main-floor spaces, while the rest of the house has converted to moderate-income rental housing. The Maryland resident-curator program is an innovative concept in preservation that encourages individuals to restore publicly owned historic houses too numerous and scattered to be maintained and that otherwise would have been lost to neglect. The Maples development in Wenham, Massachusetts, has converted a mansion and its grounds into an attractive community of housing for the elderly.

Also in the section on Newport, Rhode Island, are some interesting conversions of historic district mansions to condominium apartments. All of these large residences have been restored and preserved, and they are responsive to their community's housing needs.

Constitution Hill, Princeton, New Jersey

SITE

Constitution Hill is a 29-room Jacobean Style mansion designed by architects Cope and Stewardson in 1897 for Junius Spencer Morgan, a nephew of financier J. Pierpont Morgan. The house is sited on a 47-acre estate in Princeton, New Jersey. The house

The handsome main entrance facade of the Constitution Hill mansion now divided into six condominium apartment units, which is not evident at all from the exterior.

is located in an old neighborhood near the historic center of town and Princeton University. It is surrounded by other substantial houses on generally smaller sites. Nearby are the former homes of Thomas Mann, Albert Einstein, and Presidents Woodrow Wilson and Grover Cleveland. The house remained in the Morgan family, but rising taxes and maintenance made it impractical for them to continue to support the building as a single-family dwelling. In 1979 the family sold it to the Collins Development Corporation for conversion.

PRESERVATION ISSUE

Architect Perry Morgan of Holt and Morgan Associates, Princeton, a member of the Morgan family, conceived and designed the conversion. The consultant architect was Do Chung of Yankee Planning, Stamford, Connecticut. The mansion and its setting, at a convenient commuting distance from New York, were in an area increasingly being subdivided for single-family residential development in the late 1970s. Princeton has very strict zoning ordinances and historic preservation is given priority in town planning. A precedent for the subdivision of Constitution Hall was nearby Guernsey Hall, an 1852 Princeton landmark that contained 42 rooms on a site of only 2.5 acres. Princeton zoning at the time permitted only single-family residences in that area. A local architect, Bill Short, crusaded for its division into six condominium apartments to prevent its demolition. In 1972 the variance was finally granted.

Architect Perry Morgan wanted to preserve the Morgans' mansion and carriage house and formal garden with enough open space to keep the original setting. Rather than develop the entire parcel, the developer was able to keep 60 percent of the property as open land by clustering the new residential units at a distance from the mansion. The mansion and the carriage house were preserved by converting them into residential units.

The site plan for converting Constitution Hill to apartments and a section through the center of the property that indicates the clustering of new units and the preservation of large flowing communal open spaces. Note the sinuous road across that connects everything. This road requires far less paving than a standard road in a conventional development would.

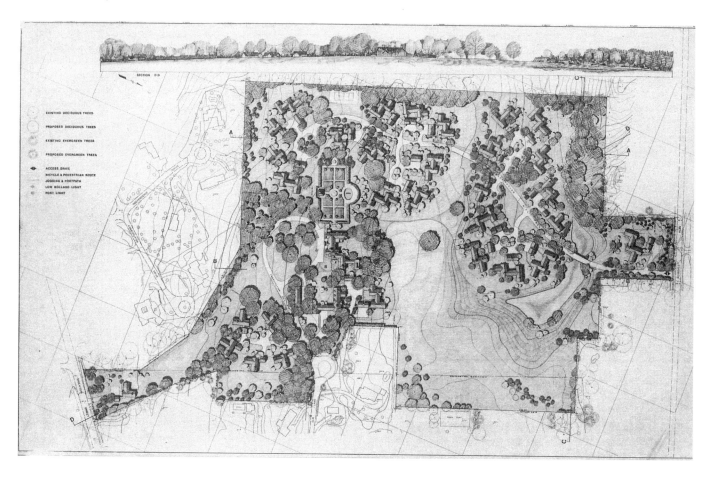

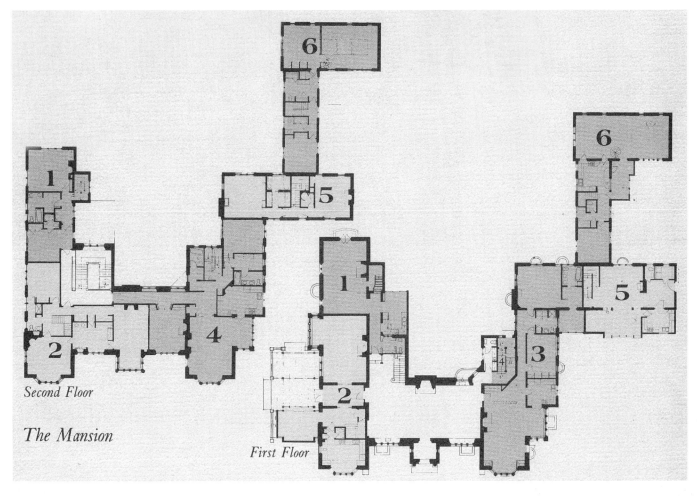

1
2
Second Floor

The Mansion

5
6

1
2
First Floor

4

3
4

5
6

The mansion itself serves as the central attraction of the development, and its architecture served as the inspiration for the new construction.

The mansion was converted into six housing units (5 two bedroom and 1 three bedroom). In was a challenge to maintain the distinctive character of the mansion's original principal spaces and parcel them out among the different apartments. Many rooms feature fireplaces, decorative plaster ceilings, and tall bay windows of leaded glass casements. The interior layout for the apartments was very complex. Four of the units have been designed as duplexes with their own internal stairs. The original 50-by 25-foot paneled and beamed ceilinged main entry hall and grand stair has been preserved as a common space and provides entrances to four of the units. It also serves as a meeting space for the condominium association. Two of the duplex units have direct outside entrances. Minor additions at ground level were executed in a buff stucco finish.

The complex division of the house was facilitated by the original brick construction of its exterior shell and some major interior walls, as well as floor spanned by steel framing and terra-cotta arches. The overlapping of the upper-level duplex apartment units did not always mirror the lower-floor plan and sometimes traversed public hallways. The basic fireproof nature of the house's original construction provided proper separation of the individual apartment units. Many mansions of this period appear on the exterior to be of substantial masonry construction but in fact have wooden floor joists and interior partitions that complicate code compliance and may require sprinklers. This is not only an added expense, but it is also difficult to conceal the sprinklers without disrupting existing finishes.

Plans for the apartments within the Constitution Hill mansion. All except units 3 and 4 are duplexes with internal stairs. The original impressive large entrance hall and grand stair have been retained for circulation, giving access to all but units 5 and 6, which have their own exterior entrances.

A side view of the Constitution Hill mansion shows a new pergola and enclosed dining area for unit 2, which has been discretely added onto an existing paved terrace. A stucco exterior covered with lattice for vines and lush landscaping create privacy for this unit.

The former stable and its walled enclosure at Constitution Hill provide privacy for a residential unit. The original large carriage doorway has been replaced with a greenhouse.

A close-up view of the entrance of one of the new Constitution Hill units is contemporary in spirit, yet echoes the brick color, texture, and character of the main house with its arched entry recess.

The carriage house and stable were converted into two residential units. Fifty-two new units were constructed on the property in a combination of 21 duplexes and 10 single-family detached homes. The design of the new units are contemporary, but some effort has been made to choose materials, textures, and colors similar to those of the mansion. They have steep roofs edged in copper, those nearest the mansion with real slate. Brick elements are constructed of warm red variegated brick with arched-topped recessed entrance doorways. The basic unit is L shaped to provide privacy for individual paved patios. Although the units are similar in plan, they are clustered in groups of five to eight with separate two-car garages for each, arranged to create some variety.

The mansion's formal gardens, lawns, a cornfield, and wooded areas were preserved. New amenities such as a swimming pool, pool house, and tennis court were also constructed in a site that screens views from the formal gardens. Constitution Hill's original entry drive, from a heavily trafficked road, had to be shifted to a minor secondary street to allow for the increased traffic volume generated by the additional residential units on the site.

SIGNIFICANCE

The Constitution Hill project preserves the mansion and offers an alternative to the rigidities of typical suburban and resort single-residence-only ordinances that produce more internal roads and monotony. It especially offers an opportunity for "empty nesters" who are accustomed to large houses to remain in the community in smaller but luxurious quarters with extensive mature traditional landscaping.

A view of new units at Constitution Hill clustered amidst existing mature trees. The flared roof brick gable ends and large chimneys, also relate to the mansion.

Squire House, Ossining, New York

SITE

The Squire House, also known as Highland Cottage, was constructed between 1872 and 1874 for a New York City merchant Henry J. Baker. Its design by S. Marvin McCord reflects the influence of the picturesque Romantic Style in the Hudson River Valley. It is also significant for being an early example of the Romantic Style and for being one of the few remaining intact residences that were constructed entirely of poured concrete. D. Amos Osbourne Squire, a prominent local physician, acquired the property about 1905. Squire had a strong interest in prison reform and was the first prison doctor in the United States, serving as the physician for Sing Sing Prison, located in Ossining. During World War I, Squire operated a hospital in the house. Squire's daughter, Evelyn Culp, is still one of its residents.

The house is located along Route 9 in Ossining, which is a busy, mixed-use area with residential and institutional buildings, abutting the town's nineteenth-century commercial district. Although many houses near Squire House are of the same era and scale, these Victorian buildings have been joined by modern multifamily housing complexes and a large school, which together have modified the residential character of the neighborhood.

PRESERVATION ISSUE

The house remained in private ownership until the mid-1980s. Squire's daughter, Evelyn Culp, lived in the large house and for years ran a business school in its basement. When in 1984 it became apparent that the Squire House had reached a critical stage of

Squire House as it appears today. Most of its original features have been preserved and restored by the Westchester Preservation League.

deterioration, the Westchester Preservation League, a then-fledgling not-for-profit preservation organization founded in 1979, acquired the title from Mrs. Culp and undertook to stabilize and restore the house, which now serves as the league's headquarters.

The house was too large to restore as a single-family residence, so the Westchester Preservation League (WPL) began exploring options. In undertaking the restoration of Squire House, the WPL was initially concerned only with a sensitive restoration and providing an appropriate use for a significant Westchester landmark. Various members of the board were community housing activists who saw the house, and its urban setting, as an ideal location for affordable housing, which is almost an oxymoron in Westchester County. As the league explored uses for the house, it determined that affordable housing was most fitting for both the house and the community.

Since the building is listed on the National Register of Historic Places and also designated a local Ossining landmark, the Westchester Preservation League has been able to raise funds from a variety of sources including New York State Environmental Bond Act and a HUD grant and loan administered through the Westchester County Community Development Office. The WPL has also been able to reach private investors through a limited partnership that took advantage of the income tax credits for historic preservation.

SIGNIFICANCE

Nearly 10 years after the acquisition, the Westchester Preservation League has almost completed the restoration.

The league was pleased to receive the Preservation League of New York State's Affordable Housing and Historic Preservation Award. In making the award, the Preservation League of New York stated said: "Squire House, built for private residential use, shows how a landmark gem can give new dignity to low-income residents, retain notable exterior and interior features, and also provide space for larger community use."

The program for the building includes affordable housing in 75 percent of the house's habitable spaces. Five out of the seven tenants in Squire House meet the HUD requirements for low- to moderate-income housing.

The house has been restored in accordance with the Secretary of the Interior's Standards for Restoration and Rehabilitation. The slate roof has been repaired, ornamental wooden buttons and bracketed cornices and window surrounds have been repaired and repainted, and elaborate porches have been restored. The wood-framed skylight that illuminated the center stairwell, long covered by a metal frame with frosted glass that created a gloomy pallor within the house, has been uncovered and repaired, substantially brightening the house.

The ground floor of the Squire House contains the office of the Westchester Preservation League, as well as a market-rate apartment created in 1986 in the former business school space and funded with conventional mortgage financing. The original living quarters of the property are used as moderate-income housing. The main floor contains public spaces including a large entry hall, living room, dining room, library, and kitchen, use of which is enjoyed by the tenants. The second floor contains four units, and the third floor contains three units. The living arrangements in the house provide shared use of ground-floor rooms. These spaces are also used by the Westchester Preservation League for meetings and events, which are often attended by Squire House residents.

Squire House has been restored without compromising the architectural and historical integrity of the building, while simultaneously providing safe, economical, and architecturally distinguished housing for people of low to moderate incomes. WPL's success in restoring Squire House for use as affordable housing belies the convention that in order to be affordable, housing must be modest and unadorned.

Knock's Folly has been restored and rescued from neglect by the Maryland Resident Curatorship Program.

MARYLAND'S RESIDENT CURATORSHIP PROGRAM

The Department of Natural Resources of the state of Maryland owns over 1200 structures, about 400 of which, on 170 different sites, have been determined by the Maryland Historical Trust to be of historical significance.

Many of the structures, such as Fort Frederick and Smallwood's Retreat, are maintained by the state as historic sites open to the public. Others are used as rental housing or houses for state employees who provide a security presence in parks. A series of about 50 Civilian Conservation Corps buildings, picnic shelters, rental cabins, and scenic overlooks, are enjoyed by Maryland's campers. Some buildings are interpreted as ruins; others can be returned to private ownership with appropriate preservation easements and restrictions. Unfortunately some buildings are deteriorated beyond the financial capability of the department's resources yet are of sufficient historic merit to warrant preservation.

It is for these categories of buildings that Maryland has developed an innovative program to restore some of the historic buildings owned by the state without using scarce state funding. With their Resident Curatorship Program, established in 1982, they have ensured the restoration of over 20 properties through the private donations of restoration and maintenance services for historic structures owned by the department.

The curators, who must show that they have experience in historic preservation and the financial ability to support their proposed undertaking, agree to restore and preserve the properties according to the secretary of the interior's guidelines for historic preservation. Proposals must include a realistic task and cost schedule that can be completed within 5 years, and generally, the proposal must represent at least $50,000 worth of improvements in order to justify a curatorship. The curator's interest in a property is only a life interest (as long as they are maintaining their obligations with regards to the property) and cannot be bequeathed.

This is a win-win situation. The curators are able to live in a historic property, built with care and craftsmanship, they could probably not have access to on the open market. The properties available for curatorship are generally in rural, tranquil locations. If they are successful, the curators can live in a unique property, mortgage and tax free. In addition, tax laws can enable the curator to deduct the costs of their improvements which are a gift to the state. The state, in turn, has a historic property appropriately restored and in use, without any public expenditure.

Although curatorships are restricted to noncommercial properties, the program provides for a long-term lease for projects involving commercial uses for historic buildings. They especially encourage such uses where the use enhances the mission of the park facilities, such as mansions that are used as inns in areas where little hotel space is available. In these cases, in addition to the obligation of restoring the property, the curator-lessee is expected to contribute a percentage of their earnings from the property to the state.

To date, over 20 properties have been restored through the Resident Curatorship Program. The following descriptions reflect the flexibility and creativity of this program, as well as the variety of historic properties it has restored.

Smith Tavern, Baltimore, Maryland

Smith Tavern is a unique example of a historic structure within a state park, restored on the exterior and adapted to the needs of its disabled occupants through the Resident Curatorship Program.

Smith Tavern, located in Gunpowder Falls State Park, Baltimore, Maryland, is a pre–Civil War structure that served as a tavern and tollhouse for the Jarretsville Pike. In the 1950s, it was gutted and remodeled by a private owner into apartments, destroying the interior integrity of the building. The state of Maryland purchased it and entered into a lease agreement with a local family. Dave Ward, one of the adult children of the family, suffered a spinal injury that left him disabled. Dave and his wife, Terri, proposed a resident-curatorship that would allow them to restore the exterior of the building while fitting the interior to showcase state-of-the-art technology for the disabled. They have completed the restoration and landscaping of the exterior at their own expense. They are now finishing the interior with the assistance of several organizations including the Volunteers for Medical Engineering, a federal grant through Baltimore County from the Department of Housing and Urban Development.

When completed, the house will not only be restored to its mid-nineteenth-century exterior appearance, it will also serve as a home for the Wards and as a model for others interested in understanding technology's ability to facilitate independent living for the disabled.

Mount Airy, Prince George's County, Maryland

Mount Airy, located in Rosaryville State Park in Prince George's County, is thought to date from the eighteenth century, when the brick wing was constructed by Benedict Calvert sometime after 1752. The Calvert family owned the property until the twentieth century and was responsible for both the Greek Revival wing and the house's name, Mount Airy. George Washington visited the house on more than one occasion, including the marriage of his stepson to a Calvert daughter. Tillie Littell Duvall, a New York artist and musician, and her husband Percival owned the house from 1903 through 1931, and during that time they entertained Presidents William Howard Taft, Woodrow Wilson, and Herbert Hoover. In 1931 the house burned, and the Duvalls sold the ruins to Eleanor "Cissy" Medill Patterson, the publisher of the *Washington Times-Herald,* who rebuilt the house in the Colonial Revival Style. Patterson had continued the tradition of entertaining presidents, and her guests included President Franklin D. and Mrs. Eleanor Roosevelt, as well as William Randolph Hearst and Alice Roosevelt Longworth. In 1972 it was sold by Ann Bowie Smith, who inherited it from Patterson, to the state of Maryland.

In 1983, when the state of Maryland felt unable to fund an adequate restoration, it was leased to a private restaurant corporation who orchestrated an extensive restoration financed through private and public grants and loans. Although this business failed, the property was restored and is now maintained by the Maryland

Mount Airy, located within a state park, has a long and complicated history combining the ruins of an eighteenth-century house incorporated within a 1930s Colonial Revival Style reconstruction. It remains a handsome testament to Maryland's innovative approach to rescuing and maintaining a large inventory of historic structures on public land.

Conservation Corps, a federally funded job skill training program for young adults. The state is exploring ways in which the property can become a self-supporting catering facility.

Elkridge Furnace Inn, Elkridge, Maryland

The Elkridge Furnace Inn, in Patapsco Valley State Park, in Elkridge, Howard County, Maryland, is a circa 1800 by Caleb Dorsey, the proprietor of an ironworks. Its site, Elkridge Landing, was once the head of the Patapsco River, but silting has long since made it unnavigable. The house was used both as a tavern and store for the ironworkers and living accommodations for the proprietor and his family. Later owners, the Ellicotts, added more stylish wings. Iron was produced there until a flood in 1868 put an end to that industry on the site. The house was a residence until the mid-1980s when it was acquired by the Maryland State Highway Administration, who intended to raze it and a number of other buildings to erect a bridge across the Patapsco River. Preservationists and environmentalists were able to stop the highway administration's plans, saving the furnace house as well as two smaller dwellings dating from the late eighteenth and early nineteenth centuries.

Because the property bordered on the Patapsco Valley State Park, the Department of Natural Resources took the property in trade for other property that the state highway authority may utilize for other road projects.

The curatorship encompasses the three buildings; two residences structured as conventional curatorships and one commercial building, the Elkridge Furnace Inn, which has a lease arrangement in which the rent can be paid in restoration services. Dan and Steve Wrecker and their wives, Donna and Patti, are the curators of the property. Their family catering business "The Wreckers, Inc.," is run out of the furnace house, which is about two-thirds complete, and they have restored the two smaller houses as their own residences. The inn now functions as a catering facility and when complete will also house a restaurant and offer overnight accommodations.

Through a public-private partnership, the property, which abuts an important state park, is preserved and actively used and will ultimately be controlled by the state, which incurred no public expense.

Raincliffe, an 1850s house, has been handsomely restored through the Resident Curatorship Program.

Raincliffe, Sykesville, Maryland

Raincliffe is located in Patapsco Valley State Park, Sykesville, Carroll County, Maryland. The house was originally built circa 1850 by an officer of the Mexican War, who called the estate "Chihuahua" after the Mexican state. A prominent two-story porch was enclosed about 1900 when subsequent owners made modifications that included a smaller pillared porch as well as several additions, now gone, in a conversion to a country hotel for Baltimore residents escaping the hot summer.

Captain Horace Jefferson, who acquired it in 1944, called the estate Raincliffe after his family estate in Wales. Nelson and Leigh Bolton became curators in 1984, and the house, now fully restored, is their residence.

OTHER RESIDENTIAL CONVERSIONS

The Maples, Wenham, Massachusetts

SITE

Wenham, Massachusetts, is a historic community, with roots going back to the seventeenth century, which has maintained its traditional New England village character. The 1920s mansion, which was the principal feature of the site until its development, is located on the main thoroughfare running through town. Main Street and the village green retain several distinctive landmarks: the white clapboard village hall, the classic First Church of Wenham with its distinctive steeple, and many fine houses, the oldest of which is the seventeenth-century Richards House, now restored as a house museum. In the eighteenth and nineteenth centuries Wenham was an agricultural community that also thrived on the sale of ice from Wenham Lake. Wenham's location 30 minutes north of Boston is now within the city's suburbs. Its location is in close proximity to beaches and coastal resorts, as well as to vacation and recreational areas in New Hampshire and Maine to the north.

PRESERVATION ISSUE

In the 1980s like many suburban towns, the longtime residents reaching retirement began to sell their houses to younger families moving into Wenham. There was nowhere in town for the older generation to move. A local church group (called Living Options for Elders, or LOFE) had been trying to develop a facility for active retirees in Wenham but couldn't find a suitable site. Then in 1989, a historic estate on Wenham's Main Street became available through bankruptcy. The 7.8-acre site was studded with fine old shade trees and rock outcroppings, and it backed up to a country club—a perfect setting for a retirement community.

At the time banks were reluctant to loan to nonprofits so LOFE approached developer James R. Brady, Jr. Brady was able to persuade his own attorney James A. Manzi to invest in the project, and he in turn was able to convince a local bank to finance the project. Brady and Manzi had to get the land rezoned as an elder housing district, which required that households include at least one person 60 or older. This process also needed approval before a town meeting. The vote was nearly unanimous because LOFE convinced the town that there was a need for this type of housing in Wenham.

The original 1920s mansion was a handsome, solid, not architecturally exceptional, Georgian Revival brick construction, which has been divided into five units with elevators in the two level units. The 50 new units were clustered on the rear 4 acres of the site so that they would retain the same sweeping lawns and setback of the original mansion. Four different layout types were created. The architectural Miquelle MZO group paid special attention to scale and massing so that the new housing units would not "overpower" the mansion itself. Clever Colonial-derived detailing and breaking up of large wall areas with breezeways, bay windows, wall dormers, and brick veneer recalling the mansion created variety and avoided repetition. The atmosphere of a small New England village is appealing to the residents who have lived in traditional style homes.

The former garages in the center of the site have been converted into a small community center, containing the on-site manager's office, mailroom, and a cozy gathering space with a fireplace. An adjoining village green and swimming pool provide for warm-weather neighborly socialization.

For the Maples project, the original 1920s mansion has been divided into five units with elevators in the two-story apartments.

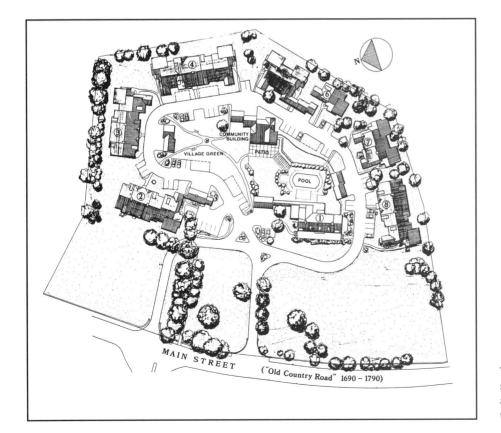

The site plan of the Maples reveals a great sensitivity to the needs of active retired persons, as well as preserving a 1920s mansion on a main thoroughfare.

The design of the new units surrounding the Maples mansion provide a variety of appealing Colonial Revival Style homes, clustered to avoid the institutional look that characterizes many developments for the elderly.

SIGNIFICANCE

The Maples is a wonderful prototype of a facility that many small towns and suburban communities need. Located in a historic district on a main road, the project has carefully retained the street scape, old stone walls and gates, and the mansion's mature landscaped setting. In many communities an elegant large mansion built in a more gracious era along a main thoroughfare is no longer desirable for a well-to-do owner, and yet it is an important landmark in the road scape. The Maples project has succeeded in preserving the mansion and fulfilling a much-needed local housing resource.

Ronald McDonald House, Philadelphia, Pennsylvania

SITE

It is hard to classify the current adaptive use of a large turn-of-the-century mansion and carriage house located in West Philadelphia, in the "center city" area. The Romanesque Revival Style, white rough-cut limestone mansion, capped with a green glazed mission-tile roof, was designed by architect William H. Decker in 1890 for William James Swain. Swain was the publisher of the *Philadelphia Ledger,* later the *Philadelphia Inquirer.*

The mansion was occupied by Swain and his family as a private residence until he sold it in the 1920s. It was bought by a long-established Philadelphia firm of undertakers, Andrew J. Bair and Son, who operated it as a funeral home until 1980.

Judging by an illustrated promotional brochure prepared for the funeral home in the 1920s, the original dignified and formal interiors were preserved along with the wood-paneled interiors, stained glass, furniture, light fixtures, decorative objects. The funeral home acquired still more "treasures" to impress their clientele.

The former carriage house, located at the rear of the site facing a secondary street, was converted to a mortuary. The transformation of a dignified old mansion to a funeral home is common throughout the United States; its sale to McDonald's in 1980 is less conventional.

Entrance hall of the Swain mansion. Through the successive ownership of the Blair and Sons, Undertakers, and the later conversion to Ronald McDonald House, the fine detailing and handsome finishes have been preserved.

PRESERVATION ISSUE

In the early 1970s McDonald's was approached through their advertising agency by a group of parents, doctors, and friends of a young Philadelphia area patient, the daughter of a popular Philadelphia Eagles football player. They described to McDonald's management the need for a facility to provide support services for the families of seriously ill children requiring hospitalization and follow-up treatments.

An aerial view of the Swain mansion showing the addition planned by Ronald McDonald House. Philadelphia architects Alesker, Reiff, and Dundon carefully studied the original detailing and proportions of the mansion and repeated the motifs on the new facade.

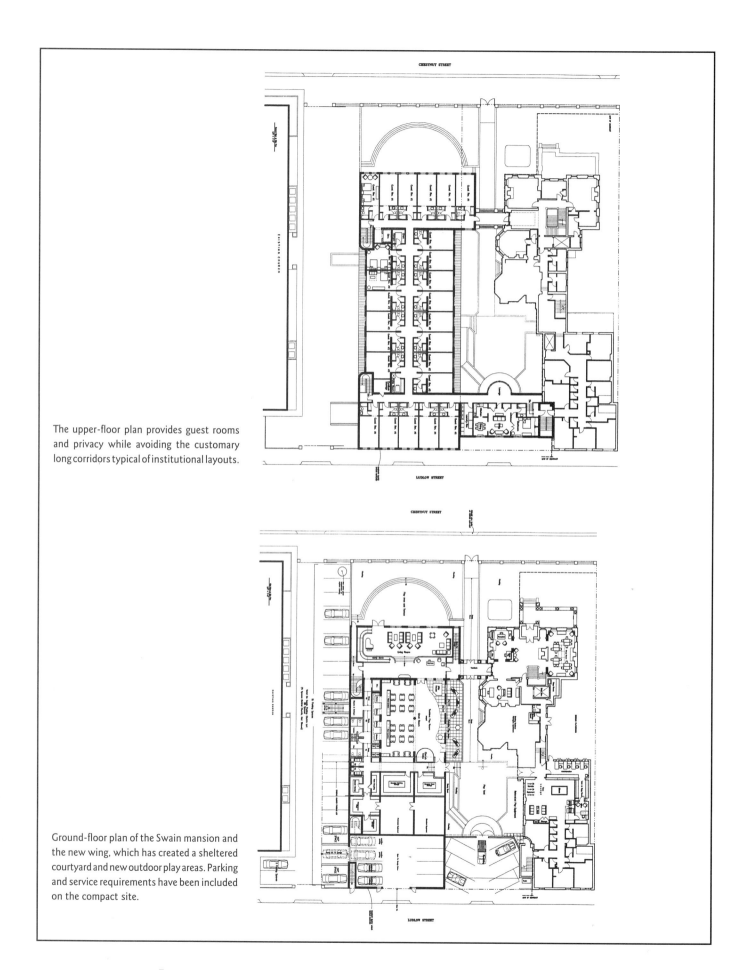

The upper-floor plan provides guest rooms and privacy while avoiding the customary long corridors typical of institutional layouts.

Ground-floor plan of the Swain mansion and the new wing, which has created a sheltered courtyard and new outdoor play areas. Parking and service requirements have been included on the compact site.

McDonald's and their restaurant owners in the Philadelphia and Delaware Valley were receptive to the proposal and supported the project. In October 1974 the first Ronald McDonald House was in operation. Almost immediately, its seven guest rooms were fully occupied, and there was always a waiting list. The success of this pilot project and its innovative concept, relying on community participation, contributions of labor, materials, and supplies, and volunteer services, has led to the establishment of more than 150 similar facilities throughout the United States and abroad.

Seeking additional accommodations, the nearby Swain mansion was acquired by the Philadelphia Ronald McDonald House and provided a total of 19 guest rooms, 8 in the main house, including a duplex resident manager's apartment in the former service quarters, and 11 guest rooms in the former carriage house. The preservation of the residential character of the mansion was important to achieve a homelike atmosphere for families and their seriously ill children, who have already spent a great deal of time in antiseptic institutional surroundings.

The elaborate principal rooms on the main floor of the mansion have been furnished as communal lounges and activities for the resident families and their children. A communal kitchen and laundry rooms permit these overstressed families to organize some modicum of household routine as well as the emotional support of others going through the same difficult experiences. This special home-away-from-home could never be provided in a typical commercial hotel or motel.

By the 1990s, a decade after the move into the Swain mansion, the facility was again inadequate to meet the demand, and more than a thousand people a year were being turned away. The Swain mansion's convenient location only a 15-minute walk from two major hospitals, including the Philadelphia Children's Hospital, was an important factor in choosing the Swain mansion initially. In 1993 when an adjacent parking lot became available through an agreement with the Church of Jesus Christ of the Latter Day Saints, a new expansion was planned.

Philadelphia architects Alesker, Reiff, and Dundon have masked a modern facility behind a sensitively designed street facade, which repeats the Romanesque arched openings of the Swain mansion on the first floor, and the nineteenth-century proportions of the second-story windows, as well as continuing the projecting band courses. The new addition maintains the same setback as the mansion and is separated from it by a recess in which the original porte-cochere now serves as the main entrance to the entire complex.

The architects have skillfully organized the interior layout of the two-story addition to provide 24 more guest rooms with private bathrooms on the second floor, and they have designed expanded lounge, communal dining, and laundry areas. New parking spaces have been created alongside the addition, as well as limited sheltered and enclosed parking at the rear. New outdoor play areas have been developed in the courtyard formed between the mansion and the new addition, and a new large semicircular flagstone-paved terrace opens from the lounge areas at grade facing the street.

A cheerful children's play area has been provided for the enjoyment of the families staying temporarily at Ronald McDonald House in Center City, Philadelphia.

SIGNIFICANCE

The Philadelphia Ronald McDonald House demonstrated an innovative adaptation of an inner-city mansion, to house an important community service facility, and renovate and add to it while respecting its architectural integrity. All major cities and smaller communities contain formerly elegant neighborhoods whose once-proud mansions have been left behind when the descendants of their affluent families moved on to newer, "more" fashionable locations.

It is interesting that the McDonald's Corporation has been able to modify its formerly rigid standards and "image" to suit the requirements of historic districts and suburban areas and under the aegis of its charitable foundation, has been able to respond so sensitively to community needs. It is a model that other major corporations might do well to emulate.

A large new residence within the farm group incorporates the form and original stone elements of the Conyers Manor garages and chauffeur's wing in a compatible style.

Recreational Uses of Mansions and Estates

The adaptation of mansions and estates as country clubs is not a novelty. The rezoning of country clubs has become a source of concern in some communities, and this aspect is discussed in the chapter on suburban zoning. Often estate lands that once functioned as gentlemen's farms are subdivided, so that the acreage with the farm group of barns, stables, and accessory structures are sold separately from the mansion. Typically, the farm group is in a greater state of neglect than the main house. Nowadays the adaptation of the farm complexes for residential or recreational uses such as skiing or polo has become quite popular.

Conyers Farm, Greenwich, Connecticut

SITE

The land for the community now known as Conyers Farm was assembled in the early 1900s by Edmund Converse, one of the founders of U.S. Steel and Banker's Trust of New York. He built a country residence patterned after an English manor, and over a 10-year period created a self-sufficient estate in excess of 1300 acres known as Conyers Manor. The manor house, built on high ground, has a commanding view of Long Island Sound as far as Manhattan. On the surrounding slopes are extensive parks, gardens, and greenhouses, and the homes Converse commissioned for other members of his family.

A small studio has been built abutting the stone ruins of a large dairy barn on Conyers Farm.

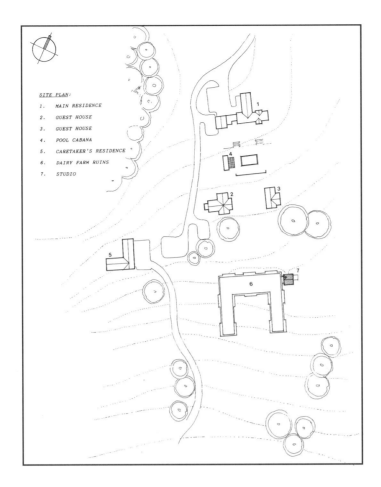

Site plan of Conyers Farm former manor farm group structures, now converted to a residence and various other accessory uses.

SITE PLAN:
1. MAIN RESIDENCE
2. GUEST HOUSE
3. GUEST HOUSE
4. POOL CABANA
5. CARETAKER'S RESIDENCE
6. DAIRY FARM RUINS
7. STUDIO

Donn Barber, a well-known New York architect, was chosen to design the manor house and the extensive farm complex. Barber was an exponent of the Beaux-Arts derived style, modern French design. He designed many banks, the Lotos Club, and institutional buildings in New York City. The estate was the largest and most complex in Greenwich, Connecticut, and at one time included more than 40 structures scattered over the site.

The landscape was planned and planted over a period of 8 years by Henry Wild, an English garden architect, who also designed gardens for the Duke of Marlborough at Blenheim Palace and for Isabella Stuart Gardner at her Brookline, Massachusetts, estate. Wild's scheme included formal gardens and a Japanese woodland garden surrounding the manor house.

The farming operations were concentrated on 200 acres of prime agricultural land lying below the manor house. Converse built a magnificent stone dairy barn and many other farm buildings. He raised poultry, cows, and pigs and produced milk, butter, and eggs stamped with the distinctive CF mark. On the high ridges extending north from the barns and into neighboring New York State were hundreds of acres of apple, pear, and peach orchards. Unlike many of his wealthy contemporaries, the extensive farming operations that also included greenhouse crops actually made money.

The property also included large stands of woodlands and the manor's own stone quarries that supplied the granite for the estate buildings. In the center of the property Converse built the manor's water supply, 100-acre Converse Lake.

Another view of the new studio on Conyers Farm that has been carefully detailed and constructed in the manner of the old stonework.

PRESERVATION ISSUE

The Converse Farm continued to operate into the mid-1930s when the property was purchased by Lewis Rosenstiel, the founder of Schenley Distillers. The present owner

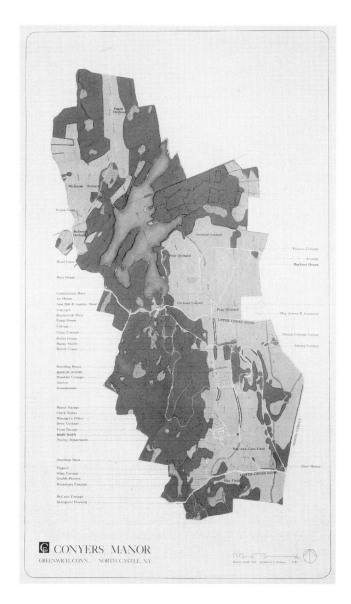

A site plan of Conyers Manor showing all the existing original structure prior to development. Robert Lamb Hart Planners and Architects prepared the layout of the Conyers Farm subdivision.

of Conyers Farm, a partnership, whose principal is Peter M. Brandt, acquired the property from the Rosenstiel estate in 1981. Since acquisition, he has developed a comprehensive concept for the subdivision plan of the estate. He is committed to the restoration of the surviving structures, many of which were in poor condition or in actual ruins, as well to the conservation of the natural environment.

Conyers Farm is planned as a private residential community with a maximum of 60 estates. These range in size from 10 to 20 acres or more. All estate owners will be members of the Conyers Farm Association which will provide: a complete road system, 5 miles of riding trails, security system, and maintenance of landscaping in common areas. Members will be bound by a set of restrictive covenants, which are intended to establish architectural controls and wildlife preserves and to prevent small subdivisions of properties and land speculation. The Conyers Farm estate has over 1000 acres of land and water in which there are four distinctive natural settings. The largest is the manor land, the original site of Converse's manor house, gardens, barns, and farm buildings. The woodlands are an established deer habitat. Mature stands of trees are interlaced with ponds, streams, and rocky outcrops. The lakefront offers broad vistas and use of the lake. The high ridges, cleared centuries ago, are traditional New England farmlands divided by old stone walls. Purchasers will be able to choose sites in one of these four settings for the construction of new residences.

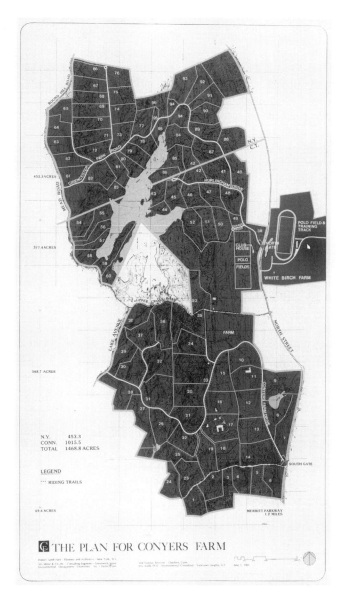

A site plan of Conyers Farm prepared by Robert Lamb Hart Planners and Architects showing the subdivision and internal road network entered at the Southern Gate. The new Polo Club located at the Northern Gate straddles an existing local road, so that members and visitors do not enter the private roads.

The main entrance to the new internal road network, the Southern Gate, is through a massive gate and its original gatehouse. At the Northern Gate the new Conyers Farm Polo Club is located. In 1984, New York architect Alan Wanzenberg designed the Polo Club. Through careful attention to the original Cotswold style cut-stone and wood-shingled detailing, he has salvaged old estate structures that were seriously deteriorated.

The Greenwich Polo Club House is a 10,000-square-foot reconstruction and addition to the shell of a stone barn that had burned in the late 1940s. The existing structure was renovated into the club room with locker rooms below. A large Shingle Style addition houses an indoor tennis court.

Dominating the estate was the manor, a 50-room mansion constructed in the manner of a Beaux-Arts French villa of the 1890s, of cut stone with a green tiled gabled roof showing wide bellcast eaves, large curved brackets, and prominent rafter ends and purlins. Two lower wings extending from the main mass of the house featured attached pergolas, and there was an impressive porte-cochere. The manor house was to have been restored, but it was destroyed by fire.

In general, the other estate buildings present a more horizontal aspect, influenced more by the English Cotswold mode and the Shingle Style. As in the manor house, they show cut-stone first stories and broad, bracketed eaves, but differ by

The Conyers Farm new Polo Club building incorporating stone ruins of an old barn.

featuring wood-shingled upper stories, wood-shingled roofs, and more asymmetrical plans.

Wanzenberg, who has a strong affinity for the Craftsman Style, since 1982 has been transforming the DeKwiatowski Farm, a site that contains the core of the original manor farm complex. The reconstructions and additions include the main residence, two guest houses, and the maintenance barn–caretaker's cottage. Within the ruins of the large dairy barn, a new studio has been added and a conservatory is planned. Two new buildings have been added: a stable, containing groom's quarters and a guest apartment, and a pool cabana. The main residence incorporates the remains of the original manor garage and chauffeur's quarters.

SIGNIFICANCE

Connecticut's long irregular coastline, with numerous small coves and harbors, offers picturesque vistas of islands and the Long Island Sound. Just as Long Island's north shore, the area shares a seafaring New England tradition dating to colonial times. In the late nineteenth century Greenwich began transforming itself into a one of America's wealthiest enclaves. Located at a convenient commuting distance to New York City, it became a fashionable community for New Yorkers prominent in social and financial circles. Sprawling mansions designed by distinguished New York architects were set in beautifully landscaped estates, the most desirable sites oriented to a water view.

Today Greenwich still retains it prestigious status, and the huge mansions are still maintained. Building sites are scarce, and thus the elaborateness of amenities provided for the new "estate owners" such as the riding trails and Polo Club could be accomplished only with low-density development and vast acreage. The Conyers Farm project should succeed in Greenwich, where it might not in other communities.

Brantwyn, Rockland, Delaware

SITE

Brantwyn, built in 1940 as the family residence of Pierre S. Du Pont III, was a 160-acre estate, called Bois des Fosses ("wood of the trenches") when in the family's ownership. The family resided there until 1988. In 1990 after the house and 60 acres were acquired by the Du Pont Company, it was renamed Brantwyn after the Brandywine area in which it is located and in which the Du Pont company achieved its first success. Since 1992 Brantwyn has served as a conference center of the Du Pont Country Club, which is located just across the road.

The eclectic Georgian Colonial Revival house, with traditional detailing and symmetrical massing, is surrounded by landscaped grounds that provide an elegant setting for outdoor events.

The Brantwyn main entrance facade has the same appearance it had as a private residence, constructed in 1940. Because of its location across the road from a corporate country club, its conversion to a conference facility was a practical adaptive use.

The Brantwyn rear facade with symmetrical flanking pavilions containing new exit stairs that were required when the mansion was converted to a conference center.

PRESERVATION ISSUE

The conversion from a residence to a fully equipped corporate conference center was done with a minimal impact on the interior spaces, although certain additions were required to satisfy safety and building codes. The original features and Georgian Revival characteristics of the house were retained and make Brantwyn a distinctive and special place in which to hold conferences and events. Mechanical systems, such as the hvac and electrical, were upgraded or added, and all renovations were designed to ensure that the house is accessible to those with disabilities. Two exterior fire stair pavilions, intended to compliment the symmetry of the Georgian Revival mansion, were added at the rear of the building.

At the ground-floor level, the family's public rooms have been converted to conference and banquet rooms. Upstairs, the family's bedrooms, sitting rooms, and dressing rooms now contain seven smaller conference rooms for groups of 2 to 20 people.

In recognition of the building's history, the rooms were named for Du Pont and Brandywine associations. The Essonne, the largest conference room and once the family living room, is named after the French government powder plant in which Irenee Du Pont learned the art of powder making. Willow Wood, the family den, is now a meeting room named after the willow wood that grew in abundance in the area, which was burned for charcoal, an ingredient required for gunpowder. Toussard Quarters is named after Colonel Louis de Toussard, an officer and hunting partner of E. I. Du Pont. Colonel Toussard and E. I. Du Pont were provisioning for a hunting trip when Du Pont became outraged with the poor quality of gunpowder available. He subsequently established a gunpowder mill that was the beginning of the Du Pont Company in the United States. Rooms such as the Lebanon Run, Governor's Station, the Boxwood Suite, and others are named after family members and estate and area place names.

SIGNIFICANCE

Brantwyn's function as a corporate country club is significantly different from traditional membership-oriented clubhouses. Within its 28,000 square feet, numerous elegant interior spaces have been redecorated so that the club can function as a conference center as well as a setting for social events. Although membership in the Du Pont Country Club is limited to Du Pont employees, Brantwyn's facilities are available to the public.

Because Brantwyn is not the main clubhouse and functions as an accessory facility, rental revenues can help offset Du Pont's costs of operating the facility.

The entry to the Swift River Inn complex is picturesque and inviting.

Swift River Inn, Cummington, Massachusetts

SITE

The Swift River Inn and Ski Touring Center is located on 600 acres in Cummington, Massachusetts. Swift River Inn's brochure describes the site as a "turn-of-the-century gentleman's dairy farm restored for guest lodging and outdoor recreation." Located in the Berkshires near Pittsfield, Swift River Inn is 30 miles from Lenox and the Lee and Stockbridge resort communities.

The site has an interesting history, beginning with its use as a farm in 1805. The property remained in the Loud family until 1916. The 254-acre farm was acquired by Alexander McCallum, a prosperous dry-goods merchant in nearby Northampton. He cleared the land and erected an impressive complex of Colonial Revival Style barns and outbuildings to accommodate his Jersey and Holstein cattle, operating it as a gentleman's dairy farm. McCallum's son inherited the farm in 1919 and sold it in 1924. The farm complex was converted to a children's summer camp, Meadowbrook Lodge, and then in 1961 it became the Science and Art Camp. In 1969 it was acquired by members of the local grange, and the McCallum farm buildings were adapted to house a summer theater, dining room, library, and dance hall. In 1973 it became the Cummington Farm Village Cross Country Ski Center. In 1987 it was purchased by a local partnership who planned to operate it as a four-season resort and to construct time-share and year-round

The former barn courtyard has been sensitively transformed into a garden, which is the central focus of Swift River Inn.

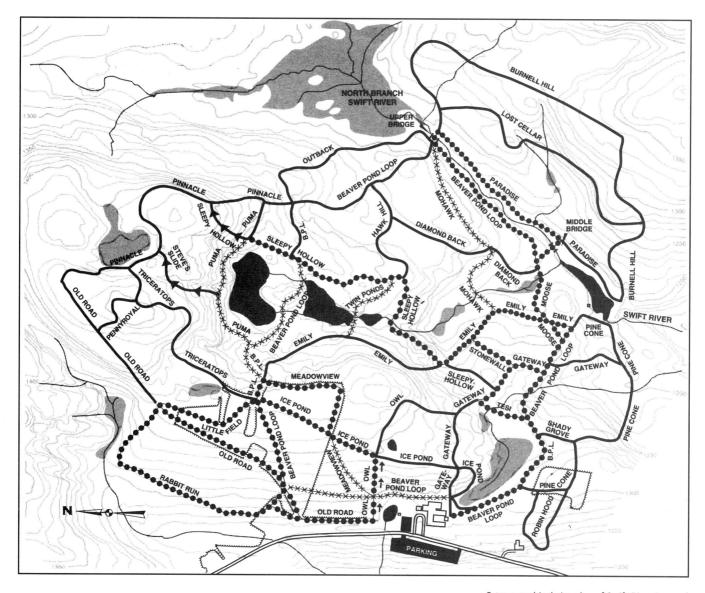

A topographical site plan of Swift River Inn and the ski touring center's 600 acres shows the extensive network of trails, graded for difficulty. The former gentleman's farm complex, now transformed as an inn and restaurant located next to the parking areas, appears diminutive in comparison to the vast site.

condominiums. The developers encountered financial difficulties, and the property was acquired at a bankruptcy sale in 1991 by Peter Laird (cocreator of the Teenage Mutant Ninja Turtles), who grew up in nearby North Adams.

PRESERVATION ISSUE

The challenge was to preserve the original character of the rustic, white-painted Colonial Revival farm group to enhance the picturesque charm of its courtyard. Because the barn complex had undergone so many adaptions over the years, considerable stabilization and upgrading of the interiors was required. The entire facility is now equipped with smoke detectors and sprinklers.

The developers were confident that there was a market for a year-round luxury facility for outdoor enthusiasts. In the summer it attracts mountain bikers, rock climbers, orienteers, and fly-fishermen. In the winter its amenities include snowmaking, an extensive 23-kilometer trail system including night skiing on 2.5 kilometers of trails, and a new plush 10,500-square-foot day lodge complete with rental-and-retail shop, ski school, ski patrol, and waxing room.

Within the main former hay barn, a cavernous lobby with a massive fireplace has been created, where piping hot snacks are available to "chilled" skiers. Nearby is a full-service restaurant, which has attracted a strong following among local residents. Those who come from further afield can stay in one of 22 guest rooms created in the former stables flanking the central courtyard. Some of the rooms contain lofts. The current arrangements can accommodate approximately 80 guests, the equivalent of a tour group. The rustic charm is enhanced by furnishings and decorative objects produced by local artists and artisans. As a result of the success of Swift River, it is probable that additional guest rooms will be built.

On moonlit nights, there are tours beyond the illuminated trails. Weather permitting, there is also ice skating. On weekends the inn provides free rides in an old-fashioned sleigh drawn by a team of Clydesdales.

SIGNIFICANCE

Most country estates contained kennels, stables, or a "farm group" for cows, horses, sheep, and chickens. The farm group along with garages, greenhouses, and recreation and service buildings were usually clustered at a distance from the main residence and formal gardens. Often when large estates are subdivided for development, the main residence and the farm group are isolated on separate parcels. Swift River Inn demonstrates a successful adaptive use of the farm group that also preserves the landscape through an extensive trail network. Modifications, additions, and minor new outbuildings are sympathetic to the architectural character of the original farm group. An exceptionally handsome graphics system of directional signs, trail markers, and maps is unobtrusive but helpfully located throughout the grounds.

Mansions as Corporate or Research Facilities

Mansions can be successfully adapted to serve as corporate headquarters for small business, but all the examples included here seem to indicate that they are often not large enough or do not provide for expansion. Mansions seem to appeal to those businesses where clients will be impressed by the character and intimacy of elegant surroundings in the reception areas, conference and dining rooms, and executive offices. The problem comes in housing the essential backup space for routine operations that are not to be seen by the visitors. Depending on the functional requirements of the corporate user, the existing residential interior configuration may be awkward or produce inefficient layouts.

Mansions that have been previously adapted for institutional use as religious retreats or boarding schools may already have some advantages because they probably have met certain code requirements. In this regard nonfireproof construction or inadequate floor-loading capacity must be investigated before applying for a variance. Especially in predominantly residential areas, it is often easier to obtain a zoning variance from institutional to commercial occupancy.

The primary concern in most communities is the number of employees, the number of visitors or clients, providing adequate parking screened from the road and neighbors, and how much traffic or how many service requirements will be generated. In residential areas with curving narrow roads, concerns about congestion or safety may be a real obstacle. If the estate is located near or on a major route, this will be less of a problem.

Penguin Hall, Wenham, Massachusetts

SITE

At the turn of the century, the quaint old fishing villages from Beverly through Gloucester on the rugged, rocky north shore coastline east of Boston were transformed into resorts and country places. In one instance Boston's Old Guard changed the name of the coastal village of Manchester to Manchester by the Sea because it sounded more

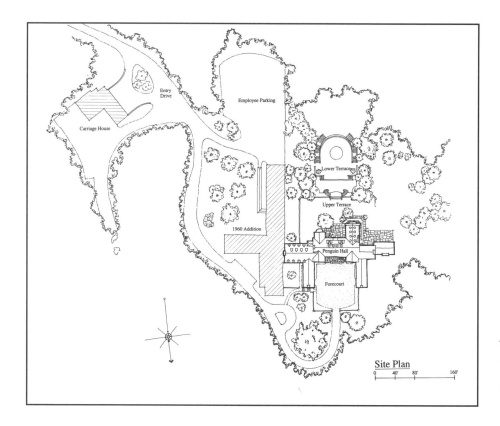

Site Plan

0   40'   80'   160'

The site plan of Penguin Hall illustrates how the mansion, its forecourt, and its terraced gardens retain the original character of the estate, while the large 1960 addition and employee parking remain distinctly separate.

like an English seaside resort. At first the Shingle Style blossomed here; later on, the whole gamut of eclectic historic revival styles began to appear. Boston's passion for horticulture produced elaborate landscaping, formal gardens, and manicured lawns. Inland communities such as Wenham and Hamilton provided the setting for fox hunts and polo fields.

In Wenham, Penguin Hall was designed by architect Harrie T. Lindeberg in 1929 for Mrs. Ruby Boyer Miller. After World War II when many mansions and estates in the area were acquired by the Catholic Church, the Church also bought this estate. During the Church's ownership of Penquin Hall in the 1960s, a large brick four-story convent wing was added to the original service end of the house. The mansion was later acquired by Commercial Union Insurance Companies who used it as a conference center in the 1970s. The zoning was changed from institutional to commercial at this time. The surrounding area continues to be a prestigious area, containing many mansions and estates, some in residential usage and others institutional. In nearby communities bordering on Wenham, subdivisions have sprung up.

PRESERVATION ISSUE

In the late 1980s the Mullen Advertising and Public Relations Agency had outgrown its previous mansion headquarters and needed to expand. Ironically it was the 60,000-square-foot former "ugly duckling" convent wing combined with the 20,000-square-foot mansion set on 50 acres that made the property attractive to the Mullens group. Harrie T. Lindeberg was a very prolific and successful architect who throughout his long career specialized almost exclusively in country houses. In 1905 to 1914, he was in a partnership with another architect, Lewis Colt Albro, with whom he had worked at McKim, Mead, and White. A "gentleman" architect, Lindeberg dominated the English-influenced school of domestic architects during the 1920s and 1930s.

In the design of Penguin Hall, Lindeberg combined elements of stripped-down Medieval and Tudor with a trace of Georgian in its symmetrical massing and handsome unadorned bold projecting pedimented main entrance door enframement. It is constructed of ashlar stone, with smooth-stone trimming multiple casement windows,

The original Penguin Hall main entrance is now approached by a ramp, which blends with the stonework of the mansion, permitting access for disabled. An elevator in the new wing, which is linked by passageways at all floor levels to the mansion, permits access to all floors.

The garden facade of the Penguin Hall mansion. The architects have designed dormers for the newly created work areas of the third floor, which skillfully blend into the existing roofscape.

some half-timbering on the service wing, and capped by a massive red slate roof. In a touch of eclectic whimsy, the main entrance door is an Art Deco confection of various metals glazed from behind, framing a large central spiderweb.

Olson Lewis Architects and Planners, Inc., has been extremely respectful to the original design of the mansion in the process of adapting it to its new use. The principal rooms of the ground floor include an eclectic mix of a Georgian paneled living room, a Jacobean paneled and beamed library, and a great hall, which have been turned into client presentation rooms. New state-of-the-art presentation and mechanical equipment were imaginatively concealed in paneling or bookcases. On the second floor former bedrooms are now used as executive offices. The introduction of office areas in the third floor necessitated the creation of dormers, which can be seen in the photograph of the rear facade. The skillful design and proportion of the dormers, which are faced with stucco and roofed to match the original roofs, blend in quite unobtrusively. A new cloisterlike corridor through the former servants' wing provided a third-floor link from the manor house to the four-story 1960s brick wing previously renovated by the architectural firm. The corridor also provided access to an elevator and an enclosed fire stair.

Although built on a hilltop, the landscaping of the 50-acre site's garden and woodlands has been restored and screens out surrounding properties.

SIGNIFICANCE

The adaptation of Penguin Hall for the Mullen Agency is significant in that it overcame several interesting handicaps that have caused difficulties in other parts of the country. First of all, local zoning permitted its usage for a commercial purpose. The mansion had gone through several previous institutional uses and survived with its original detail and character intact. The existence of the serviceable, but not attractive, 1960s wing was essential because it offered backup staff space the mansion itself could not contain. The mansion provided the ideal setting and attractive showplace for the client presentations and executive offices that this sophisticated, discrete, and highly successful advertising agency sought. If the 1960s addition had not existed, no doubt a structure more sympathetic to the original character of the mansion could have been constructed, but at a greater cost, which might have dissuaded the agency from acquiring it.

Often restoration purists demand that later additions must be removed in order to restore the original appearance and setting of the mansion. There are architecturally exceptional and historically significant mansions and estates replete with their collections and furnishings that should be restored and maintained as house museums. But there are also many mansions of the golden age that can be adapted to productive and self-sustaining new uses.

The principal entertaining rooms of the Penguin Hall mansion now provide dramatic settings for client presentation rooms.

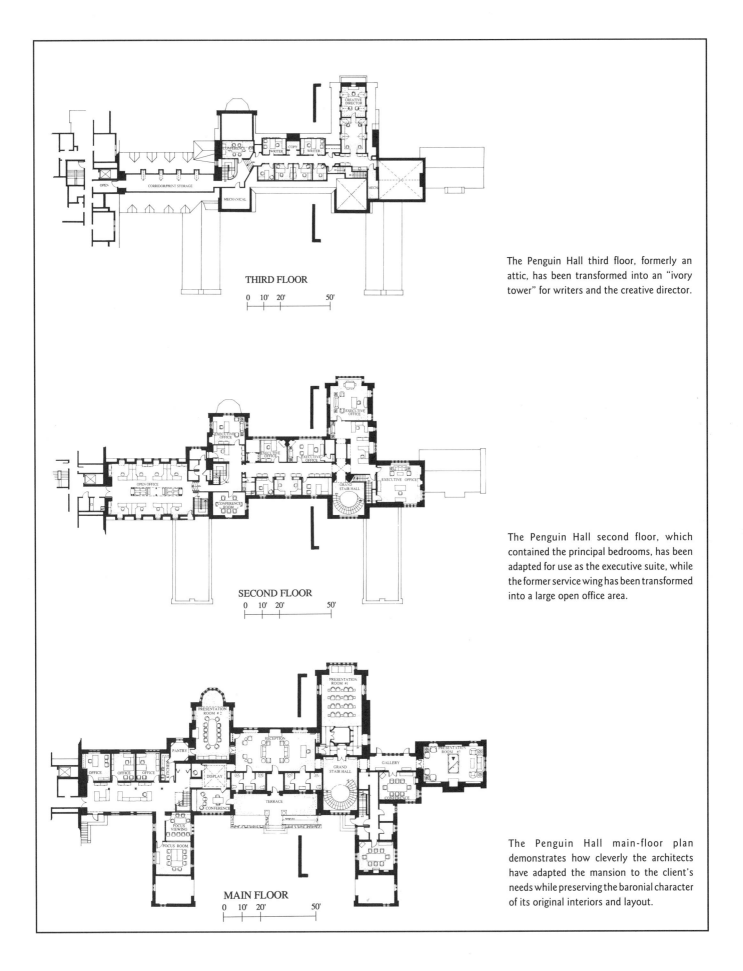

THIRD FLOOR

0   10'   20'   50'

The Penguin Hall third floor, formerly an attic, has been transformed into an "ivory tower" for writers and the creative director.

SECOND FLOOR

0   10'   20'   50'

The Penguin Hall second floor, which contained the principal bedrooms, has been adapted for use as the executive suite, while the former service wing has been transformed into a large open office area.

MAIN FLOOR

0   10'   20'   50'

The Penguin Hall main-floor plan demonstrates how cleverly the architects have adapted the mansion to the client's needs while preserving the baronial character of its original interiors and layout.

The original quaint gatehouse of the Pleasantdale Farm estate gives no hint to the visitor of the corporate conference center that lies at the end of a winding road through a beautifully tended landscape.

Pleasantdale Farm, Essex Fells, New Jersey

SITE

The setting of Pleasantdale Farm is an idyllic 85 acres of forested hilly terrain adjacent to the Essex Fells Country Club. On the other boundary is a development of modest suburban homes. Originally acquired by Dr. Charles W. Nichols, a founder of the Allied Chemical Corporation, as a summer vacation site, it was gradually transformed into a gentleman's country estate in the early 1930s by architect Augustus N. Allen. The gatehouse, main house, and outbuildings are a superbly picturesque evocation of a French Norman farmhouse complex. It is a fairly large house whose massing is broken

Parking areas added to the original Pleasantdale Farm site have been discretely hidden away from the entrance pavilion, preserving the original intimate forecourt of the picturesque sprawling French Norman Style mansion.

The vaulted ceilinged music room, which retains its original built-in organ console and massive hooded fireplace preserves much of the elegant residential splendor of the principal entertaining rooms of Pleasantdale Farm.

down into a series of towers and pavilions linked by slate-roofed gabled wings, providing a deceptively intimate and comfortable scale of interior spaces. An enclosed greenhouse leads to a Mediterranean tiled-indoor swimming pool, and a rustic heavy timber framed barnlike entertainment space.

PRESERVATION ISSUE

The house was acquired by the Allied Corporation in 1963, and it functioned for many years as an executive retreat, location for board meetings, corporate conference center, and guest house. The author was a consultant to the attorneys called in the early 1980s when Allied had decided to increase the size of the conference center in order to provide additional sleeping accommodations.

While the size and configuration of the main house and accessory structures provided adequate meeting and recreation space for most of Allied's conference requirements, the ratio of sleeping accommodations was usually insufficient. Reusing the existing bedrooms and servants' quarters, the house could provide a total of 22 guest rooms of varying sizes accommodating up to 34 guests.

Because Allied has a national, as well as international, organization, these limitations resulted in an awkward situation where out-of-town attendees would stay overnight but local participants would have to return home. The conference organizers felt that this imbalance defeated the esprit de corps they were trying to achieve.

In order to construct the additional dormitory structures, Allied applied for zoning permission to modify its status as a corporate conference center. The adjacent property was a long-established golf club, and large nearby tracts were already being developed as corporate headquarters. Only the adjacent owners of small residences remained to be convinced. They had long considered Pleasantdale Farms as a bucolic private park, and they were alarmed at the prospect of the increased traffic that an enlarged conference facility might generate. In consultation with Allied's attorneys, we made a public presentation and convinced the zoning board and the neighbors that the conference center was a far more benign usage than the intensive residential development that the existing zoning would have permitted. The permission was granted, and the new contemporary-styled dormitories providing a few meeting rooms and 24 additional guests rooms were built as a satellite facility at a discrete distance from the original residential complex.

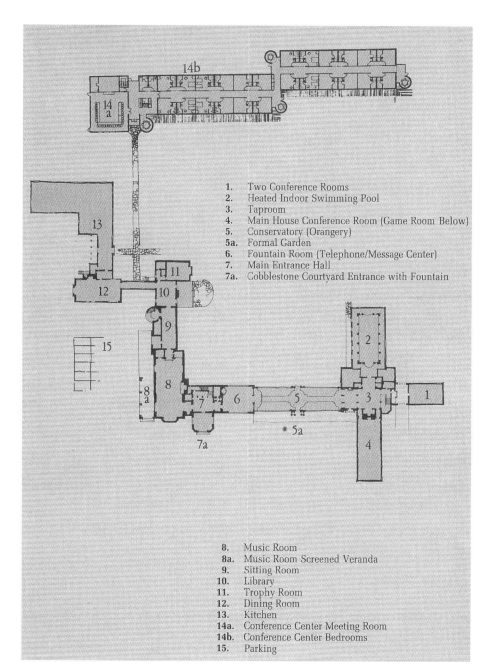

1. Two Conference Rooms
2. Heated Indoor Swimming Pool
3. Taproom
4. Main House Conference Room (Game Room Below)
5. Conservatory (Orangery)
5a. Formal Garden
6. Fountain Room (Telephone/Message Center)
7. Main Entrance Hall
7a. Cobblestone Courtyard Entrance with Fountain

8. Music Room
8a. Music Room Screened Veranda
9. Sitting Room
10. Library
11. Trophy Room
12. Dining Room
13. Kitchen
14a. Conference Center Meeting Room
14b. Conference Center Bedrooms
15. Parking

The ground-floor plan of the Pleasantdale Farm mansion does not contain any sleeping accommodations (guest rooms occupy the second floor). At the rear, linked by a flagstone-paved path, are the new conference center sleeping accommodations, interspersed with small circular conference areas, echoing the turretlike form of the staircase tower adjacent to the sitting room of the mansion.

SIGNIFICANCE

Many large corporations rent conference accommodations as needed. Allied Corporation felt that commercial conference centers were often distracting, and it preferred to maintain its own facility. Located near the company's main headquarters in Morris Plains and nearby Newark Airport, Pleasantdale Farm was a convenient site for visitors. Much of the economy of running such an elaborate estate is aided by the nearby corporate headquarter's existing catering staff and groundskeepers. Chosen as a practical corporate model for the sympathetic reuse of a suburban estate, beginning in the 1960s and expanded in 1982, Pleasantdale Farm was listed for sale in *The New York Times* in June 1992 and was still on the market at the time of this publication. The changing corporate climate of the 1990s and the growing value of its 85-acre site may have been factors in Allied's decision to sell it.

Hewitt Associates, a consulting firm, has established its headquarters in a 1916 English Tudor Revival mansion, Rockledge, in Norwalk, Connecticut. This view is of the rear facade facing the garden.

Rockledge, Rowayton, Connecticut

SITE

Rockledge was built in 1916 by James A. Farrell, to replace his summer home that had burned a few years earlier. Farrell had risen from laborer to head of U.S. Steel and was the founder of Farrell Steamship Lines.

He was a leader of the elitist Irish-American Society, as well as the First Irish Families (FIFs), a group proud of their Celtic heritage and loyal to their church. Rockledge stands as a symbol of this struggle for a well-deserved niche in our society. Farrell was among the first to climb to the top of the economic ladder without denying his Irish ancestry.

Rockledge is a massive (74 room) English Tudor Revival masonry house with a slate roof and limestone trim. The building's stained glass front door depicts saints and symbols from Celtic mythology. Farrell designed an iron door using ancient Irish iconography that was executed by Philadelphia sculptor Gordon Youlte.

PRESERVATION ISSUE

The Farrells died in 1943, and the property has enjoyed three subsequent uses. It was initially purchased by the Sperry-Rand Corporation for use as a headquarters and research facility. The UNIVAC computer was developed in the estate's original stable sited across the street, which has become the Rowayton Community Center and Library. General Douglas MacArthur, while he was associated with Sperry-Rand, had his office in Rockledge. His desk is now the reception desk in the main foyer.

Sperry-Rand used the property until 1964, when the main house became the Saint Thomas School for Girls and the community acquired the stable across Highland Avenue. The school merged in 1975 with another local school, and the Continental Group purchased the estate for use as headquarters and a conference center. Continental had the building listed in the National Register of Historic Places in 1977. After lengthy and contested proceedings, Continental succeeded in having the property rezoned for office use, only to determine that the site was too small for its increasing needs. Rockledge was purchased by Hewitt Associates, a consulting firm, in 1979.

The dark woodwork of Rockledge's former library's bookcases and the light-colored decorative plaster ceiling provide a dramatic setting for a large conference room with modern furnishings.

Hewitt Associates restored the mansion and built a low-rise modern office building on the site that is obscured by trees and plantings. Rockledge's drawing room and dining room and garden terrace are used daily by the staff as a dining room. The library and billiard room serve as conference rooms, as do the primary bedrooms on the second floor. The rear of the second floor and the third-floor space are mainly used as offices.

New, updated mechanical and safety systems were invisibly incorporated into the restoration, and the metal windows and leaky exterior and roof were carefully and sensitively restored.

The estate feeling was carefully preserved. The original drive was maintained, with the gatehouse now serving as a guest house for business travelers. Limited visitor parking is off to the side, and visitors enter through the main entry porch. The new building is executed in glass and is not obvious because it reflects the estate's plantings. It is behind this new building that the parking for employees is accommodated.

Hewitt Associates now needs more space. Since their agreement with the city of Norwalk does not allow for further expansion, they are investigating off-site space, but they intend to keep Rockledge as their eastern headquarters.

Hewitt Associates has maintained the traditional character of Rockledge's principal rooms, for conference rooms and staff dining rooms, and portions of the second and third floors as offices.

Ensign House, Simsbury, Connecticut

SITE

The Ensign House was built in 1909 to 1910 by Joseph Ralph Ensign, a principal and eventual president of the firm of Ensign-Bickford, a manufacturer of mining safety fuses. Ensign, in addition to being a successful industrialist, was involved in many Simsbury institutions, serving on the school and cemetery boards and as a local legislator. Ensign was an original incorporator of the Simsbury Electric Company and the Village Water Company.

The house is the third on the family's site assembled by Joseph Toy Ensign, Joseph Ralph's grandfather, in the 1850s, in the heart of Simsbury. As was common in the nineteenth century, the family lived up the hill from, but in close proximity to, their factory. The asymmetrically massed house, constructed of reddish-brown stone with a red clay tile roof, supported by deep, bracketed, flared eaves is an eclectic amalgam of period revival styles popular at the time. It was built by a local stonemason, William Mansfield Ketchin, who probably also served as its designer.

Located at the crossroads of Simsbury's main streets, the area has remained primarily residential, despite the proximity of the Ensign-Bickford manufacturing facility. In the 1970s, a small shopping center was built, and another of the Ensign family residences was converted to a medical office, although it retains its residential character.

In the 1960s and 1970s, the house served as the parish house for the First Church of Christ United, who built a large addition at the rear of the property. Although the area is dominated by residences, the large size of the addition precluded its re-use as a single-family dwelling.

In 1984, a developer purchased the property with the intention of building commercial office space, but in 1985, the Connecticut National Bank, now Shawmut Bank, acquired the house and converted it into its Simsbury branch.

PRESERVATION ISSUE

James Cassidy, vice president of the Hartford architectural firm of Jeter, Cook and Jepson, served as project manager for the renovation, which took 3 years. The bank did not require all of the available square footage on the main floor and basement of the new addition, so those spaces have been converted to tenant space. By confining the bank's

Ensign House's new entrance courtyard incorporates a ramp providing barrier-free access and masks some of the flat-roofed boxiness of the 1960 parish hall addition.

functional needs to the original residential section and only a portion of the addition, the architects and client were successful in preserving original architectural details of the interior. Fireplaces, wood paneling, wood moldings, and a magnificent staircase were all preserved, and the integrity of the original room design was respected. The living room, dining room, parlor, reception room, and library have been adapted for banking use without displacement of interior walls. Part of the addition constructed by the church in 1961 serves as the main banking room where teller stations are sited.

The church had compromised the residential character of the site with the addition of a large parking lot in front of the main entry. In the bank conversion, the parking lot was relocated to a less visible site, and the area was relandscaped. The 1961 addition, which was built with materials incompatible to the house, was repainted and reroofed to lessen its visual impact.

A prominent two-story bay window, long obscured by overgrown plantings, is now visible. The original residential entrance is visible from the main access route, but a side entrance, with an adjacent courtyard connecting the 1961 addition and equipped

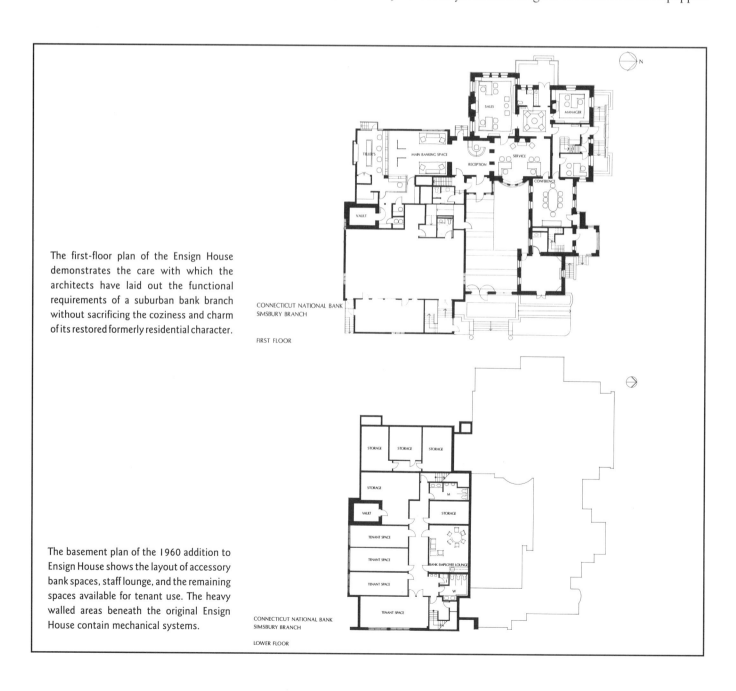

The first-floor plan of the Ensign House demonstrates the care with which the architects have laid out the functional requirements of a suburban bank branch without sacrificing the coziness and charm of its restored formerly residential character.

The basement plan of the 1960 addition to Ensign House shows the layout of accessory bank spaces, staff lounge, and the remaining spaces available for tenant use. The heavy walled areas beneath the original Ensign House contain mechanical systems.

with access ramps, now serves as the main public entrance to the bank and the tenant spaces.

This exterior view restores the "cozy stone cottage" look of the original Ensign House, while operating as a suburban branch bank in the midst of a residential community.

SIGNIFICANCE

The Greater Hartford Architecture Conservancy conferred a merit award on the Ensign House for substantial rehabilitation in 1988.

The conversion of the Ensign House to a bank is an interesting project because the original residence, in a not atypical occurrence, had already been compromised by its earlier institutional additions. By skillfully masking the bulk of the addition, shifting the main entrance to a new intimate courtyard, and relocating and screening the parking lots, the architects have restored the original charm and character of the residence and improved its relationship to its surroundings.

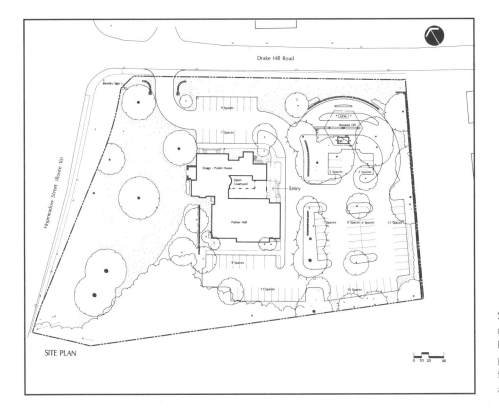

Site plan of Ensign House, which was formerly modified as a parish house and now contains a branch bank and other commercial space. The parking lots have been landscaped, and a new free-standing gazebo shelters a drive-in teller and ATM.

Jones Laboratory (1893) was the first research building built on the site overlooking Cold Spring Harbor. In 1975 architect Charles Moore restored its original interior shell of wooden scored boarding and designed modern freestanding laboratory modules.

Cold Spring Harbor Laboratories, Cold Spring Harbor, Long Island, New York

SITE

Together Nassau and Suffolk counties on New York's Long Island represent the largest aggregation of mansions and estates in the nation. Many mansions remain today, taking into account demolitions in the period following World War II, and the increasing suburbanization of the once-rural character of small villages and farmland. The same period saw considerable changes in the lifestyles of the wealthy for whom the maintenance of mansions and large estates, the domestic staff, the estate managers, the groundskeepers, the greenhouses, the luxurious entertainments, the facilities for the sporting life—for example, stables for polo—were no longer affordable, even for their own children. Transition was inevitable but complicated because of strict local control in well-to-do exclusive villages. It is interesting to compare three different adaptations of mansions to nonresidential use.

Cold Spring Harbor Laboratories has had a remarkable evolution since its founding in 1890 as the Biological Laboratory of the Brooklyn Institute of Arts and Sciences, as a field station for marine biology. Its origins and siting within the community are different from the circumstances of other Long Island mansions. Though the population at the labs has grown from 65 to 575 over the last 20 years, this growth is not evident outside the 100-acre enclave of the "Village of Science." It is located along a winding old scenic route on the edge of picturesque Cold Spring Harbor, which is filled with sailboats and watercraft in season.

The origin of the laboratory site begins with a local family in the eighteenth century. The Jones family harnessed the water power of the springs to operate a gristmill, a sawmill, a tannery, a linen paper mill, and woolen mills. With the demise of milling, the family established in 1836 the Cold Spring Whaling Company, which converted many of the old mill buildings.

Davenport House, a Victorian Stick Style "mansion," was built in 1884 for Frederick Mather, the first director of the fish hatchery of the New York State Fisheries Commission (which still operates across the road). John D. Jones, who later helped found the biological laboratory, donated the land and materials for its construction on the site of the family homestead. In 1904 it was transferred to the Carnegie Institution as a director's residence. Since 1934 it has been used as a residence hall.

PRESERVATION ISSUE

Because the Cold Spring Harbor Laboratories had its origins more than a century ago, it has had greater community acceptance than if a proposal for a modern research facility were made today. This doesn't mean that there has always been universal or immediate acceptance for the laboratories' expansion plans over the years. The laboratories have been very astute in the cultivation of a good relationship with the community and neighbors over the years and have been quick to anticipate their concerns. The Cold Spring Laboratories offer regular public tours so that nearby residents and visitors can observe for themselves the nature of the scientific research under way. The laboratories also engage local residents' interests and support through dinner parties where community members may host distinguished visiting scientists. Because the laboratories are tax-exempt, they have to negotiate with the local schools to provide for a limited number of staff children's education. When the agreed-upon amount was exceeded, the laboratories made a voluntary payment. Plans for a new child-care center for staff children will require a public review. The laboratories will call upon the goodwill it has earned in the community to assist in supporting the approval of these plans.

With the increasing public awareness of environmental matters and pollution, it is natural that members of the community have expressed concern over possible contagion from the disease research, animals, possible toxic fume emissions, and waste water disposal. The laboratories have gone to great lengths, and perhaps to excess, to demonstrate that they have taken adequate precautions.

The laboratories are unique as an institution because, even as they have grown over the years, they provide intimate and beautiful campuslike surroundings in which

Davenport House at the Cold Spring Harbor Laboratories complex is an 1884 Stick Style mansion built for the first director of the New York State fish hatcheries. The house has gone through many internal changes. The exterior, with its distinctive nineteenth-century color scheme, was restored in 1980.

An aerial view of the Cold Spring Harbor Laboratories showing the campuslike layout of individual structures, which have evolved over a century of development.

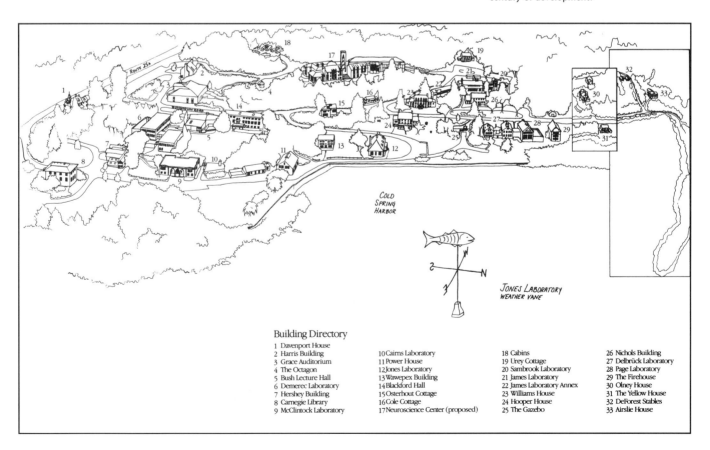

Building Directory

1 Davenport House			
2 Harris Building	10 Cairns Laboratory	18 Cabins	26 Nichols Building
3 Grace Auditorium	11 Power House	19 Urey Cottage	27 Delbrück Laboratory
4 The Octagon	12 Jones Laboratory	20 Sambrook Laboratory	28 Page Laboratory
5 Bush Lecture Hall	13 Wawepex Building	21 James Laboratory	29 The Firehouse
6 Demerec Laboratory	14 Blackford Hall	22 James Laboratory Annex	30 Olney House
7 Hershey Building	15 Osterhout Cottage	23 Williams House	31 The Yellow House
8 Carnegie Library	16 Cole Cottage	24 Hooper House	32 DeForest Stables
9 McClintock Laboratory	17 Neuroscience Center (proposed)	25 The Gazebo	33 Airslie House

Architect Charles Moore has designed a delightful wood lattice gazebo overlooking Cold Spring Harbor, sitting over the water treatment plant, disguising its utilitarian function.

The Grace Auditorium, designed by the architectural firm of Centerbrook Moore and Grover in 1986, is built into the hillside to minimize its bulk. It contains reception, administrative, and conference facilities for the Cold Spring Harbor Laboratories. The auditorium opens out onto a patio and terraced hillside garden, which can serve as an outdoor amphitheater.

the scientists and their families can live and work. The brilliant geneticist Dr. Thomas Watson, who is the director of the laboratories, and his wife Elizabeth have a personal commitment to preserving the charm of the old structures on the site as well as to commissioning the best contemporary architects to create new structures that fit comfortably into the existing ensemble.

SIGNIFICANCE

The Davenport House still sits prominently on a hilltop rise visible to passersby in the context of its original landscape of mature trees and overlooking Cold Spring Harbor. Unlike other "roadside" mansions, it has been adapted to serve the needs of a prestigious center of scientific research. Later structures constructed on the site have been kept at a considerable distance back from the house and have been screened by landscaped parking areas. Cold Spring Harbor Laboratories are a unique and well-endowed institution that is not easily replicated, but the laboratories do demonstrate that an institutional use on large acreage can fit in comfortably with residential neighbors, especially along stretches of formerly bucolic, meandering country roads that have become heavily traveled. Most suburban communities have been accepting of mansions converted to religious and educational purposes, but less enthusiastic about commercial or scientific research facilities.

CHAPTER 8

Adapting Mansions to Suburban and Urban Cultural Facilities

Many of the past options for the preservation of mansions and large estates are no longer realistic. Contrary to the original intent of their donors, institutional owners of religious retreats, boarding schools, and university study centers are putting these properties on the market. Most of these estates were exempt from property taxes and local residents and neighbors were not able to visit their grounds. The transformation of large rural and suburban mansions and estates into cultural centers does allow public participation and enjoyment without the loss of large acreage or creation of new subdivisions. Depending on the location of the property, exhibitions and cultural events may increase local traffic and parking problems and become a source of irritation to neighboring property owners.

Estates as Rural or Suburban Cultural Centers

As the case studies indicate, well-intentioned families who have donated and even endowed mansions and estates complete with original furnishings and collections to foundations, institutions, the National Park Service, and the National Trust for Historic Preservation discover that eventually maintenance and operating expenses outstrip income.

Despite the additional wear and tear that increased visitation may entail, it seems to be the only way to provide additional income and donations—especially in the 1990s, as competition for declining government funding and private donations is rampant. House museums which were once static have been forced to introduce more cultural programming, changing exhibitions, and gift shops targeted to appeal to a broader public. Many communities have promoted historic properties as a boost to the local economy through increased tourism.

The traditional training of museum administrators, which emphasized scholarship and connoisseurship, did not include the business management, fund-raising, and promotional skills which are now required. Due to the shortage of experienced museum professionals, many smaller rural and suburban historical sites and cultural programs are at a disadvantage in the present competitive atmosphere.

Aspet, Saint-Gaudens National Historic Site, Cornish, New Hampshire

SITE

Quite unlike the industrialists who built the turn-of-the-century seasonal resorts of the rich, many of the most influential proponents of the "American Renaissance" were an elite group of New York–based architects, writers, and musicians who established for themselves three artistic colonies in New Hampshire, at Cornish, Peterborough, and Dublin. This group was receiving the commissions for mansions and monumental projects of the "the gilded age."

For themselves they created an ideal setting in which to experiment with their interest in classical themes. The result was a curious mix of traditional New England Colonial villages and farmhouses that were gradually transformed with Italian Renaissance gardens, sculpture, and houses.

The central figure among this group was Augustus Saint-Gaudens, an Irish-born American sculptor. Saint-Gaudens arrived in Cornish in 1885, and at first rented and later bought "Higgens Folly," a former tavern, to remodel it for his use as a summer retreat to provide an escape from hot New York summers. Immediately upon purchasing the house, which he called Aspet, he converted the barn to his studio and commenced work on his "standing" Lincoln, for a park in Chicago.

Saint-Gaudens' arrival in Cornish marked the beginning of the Cornish Colony. His associates, Frederick MacMonnies, Philip Martiny, Herbert Adams, Frances

Overleaf Aspet, Saint-Gaudens' summer home and studio, is the result of adaptations of the original structures on the site, an old tavern and a barn.

The interior of the high-ceilinged studio at Aspet, with a portion of the adjustable light shutter visible and a vista through the doorway of the porch and portico.

Grimes, James Earle Fraser, Elsie Ward, and his brother, Louis Saint-Gaudens, were among many young sculptors who studied with the artist.

The artistic circle of American artists, poets, and writers who were attracted to Cornish as a summer retreat grew to include George de Forest Brush, Thomas W. Dewing, Henry O. Walker, architect Charles A. Platt, Steven Parrish, Maxfield Parrish, Charles Dana Gibson, playwright Louis Shipman and his wife, landscape architect Ellen Shipman, Percy MacKaye, William Vaughn Moodey, and novelist Winston Churchill.

Saint-Gaudens used the house as a summer home from 1885 through 1897, when he went abroad for 3 years. Before departing, he gave up his New York City house and studio but kept the house in Cornish. Upon his return, he made it his permanent home and resided there until his death in 1907.

One of the most extraordinary events to take place on the grounds was the "Masque of the Golden Ball" in June 1905. To celebrate the twentieth anniversary of the founding of the Cornish Colony, 70 members of the colony participated in the elaborate costumed production aided by members of Boston Symphony.

PRESERVATION ISSUE

During his tenure at Aspet, Saint-Gaudens made many changes to the house and site. Saint-Gaudens hired New York architect George Fletcher Babb to remodel the austere brick house, built circa 1800, adding a coat of white paint, terraces, and an Ionic-columned porch on the western elevation to take advantage of the prevailing breezes and the view of the Connecticut River. The attic was made usable with the addition of dormers, the interior was reconfigured, and a new wing was added. The grounds were transformed by Saint-Gaudens from pasture into a planned landscape with pools, hedges, lawns, gardens, and even a nine-hole golf course. A formal garden was planted between the house and barn. The barn was converted into a studio by adding an enormous north-facing skylight at the rear and a lantern above the roof with movable panels to adjust the light. A vine-covered pergola supported by classical columns surrounded three sides of the studio.

At Saint-Gaudens' death in 1907, his widow and son ensured that the property would be preserved as a memorial to the artist. They deeded the property to a group of trustees, which was chartered by the state of New Hampshire, and since 1964 the National Parks Service has maintained and interpreted the property.

Since its acquisition by the National Park Service (NPS), many programs have been created to enhance the visitors' experience. The Ravine Trail, which descends to a brook, allows visitors to explore the wooded areas of the site. A more recent addition to the Saint-Gaudens site is the Blow-Me-Down Pond Natural Area, which contains more than 80 wooded acres protected by the NPS. Included are Blow-Me-Down Pond and the surrounding wetlands, as well as a dam, a stone bridge, and a grist mill designed by McKim, Mead, and White in the 1890s. One doesn't usually think of this famous architectural firm designing a rural grist mill, but Stanford White and Saint-Gaudens collaborated on many major commissions. The architectural firm designed the pedestals or bases for some of Saint-Gaudens' monumental sculptures and commissioned him to execute decorations such as those in New York for Henry Villard's mansion.

SIGNIFICANCE

Although artists no longer congregate in Cornish, the Saint-Gaudens' National Historic Site allows a visitor to experience the home and workplace of the American sculptor who inspired the vitality of the artistic colony at Cornish.

The National Park Service has been meticulous in the restoration, repair, and maintenance of the historic structures on the grounds. The site is open from May through October. The NPS provides an excellent interpretive tour of the buildings and site orientation. There is an annual sculptor-in-residence program set up in Saint-Gaudens' original ravine studio. There are also changing exhibitions of contemporary art in the gallery. Sunday afternoon concerts are held in the "little studio."

The National Park Service has also been active in the conservation of the original surrounding land and by the addition of the Natural Area, has provided 2 miles of hiking trails by clearing old cart trails. The site attracts in excess of 40,000 visitors each season. John Dryfhout, superintendent of the site, has been candid about several issues they face that include: lack of adequate visitor reception facilities; lack of a museum-gallery collection facility; lack of bus and handicapped-accessible parking; lack of an adequate maintenance facility; and the need to extend the site boundaries to protect park resources and buffer neighboring development.

Aspet's old barn was converted to a studio by creating a long shaded porch and surrounding it on three sides with a vine-covered pergola supported by stout classical columns. A shingled covered lantern was constructed on the roof to provide the sculptor with natural daylight.

Lyndhurst, a mid-nineteenth-century Gothic Revival Style Hudson River mansion, is now restored and operated by the National Trust for Historic Preservation.

Lyndhurst, Tarrytown, New York

SITE

Lyndhurst is a fine Gothic Revival Style mansion designed by Alexander Jackson Davis. It is a rare surviving nineteenth-century mansion typical of the villas that once lined the eastern shore of the Hudson River. Although its landscape is virtually intact, its desirability as a private residence has been compromised by the increased commercialization of Route 9 on which it fronts and its proximity to a major Hudson River crossing, the Tappan Zee Bridge, built in the 1950s. It abuts a corporate research facility, which acts as a visual buffer to the bridge approaches.

Davis originally designed the house, then called Knoll, in 1838 for William Paulding as his retirement home. Paulding was a general in the War of 1812 and a past mayor of New York City. In 1864, the estate was acquired by George Merrit, a New York City merchant who renamed the house Lyndhurst and commissioned Davis to enlarge it. These alterations included raising the roof line of the original section and adding a new wing and an imposing tower and a porte-cochere. During this phase, Davis designed furniture for the house, some of which is still on display.

Merritt also added and enlarged outbuildings at Lyndhurst, possibly with designs by Davis. It was at this juncture that the gate lodge and carriage house and stables were enlarged. Merritt also built the main carriage house building to accommodate grooms' quarters, stalls, and carriage sheds. Built of brick, the complex forms an enclosed courtyard.

In 1880, the estate was purchased by railroad tycoon Jay Gould who, with the exception of the construction of an enormous cast-iron framed Lord and Burnham greenhouse, made only minor changes to the house and grounds. His eldest daughter, Helen Gould Shepard, maintained the property from 1913 through 1938 and built numerous outbuildings including a bowling alley, swimming pool building, laundry, and school room, the Kennel, and the recently restored "Rose Cottage," a children's playhouse. After her death, her younger sister, Anna, Duchess of Talleyrand-Perigord, who resided in Manhattan, maintained the estate until her death in 1961 when she donated it to the National Trust for Historic Preservation, complete with most of its original furnishings. It is now operated by the National Trust as a historic house museum.

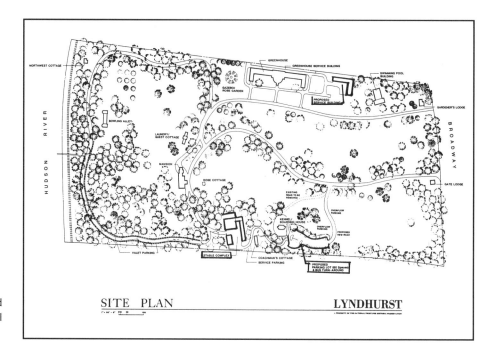

SITE PLAN   LYNDHURST

A site plan of Lyndhurst's extensive landscaped grounds indicating the location of the original stable complex.

PRESERVATION ISSUE

Lyndhurst, like most historic houses, was designed as a residence, not a museum. Its popularity has drawn so many visitors that the house has outgrown the capacity of its reception hall. Lyndhurst has a long-standing need for a visitors' center that can accommodate the greeting and orientation of large groups of visitors. In addition, Lyndhurst requires tremendous financial resources for both its interior and exterior upkeep, some of which is earned by making the estate and grounds available for special events. In order to minimize the impact on the historic house, rental for events such as weddings is confined to the porch and grounds, greatly limiting the period in which the property can be rented. The 12 evenings available between the months of May and September and the July use of the property for outdoor concerts are Lyndhurst's only opportunity for earning such rental income.

Many of the outbuildings on the estate are used either as staff residences or offices, but most are too small or in some other way inappropriate for public accommodation. The estate, however, has an underutilized resource, the carriage house complex, located at a convenient distance from the mansion, which will serve as an education and

A period view (1865 to 1870) of the Lyndhurst carriage house, which is proposed to be converted into a Heritage Education Center.

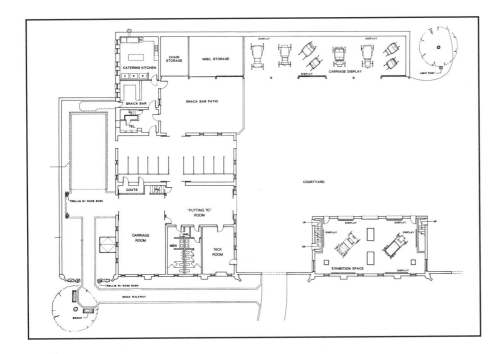

A detailed plan of the proposed Heritage Conservation Center, which will be created in the former stable complex.

visitor center, providing public conveniences and a catering facility. It's location, at a discrete distance from the house, will preserve the original ambiance of the mansion. In addition to providing interpretation outside of the mansion, it will limit the wear and tear on the historic interiors while allowing more people to tour the house.

In its over 30 years of operation, the carriage house and stable complex have been the only outbuildings open to the public. For many years, the National Trust's Restoration Workshop was operated from the garage of this complex. The carriage house now contains a minimal carriage display, maintenance shops, and a storage facility, but it is presently being turned into an education and visitor center.

The tack room, which seats 40, will be used as an orientation site for visitors, the large carriage room can be utilized by school groups, and many spaces will be available for special events. Modern restrooms will be located in this area. The garage that once housed the Restoration Workshop will house permanent and changing exhibition spaces. To ensure that the original purpose of the complex is clear to visitors, carriages will be displayed in the sheds off the main courtyard.

Lyndhurst is a large estate situated outside of Tarrytown's commercial area. The installation of a small restaurant—utilizing the stable stalls as booths, with tables in the outdoor courtyard in good weather—will provide both additional revenue for the house museum and will encourage the use of the carriage house complex for special events.

Income from the carriage house facility will support the operation of the Heritage Education Center.

SIGNIFICANCE

Because of its elaborate interiors and intact collection of original furnishings, any attempt to adaptively reuse the Lyndhurst building would have required a great sacrifice of its integrity. Fortunately, its large, landscaped grounds, which are in essence the original site, provided ample space on which several accessory structures could be located.

The cost of upkeep and maintenance of this property makes it desirable to encourage greater visitation. The mansion is conveniently located to serve the tri-state area. In establishing an education-visitor center in the carriage house complex, Lyndhurst will be able to accommodate more visitors, improve the interpretative experience for both individuals and large groups of visitors, and derive increased revenues to offset operating expenses.

View of the rear, garden front facade of The Mount. The tent-covered terrace is now used as an outdoor performance area for Edith Wharton's works.

The Mount, Lenox, Massachusetts

SITE

Although the Berkshires attracted the fashionable summer crowd, many including Edith Wharton established themselves here as a more bucolic alternative to the rigorous and confining rituals of Newport society. In contrast to the limited sites available at the seashore, the open rolling countryside of the Berkshires provided large expanses of relatively inexpensive woodland tracts and farm fields. Large estates could be laid out that typically would include a farm group as well as formal gardens offering both privacy and magnificent scenic vistas.

The historic estate planned by Edith Wharton with architects Ogden Codman, Jr., and Francis L. V. Hoppin and her niece landscape architect Beatrix Farrand is essentially intact. Both the house and the grounds have survived with no significant alterations to the 1902 design. The estate of 130 acres, now reduced to 50 acres, which includes a stable and gatehouse also built in 1902, were in a state of extreme neglect by 1971 when the entire estate was designated a National Historic Landmark. The Edith Wharton restoration group was founded in 1980.

PRESERVATION ISSUE

The scenic Berkshire Hills of western Massachusetts attracted Nathaniel Hawthorne and Herman Melville as a rustic retreat prior to the Civil War. By the 1870s the summer people discovered the picturesque eighteenth-century villages of Lenox and Stockbridge, which provided accommodations at inns. As the popularity of the place attracted the well-to-do from New York and Boston, they set themselves up in the grand manner by constructing extravagant cottages.

The Stockbridge Casino, the social and cultural center of the resort colony, was relocated in 1926 and transformed into a nonprofit theater in 1928. The playhouse is now known as the Berkshire Theater Festival. In the depression years of the 1930s, the Berkshire Symphonic Music Festival was established, the precursor of today's Tanglewood Music Festival.

With such an established audience for cultural pursuits, it was logical to emphasize the performing arts aspect of The Mount. Gradually The Mount has garnered its own dedicated supporters, and major stabilization and restoration projects are under way. Catching up with years of neglect of the wood-framed stucco residence has been the first priority, and the full potential of the grounds and the barn group have yet to be realized. A successful shop and bookstore, located in the house, specializes in Edith Wharton's literary *oeuvres*. In the future a restaurant or cafe in the large barn would be a useful adjunct to visitors and performance patrons and a source of additional revenue.

SIGNIFICANCE

A great deal of the success that has been achieved in the rescue of Edith Wharton's Mount is due to its fortunate location in the thriving Berkshire resort town of Lenox. Far more dynamic than a house museum, the use of the estate as a summer theater for the performance of Edith Wharton's work is especially appropriate. The Mount was a source of inspiration for backgrounds in her own fiction, and it brings to life for a contemporary audience the turn-of-the-century world she portrayed in her writings. The use of The Mount as a setting is also intriguing because of her interest in architecture, interiors, and gardening. Together with Newport architect Ogden Codman, Jr., their books *The Decoration of Houses* (1897) and *Italian Villas and Their Gardens* (1904) were of considerable influence on the taste of wealthy Americans who created the golden age of great estates and gardens.

Many of the fashionable charitable fund-raising events now organized on the estate to benefit the restoration of The Mount would seem familiar to Edith Wharton—the Lenox Garden Club, the Annual Berkshire Cottages Tour, and the Parade of Champions Dog Show. The Mount is also used as the setting for fashionable weddings.

The large carriage house, located at a distance from the mansion, offers adaptive-use possibilities that could provide a source of income to contribute toward the repairs and restoration of The Mount and its operating costs.

Chesterwood, Stockbridge, Massachusetts

SITE

Chesterwood was the estate of the renowned American sculptor Daniel Chester French and served as his summer home and studio for 33 years, from 1897 until his death in 1931.

Sculptor Daniel Chester French's studio at Chesterwood.

The garden facade of Daniel Chester French's residence. A stucco-faced structure which is part of architect Henry Bacon's ensemble at Chesterwood.

French chose the 150-acre former Marshall Warner farm property because of its magnificent view of Monument Mountain. Unlike his wealthy neighbors who occupied their enormous Berkshire "cottages" after the Newport season for the late summer and early autumn, French used this estate as a working environment, spending 6 months a year in Stockbridge. French commissioned New York architect Henry Bacon to design a studio on the foundations of an old barn.

As was common in the Beaux-Arts tradition, the sculptor and the architect often collaborated on projects. When Henry Bacon designed the Lincoln Memorial in Washington, D.C. (1911 to 1922), its focal point was Daniel Chester French's monumental sculpture of seated Lincoln.

The studio interior maintains the ambiance of the renowned sculptor's working place. His tools and plaster models are on display.

The studio is vaguely Italianate in style with its flairing roof terminating in deep bracketed eaves protecting its stucco walls. The family lived in the original farmhouse until 1891 when it was replaced by another building designed by Bacon, an eclectic amalgamation of Georgian Colonial Revival in the same gray stucco as the studio. French salvaged some old wood paneling from the farmhouse to be incorporated into the study of his new house.

French was an avid gardener and designed the landscaping himself. His studio's reception room and adjacent veranda served as a place to entertain guests and clients, and the estate's formal gardens were adjacent to his studio, rather than, as might be expected, to the house.

PRESERVATION ISSUE

After French's death, the house was retained and used by his family. In 1955, his daughter Margaret French Cresson took the initial steps to ensure that Chesterwood would be preserved for public benefit, deeding the property to The Trustees of Reservations. Seven years later, the family created the Daniel Chester French Foundation to maintain the property as a museum and memorial to French, and in 1968, the property as acquired by the National Trust for Historic Preservation, which operates it as a museum. Throughout, Mrs. Cresson maintained a life interest in the property until her death in 1973. The property was opened to the public in 1974.

Conversion of the site to a museum has necessitated changes in the uses of most of the buildings. French was an avid gentleman farmer as well as a gardener, and the property includes a barn that once housed his farm animals. The barn now serves as a gallery for plasters made by French, as well as some of his early works in their final form. The building also houses some of the work of Mrs. Cresson, who was an artist in her own right. A pictorial history of the *Minute Man,* one of French's earliest and best-known sculptures, is also on exhibit in the barn.

French's studio serves both as a museum for plaster casts and an interpretive site for the life and work of the sculptor. It is still furnished both as a working studio and the reception room where French entertained his clients and social guests.

Only the ground floor of the main house is opened to the public. Although it reflects Mrs. Cresson's residence, it will eventually be interpreted in the period from 1925 through 1931, which were French's last years in the house. The upper stories serve as administrative offices and archives.

The estate's original garage and maintenance sheds now serve as the gift shop and public facilities. The property is open to visitors from May through October. Various annual special events are held on the grounds of Chesterwood: the Antique Auto Show, the Flower Show, the Outdoor Sculpture Show, and Christmas at Chesterwood.

SIGNIFICANCE

Chesterwood is more than a house museum; it is a vast archive of the works and lifestyle of one of America's great sculptors. The impression of seeing his works and studies at the site where they were created is very different from the experience of seeing the monumental sculptures as part of a great museum collection. Chesterwood combines both process and context, which attracts the knowledgeable as well as the casual visitor.

Stockbridge is also the home of the Norman Rockwell Museum, which has recently been expanded. Edith Wharton's estate The Mount, in nearby Lenox, is under restoration and offers performances of her novels. At Naumkeag one can visit a surviving "cottage" with its exquisite garden, which is maintained by The Trustees of Reservations. The Berkshires were once an exclusive resort. The growth of Tanglewood as a major musical festival has made this amazing concentration of historic sites accessible to a huge popular audience interested in cultural pursuits. This large number of visitors helps to justify the cost of operating and maintaining these landmarks. In addition, clearly these very special sites give a tremendous boost to the local economy, including hotels, restaurants, resorts, and service industries.

View of Spencer Trask's Saratoga mansion Yaddo as seen from the formal gardens and reflecting pool, which are seasonally open to the public. In the fall of 1993, public tours of the mansion were begun for the first time.

Yaddo, Saratoga Springs, New York

SITE

The curative benefits of the mineral waters of Saratoga Springs were known to the Native Americans. Colonists attempted to construct a spa at the springs, but the establishment of the spa was interrupted by the Revolutionary War. The project was abandoned until 1802 when Gideon Putnam constructed the first major hotel at the springs. In increasing numbers, visitors were drawn to the area, and by the time of the Civil War Saratoga Springs had become the social center of the North. The Grand Union Hotel, horse racing, the Leland Opera House, and gambling at the Canfield Casino gave Saratoga its reputation as the "Queen of the Spas" for mid-Victorian America. The racing events in August were the highlight of the social calendar. The wealthy began constructing mansions in the area. Katrina Trask, an accomplished writer of the 1880s and 1890s, and her husband Spencer, a New York City financier, built themselves a bulky, rock-cut stone mansion with a tower and battlements of Norman inspiration. The mansion was the focus of a 500-acre estate, which included four lakes. In 1899 Spencer Trask gave his wife a gift of formal gardens, oriented to be seen from the terrace of the house which was set atop a hill. The gardens were designed in the Italian manner, complete with a Florentine fountain, statuary, and four rose beds, containing varieties of red and white roses, and pergolas covered with roses.

PRESERVATION ISSUE

At Yaddo, their summer home, the Trasks entertained leading figures in politics, commerce, and increasingly, the arts. Having no direct heirs (all four of their children having died of illnesses in childhood), the Trasks decided to establish a permanent legacy for future creative individuals. In 1900 Yaddo was incorporated by the Trasks and several close friends and advisors. After Spencer's untimely death in a train wreck in 1909, Katrina closed the mansion and moved into the superintendent's house in order to conserve funds for the institution's future. During World War I, she questioned the meaningfulness of an intellectual and artistic retreat in the midst of devastation. Having suffered such personal loss in her own life, she determined to pursue her original commitment with almost religious zeal. She died in 1922, and the first guests arrived at Yaddo in 1926.

Since that summer with just a few writers and artists in residence, more than 3000 artists have enjoyed the peace and guaranteed privacy that nurtures serious creative work.

The program still flourishes, with approximately 175 artists spending time at Yaddo each year. Just a few of the renowned artists who have joined the roster of Yaddo's former guests include John Cheever, Langston Hughes, Katherine Anne Porter, Saul Bellow, Aaron Copland, Leonard Bernstein, Philip Guston, and Milton Avery.

Additional studios have been located beyond the mansion in converted barns and an old family chapel. Yaddo functions year-round, and the size and layout of the estate permits public visitation of the gardens, as well as many weddings, from May through August, while preserving the privacy of guest artists-in-residence.

Until the decade of the 1970s the Trask endowment was sufficient to cover all costs, but that financial picture has changed with increasing costs of operation and inflation, together with deferred maintenance, which has resulted in the need for extensive repairs, and rehabilitation of the mansion and other estate structures.

Fund-raising appeals and former guests' contributions have helped as well as grants from the National Endowment for the Arts and the New York State Council on the Arts. In the fall of 1993 Yaddo opened the mansion for the first time to the public for tours. The reason is more for public relations than fund-raising, with the admission fee initially set at $12. Yaddo's directors hope that the tours will lead to future gifts.

SIGNIFICANCE

The case of Yaddo demonstrates, as do so many of the other successful examples presented thus far, that it is the determination of the estate owners not only to donate the estate itself and provide an endowment but also to give some direction as to its future institutional use that renders preservation possible. Unfortunately, many of the religious, charitable, and educational institutions who, in the past have accepted estates, have not demonstrated a serious commitment to stewardship. Many of the mansions now requiring rescue have been through this cycle.

Ragdale, Lake Forest, Illinois

SITE

A young Chicago architect, Howard Van Doren Shaw, and two friends sought land for a rural retreat for the summer within easy reach of Shaw's office in Chicago. The community of Lake Forest had been linked to Chicago by the Northwestern Railroad

Ragdale, Chicago architect Howard Van Doren Shaw's 1897 Arts and Crafts Style summer residence, has been transformed into a retreat for artists, writers, and composers.

since 1855, making it a convenient and quick commute. The three friends bought a 53-acre parcel in Lake Forest, and they divided it into thirds. Shaw's portion contained an old farmhouse and a barn. Not long afterward he bought some additional acreage beyond the Skokie River, enlarging his holdings to 50 acres. Shaw's farm acreage was open land with an old apple orchard and a few scattered trees merging into a meadow and the undisturbed portion of the original prairie.

Shaw was backed by his father, a prosperous dry-goods merchant, who offered to pay for the house. As a young architect, Shaw was intrigued by the arts and crafts movement begun in England by Ruskin and William Morris. In 1897, the same year he built Ragdale, the Chicago Arts and Crafts Society was founded, which included among its members Frank Lloyd Wright.

Howard Van Doren Shaw welcomed the opportunity to build for his own family his first house in the Arts and Crafts mode, unfettered by his conservative clients' demands for opulence. Howard Shaw named his new country house Ragdale after an old Tudor house in Leicestershire, England. Shaw had traveled extensively for a year and a half in Europe following his graduation from Yale and then MIT. As was the practice of the period, he sketched buildings as he traveled. Familiar with the originals, he sought to achieve the effect of a charming Cotswold cottage with stucco and timber.

Shaw was also a planner, concerned with the community. Elsewhere in Lake Forest, he later designed many country houses, parts of Lake Forest College, and, most notably, Market Square. This English Style village square built in 1916 was among the first consciously planned town centers in the United States.

In designing Ragdale, he aimed for informal country surroundings for his house, not the traditional landscaping of a well-groomed estate. The family indulged in artistic pursuits, and their circle of friends included Carl Sandburg and Vachel Lindsay. In 1912 Shaw designed Ragdale Ring, a circular garden theater seating 250, for his playwright wife Frances.

PRESERVATION ISSUE

Howard Van Doren Shaw died in 1926, and his wife in 1937. Successive generations of the family occupied the house, making relatively minor modifications inside and out. In 1976 Shaw's granddaughter Alice Ryerson Hayes started the Ragdale Foundation and was its director for many years. For the first few years the family continued to occupy the house in the summer and began to invite writers to use it during the rest of year. In 1980 the foundation bought back the barnhouse (a renovation combining the old farmhouse and barn), and refurbished it and the main house in order to accommodate more artists- and writers-in-residence. Other accessory structures were also adapted as artists' studios. In 1986 the foundation donated the two residences to the city of Lake Forest. It accepted the responsibility for the maintenance of the two buildings and the grounds immediately around them, and the following year the garden was added to the city's property. The city agreed that the Ragdale Foundation could continue to operate its program in the buildings for 25 years. Ragdale now provides annually residencies for more than a 150 artists, writers, and composers lasting from 2 weeks to 2 months.

The foundation has shared the use of the public rooms for meetings and seminars and other public events. From time to time there are large open houses so that the public can visit the house. In the basement of the house are now the offices of the Lake Forest Open Lands Association, which owns almost all of the original Ragdale land. The house now overlooks a large nature preserve, which maintains the original character of the prairie, woods, and meadow and provides a rural context as a buffer to the future suburban commercial development of its surroundings.

SIGNIFICANCE

The active role of Howard Van Doren Shaw's descendants in the transition of Ragdale from family home to an unpretentious artists' and writers' retreat has made possible the preservation of Ragdale's original contents, artworks, and family lore associated with the long history of the family's involvement with cultural pursuits. Establishing the active participation of the family, the foundation, the city, and a nature conservancy is a considerable achievement.

Impact of Adaptive Reuses on Neighbors

Owners of isolated mansions and estates may have a more difficult time finding a suitable museum or adaptive use to replace the original single-family occupancy, but they usually face fewer conflicts with neighbors and zoning ordinances. In more fashionable suburban and resort communities, often problems with the neighbors inhibit successful cultural programming and restricted visitor access.

In most cases mansions and estates owned by government or not-for-profit cultural organizations charge an admission fee to defray some of their operating and maintenance costs. Special programs, concerts, exhibits, lectures, and benefits are essential to attracting visitors and providing financial support. However, even if the site is large enough to absorb the parking requirements, the traffic generated on existing narrow roads may cause congestion and nuisance for the neighbors.

Sagamore Hill, Teddy Roosevelt's mansion in Oyster Bay, Long Island, and Thomas Edison's mansion Glenmont in Llewelen Park, New Jersey, have been a headache to the National Park Service because of complaints from adjacent neighbors about visitors who snoop around their exclusive neighborhoods. Although heavy visitation and group tours are encouraged at Edison's laboratories in nearby West Orange, a National Historic Site, tours of his mansion are not publicized.

Riverdale, New York, is a strangely bucolic community that overlooks the Hudson River; it was originally part of Westchester County and annexed to Greater New York only in 1898. The establishment of New York's first planned "villa suburb" coincided with the arrival of the railroad along the Hudson in 1852, and it was originally conceived of as a summer colony. Gradually large mansions and estates were created along the river, and picturesque Tudor apartments appeared in the 1920s. Riverdale managed to retain some quality of isolation until 1939 when the infamous power broker Commissioner Robert Moses ran the Henry Hudson Parkway through Riverdale and constructed a bridge traversing the Harlem River Ship Canal and connecting it with Manhattan.

Sagamore Hill, Teddy Roosevelt's rambling Queen Anne Shingle Style mansion, in Oyster Bay, Long Island, is a vibrant house museum with all the family's original furnishings. The mansion offers the visitor a genuine glimpse of the golden age.

Glenmont, Thomas Edison's Queen Anne Style mansion, replete with its original furnishings, provides an intimate view of the great inventor's sedate domestic surroundings.

After a succession of occupants, Wave Hill now operates as a performing arts center and gallery on a magnificent site overlooking the Hudson River. It also provides a park and arboretum open to the public.

Following a pattern discussed in the section on suburban zoning, property owners along the parkway route sold off strips of land to developers who constructed large modern apartment houses. Many of the estate owners sold their properties, and others donated them to large institutions such as Columbia University who, they hoped, would maintain them. Ultimately they would be sold for residential development. In the 1960s the Perkins family gave their estate Wave Hill to the city of New York. Wave Hill is administered by the New York Parks Department as a park, museum, and environmental center. There is no public transportation nearby, and as its popularity increased, the number of visitors' cars exceeded the limits of the parking lots, with the result that visitors were parking along the narrow roads. Feeling threatened by all these encroachments, the remaining mansion and house owners banded together and had their enclave declared a "natural area." In the 1970s several individual buildings were designated as individual landmarks, and finally in the 1990s a historic district was created.

Wave Hill's wealthy neighbors have refused to allow public transportation direct access or to permit the enlargement of the parking lots. Built atop a promontory across the road from Wave Hill is the Campagna house, an imposing 24,000-square foot Tuscan villa designed in 1922 by architect Dwight Baum who was highly regarded for his residences and their gardens as well. Some of its original acreage was sold off earlier as home sites. The current owners purchased it as a residence in 1980. In 1991, after several years of marketing, the Campagna owners finally found a serious buyer; a food corporation wanted it for their headquarters. It became the source of a community dispute over the required commercial zoning variance and was mired in litigation that ruined the sale. In the fall of 1993 it was designated as a New York City landmark and has been sold to a religious group that immediately proceeded to challenge the restrictions imposed.

Large Mansions as Urban Cultural Facilities

Typically the mansion is the focus of a large American estate from which the gardens and landscaping extend out into the surrounding acreage. Even on the outskirts of urban areas such as Rock Creek Park in Washington, D.C., or in resorts such as Newport, Rhode Island, or Palm Beach, Florida, where the acreage is quite limited, walled compounds contain a superbly cultivated miniature world within their confined sites. During the golden age, in urban areas the mansion was often "the house in town" with little more greenery than a small lawn or rear yard that sufficed for a family who could afford to maintain spacious residences set in extensively landscaped estates in one or more seasonal resort areas.

Whereas the country mansion shorn of its gardens and acreage presents a formidable preservation challenge, the urban mansion, which may be a white elephant of equal size, relates to its surroundings in an entirely different way. Being overshadowed by towering new neighbors is more of a problem. Even though most of these institutional adaptations initially try to accommodate their new usage within the confines of the existing mansion, this is seldom a satisfactory long-term solution. Growth and change soon exceed the limitations of the original residential volume. Unless additional vacant land or adjacent structures are available for expansion, the entire investment in restoration and adaptation may have to be abandoned in order to seek adequate space by moving to another site.

Several of the following examples represent the large urban mansion prototype adapted to cultural uses.

Hackerman House, Walters Art Gallery, Baltimore, Maryland

SITE

Baltimore's Mount Vernon Square is one of America's most beautiful urban spaces. During the 1950s its architectural and historic integrity were threatened by the expansion needs of Walters Art Gallery whose proposed 1930s addition was thwarted during the great depression. Concerned local citizens demanded the retention of the grand nineteenth-century townhouses, including William Walters' own, where the nucleus of the museum's collection originally resided. Fortunately in the 1970s a site away from the square was found to add a contemporary wing equal in bulk to the original museum. Despite the added gallery space, the Walters still did not have the appropriate setting to display its own impressive Oriental collections, hidden away in storage since the 1930s.

After several successive cycles of neglect, the Thomas-Jencks-Gladding house, a 22-room 1851 Italianate villa on Mount Vernon Square, was rescued by a local philanthropist, Willard Hackerman, and donated it to the city of Baltimore with the

View of rear and side facades of the Hackerman house, located on Baltimore's historic Mount Vernon Place and now linked to the Walters Art Gallery.

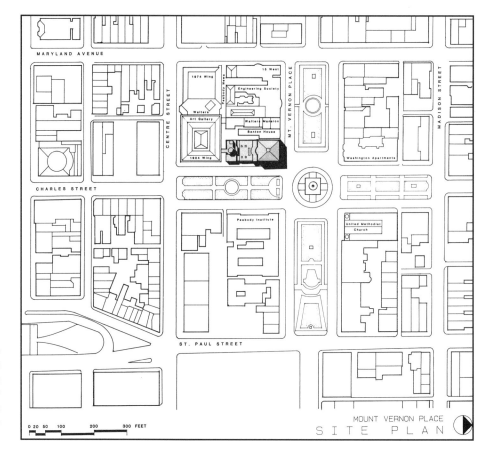

Site plan of Mount Vernon Place showing the relationship of the Hackerman house to the Walters Art Gallery and its immediate neighborhood. It is one of the four architecturally significant landmark structures that anchor the corners surrounding the historic 1829 Washington Monument.

proviso that it be preserved for public use. Many groups bid for the property with proposals for conversions. In 1985 the Walters Art Gallery was awarded the villa, now rechristened the Hackerman house, based on its plan for a museum annex.

With great ingenuity, the Baltimore architectural firm of Grieves, Worall, Wright and O'Hatnick, has linked the neighboring nineteenth-century Hackerman house to the original Walters Art Gallery, a Delano and Aldrich designed Renaissance palazzo of 1904, which the same firm updated in the 1988. Unlike the earlier 1970s "modern" addition to the Walters by the Boston architects Shepley, Bulfinch, and Abbott, this expansion did not involve demolition. The Hackerman mansion's coach house and stable yard adjoined the original Walters Art Gallery, facing landmark Mount Vernon Place's focal 1829 Washington Memorial Column.

PRESERVATION ISSUE

The free-standing Hackerman house was located on top of the hill on Mount Vernon Place separated from the Walters Art Gallery by its coach house and yard. Designing a connection between the two was complicated by the differing floor levels in each and

A longitudinal section showing the Hackerman house and a portion of the Walters Art Gallery. Despite the sloping site, linking the two structures would have been relatively straightforward were it not for the neighbors' desire to preserve the freestanding character of the mansion. The architects were forced to develop a more circuitous route for visitors.

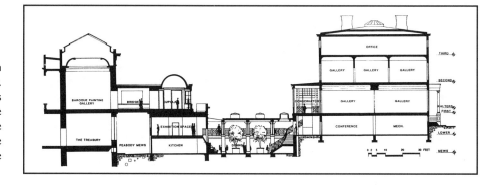

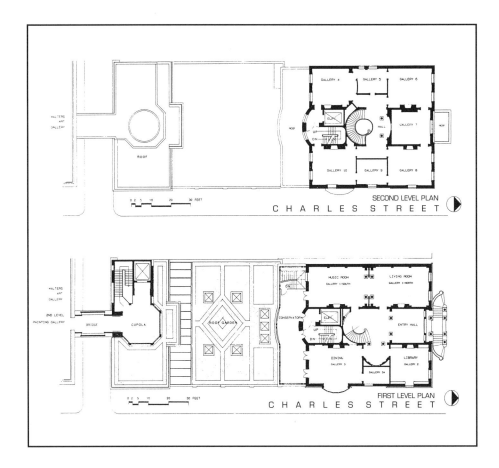

SECOND LEVEL PLAN
CHARLES STREET

FIRST LEVEL PLAN
CHARLES STREET

The first- and second-floor plans of the Hackerman house showing its relationship to the Walters Art Gallery. In order to connect the two, a visitor must descend, traverse the former yard, now the café, and ascend to the first floor. This required two new stairs and two new elevators to provide barrier-free access.

the need to provide handicapped access for visitors. The architects' first scheme linked the structures at the "parlor floor" level of the villa, which would have compromised the glazed conservatory, part of a major renovation by New York architect Charles Platt in the early 1900s. Also concerned about the obstruction of their view of Mount Vernon Place, the neighbors pressured the museum to go back to the drawing board.

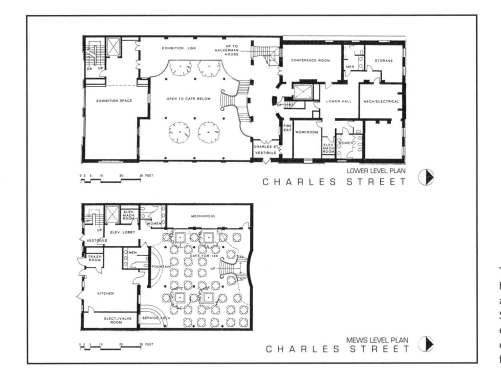

LOWER LEVEL PLAN
CHARLES STREET

MEWS LEVEL PLAN
CHARLES STREET

The plan for the lower level, which is at the basement level of the Hackerman house, provides a direct outside access to the café from Charles Street, as well as a fire exit and mezzanine exhibition areas. The mews level is now an elegant café with a fountain set against the brick facade of the original mews carriage house.

The Hackerman house's high-ceilinged double parlor, with elegant Greek Revival Style decoration, provides a fine background for free-standing vitrines displaying the Walters Art Gallery collection of fine Oriental porcelains.

Ultimately this demand led to an imaginative resolution: By excavating the former stable yard and roofing it over at the height of its original street wall, a skylit space for a new café-restaurant, the Pavilion, was created. To provide barrier-free access, small elevators were installed in both the museum and Hackerman house. The café, with its centerpiece fountain, has its own sidewalk-level entry and has become a popular local gathering place attracting museum visitors and generating additional revenue for the Walters Art Gallery.

SIGNIFICANCE

The Walters Art Gallery project demonstrates that in order to survive, an old cultural institution needs to grow and adapt sensitively to its contemporary audience and its surroundings.

The linking of the Hackerman house to the Walters Art Gallery is a tremendous success in several important ways. The whitewashed interiors (except for the former dining room retaining a handsome dark nineteenth-century painted ceiling treatment) emphasizes the classic elegance and simplicity of the original architectural detailing, including the moldings, ceilings, and decorative plasterwork. The individual room

The Hackerman house's former dining room, which still has its original stencil-decorated ceiling, provides a handsome setting for Japanese objects.

The Hackerman house second-floor exhibition space, converted from the former bedrooms that have lower ceilings than the first-floor rooms and less elaborate architectural detail, provide an ideal setting for the display of ancient earthenware, terra cotta, and bronze objects. The large undraped windows provide an excellent vantage point for viewing historic Mount Vernon Place.

settings provide a handsome and nondistracting backdrop for a collection of approximately 1000 works of Chinese, Japanese, and Indian art. Many are small and have been reinstalled in refurbished glass vitrines originally commissioned for the Walters family to house their treasures.

Combined with tinted ultraviolet light–filtering glass to prevent fading, the traditionally draped windows facing Mount Vernon Place allow the visitor to experience the relationship of the grand townhouses facing this historic Baltimore square. The use of the house as an extension of the Walters Art Gallery justifies the preservation of this elegant mansion, which is a key architectural anchor within the street scape of this historic district and a pendant to the venerable Peabody Conservatory opposite it. The resulting scheme handsomely preserves the villa and the historic street scape of Mount Vernon Square and provides an elegant, though not inexpensive, addition to the Walters Art Gallery. The city and the Walters Art Gallery investment in the Hackerman house annex as well as the elaborate privately financed refurbishing of the dowdy nearby Peabody Court Hotel has sparked a renaissance in this neglected but architecturally, culturally, and historically significant center-city Baltimore neighborhood.

Evergreen, Johns Hopkins University, Baltimore, Maryland

SITE

Evergreen was built as a villa on the outskirts north of Baltimore in the 1850s. The details of its construction and original architect are no longer known. A great deal of documentation exists concerning the extensive additions by two generations of the Garrett family who owned it from the 1870s until the early 1940s.

PRESERVATION ISSUE

John Garrett bequeathed Evergreen to Johns Hopkins University in 1942, complete with its extensive library and rare-book collections along with all of its decorative arts, furnishings, and paintings. Ten years later following her death, his widow Alice established and endowed the Evergreen House Foundation. The house now functions as a research center and house museum. The introduction of visitors as well as the conservation requirements of the library and the collections have necessitated an elaborate upgrading of building systems, fire protection, and climatization.

One of the most distinctive features of Evergreen is the intimate theater, created out of a former gymnasium and school room, which continues to function for perfor-

The main portico of Evergreen House, an 1850s Greek Revival mansion, is located on an estate in Baltimore, which was donated by the Garrett family to Johns Hopkins University. The mansion now functions as a research center and house museum.

The charming theater, a 1920s renovation, occupies portions of a late-nineteenth-century addition to Evergreen House. It is a unique example in the United States of decorations, including two stage sets by Leon Bakst, the renowned designer for the Ballet Russe. Architects Mesick, Cohen, and Waite have restored and upgraded the wooden structure, which still functions as a setting for intimate performances.

mances. The theater and its lobby are unique because they were decorated and designed in 1922 by the famous designer of the Ballet Russe, Leon Bakst, who also designed two stage sets.

SIGNIFICANCE

The Garretts planned the transition of Evergreen for its donation to Johns Hopkins University. The task of displaying and preserving diverse collections in a residential setting is far more of a challenge than it would be in a museum setting, especially where wooden floors, paneling, and other nonfireproof decorative finishes may put the contents at risk. In a residential setting, it is awkward to introduce display cases, which would permit a means of providing specialized temperature and humidity control. It is impossible to provide a uniform ideal conservation environment for all different materials, including textiles, paper, wood, and leather. The introduction of some conservation measures such as ultraviolet light filtering on windows is relatively unobtrusive.

Often satellite campuses and estates remote from the main campus become a tremendous administrative and maintenance burden to the conventional university buildings and grounds staffs. Elaborately furnished historic houses cannot be subjected to routine institutional maintenance and may require highly specialized museum care techniques.

Eastman House, Rochester, New York

SITE

George Eastman admired a house built in Buffalo by McKim, Mead, and White, yet he commissioned a Rochester architect, J. Foster Warner, to built a substantial Georgian Colonial Revival mansion, and in an unusual arrangement he engaged McKim, Mead, and White to design the interiors and detailing. In 1902 Eastman had purchased an 8½-acre site on Rochester's prestigious East Avenue "millionaires' row." A life-long bachelor Eastman lived with his mother in a nearby substantial Richardsonian Ro-

Eastman House's restored main entrance facade and portico as seen from East Avenue, Rochester's prestigious "millionaires' row." The International Museum of Photography of the George Eastman House has removed its collections to a modern archival storage facility constructed at the rear of the site. This has permitted the mansion's principal rooms to be restored as a house museum.

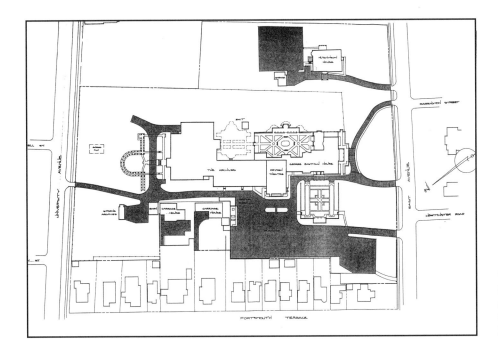

A site plan of Eastman house and the adjoining properties, showing that preserving the original semicircular pergola, which was once the terminus of the garden vista, determined the location of the new archival facility.

manesque house. At the time of its completion in 1905, the 35-room mansion of 35,000 square feet was the largest private residence in Monroe County. Rochester has a strong horticultural tradition and Eastman's father had been a nurseryman turned businessman so he consulted architect Claude Bragdon on the design of the west garden. The general plan was laid out by landscape architect Alling de Forest who managed to locate on its compact site a vegetable garden, a greenhouse, a decorative cutting garden for flowers, a barn for horses, cows, and chickens, and a carriage house.

PRESERVATION ISSUE

After Eastman's death in 1932, the mansion was bequeathed to the University of Rochester and served as the residence for its presidents until 1947, when it was incorporated as the site of the International Museum of Photography of the George Eastman House. The museum houses the world's largest collection of photographs, as well as one the great archives of motion pictures. Over time the museum and its photo collections gradually expanded to fill the entire house.

In the mid-1980s a major local as well as national controversy erupted over the proposed transfer of the photography collections to the Smithsonian. Eventually community pressure prevented the removal of the collections from Rochester, and the issue was resolved. A $10 million fund-raising campaign and a $16 million endowment from Kodak enabled the photography museum to commission a new wing. Because Eastman experimented with film, the mansion is of fireproof construction, unusual for mansions of this period.

In 1989 a new large modern archival storage building was constructed behind the house, at the rear of the lot. In order to reduce the bulk of the new addition and still provide sufficient space, some of the archival storage and offices were located underground, preserving the garden above. The modern addition is able to provide the specialized climatization for the precious film collection. Much of this old material is not only brittle but also highly flammable. A prior addition contained exhibition spaces and auditoriums. Recognizing the need for continuing financial support, the new wing also provides additional exhibition space, a gift shop, a monumental peristyle hall, and a catering facility that permits the entire complex to host conferences and receptions. This trend is growing all over the country. New York's world-renowned Metropolitan Museum earns substantial income from corporate and convention groups holding

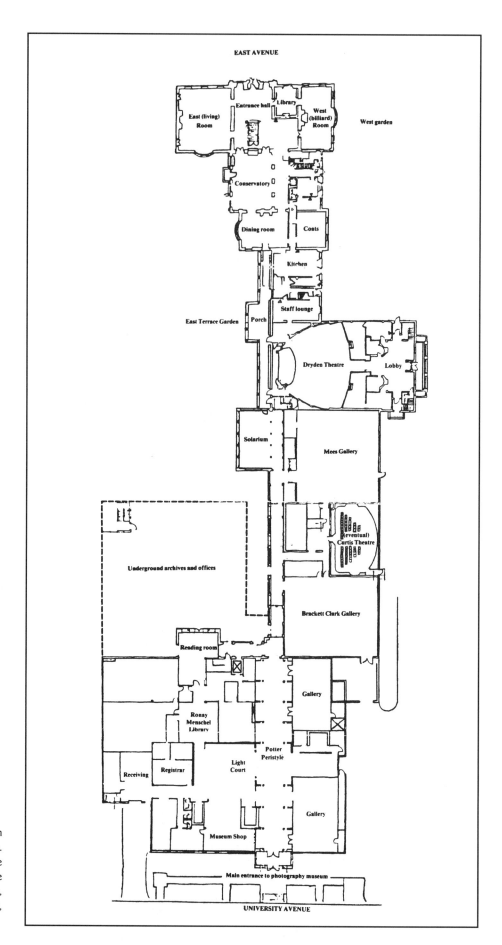

EAST AVENUE

East (living) Room

Entrance hall

Library

West (billiard) Room

West garden

Conservatory

Dining room

Coats

Kitchen

Staff lounge

East Terrace Garden

Porch

Dryden Theatre

Lobby

Solarium

Mees Gallery

(eventual) Curtis Theatre

Underground archives and offices

Brackett Clark Gallery

Reading room

Gallery

Ronay Menschel Library

Receiving

Registrar

Light Court

Potter Peristyle

Gallery

Museum Shop

Main entrance to photography museum

UNIVERSITY AVENUE

Ground-floor plan of the International Museum of Photography at the George Eastman House. Starting from the Dryden Theater, successive additions have extended from the rear of the original mansion almost to the rear of the lot, linked by a glazed (or glass-enclosed) corridor, running alongside the formal gardens.

View from original Eastman mansion, looking out over restored formal terrace garden. In the distance is the new archival storage addition. In order to reduce the bulk of the new facility and keep it at a distance from the original mansion, an underground extension lies just beyond the stone balustrade.

receptions in its vast spaces. Special areas of the museum have been developed to attract visitors including a rooftop sculpture terrace overlooking Central Park.

After the collections were removed to the new wing, the focus shifted to restoration of the interior. The mansion was structurally sound but required extensive cosmetic restoration. Over the years the house had been altered, and much of Eastman's furnishings were dispersed. Architectural historian William Seale, a specialist on historic interiors who has documented and written on the White House, was hired as a consultant for the interior restoration. Fortunately Eastman had extensively photographed the house over the years, so there were scrapbooks available for reference. Because the photographs were black and white, one of Seale's greatest challenges was to recreate the original color scheme. The object of the restoration was to re-create the period atmosphere of Eastman's time. A major effort has resulted in the retrieval of many original pieces. Some light fixtures and other decorative elements have been reproduced. Thus far only the main ground-floor rooms have been furnished. The second floor is devoted to exhibition space on George Eastman, his life, his work, and his philanthropy. The third floor, formerly Eastman's private domain, is currently being used as office space.

The original conservatory, formal gardens, reflecting pool, and pergolas are also being restored to their appearance during Eastman's lifetime. Because the lot ran through the block to University Avenue, it was possible to create a new main entrance to the photography museum at the rear. The site planning has carefully screened the new addition, service, and visitor parking areas from the traditional approach route along East Avenue.

SIGNIFICANCE

The preservation of George Eastman's house has a triple benefit to Rochester:

1. It preserves the legacy of one of Rochester's most world renowned citizens and the company he founded which is still headquartered in the city.

2. It secures the future of a unique and world-famous photo collection and makes it available to scholars and the general public.

3. It visually anchors a significant stretch of Rochester's most prestigious historic district, which is undergoing a transformation to institutional and commercial usage while trying to preserve its original elegant residential character and its dignified architectural ambiance.

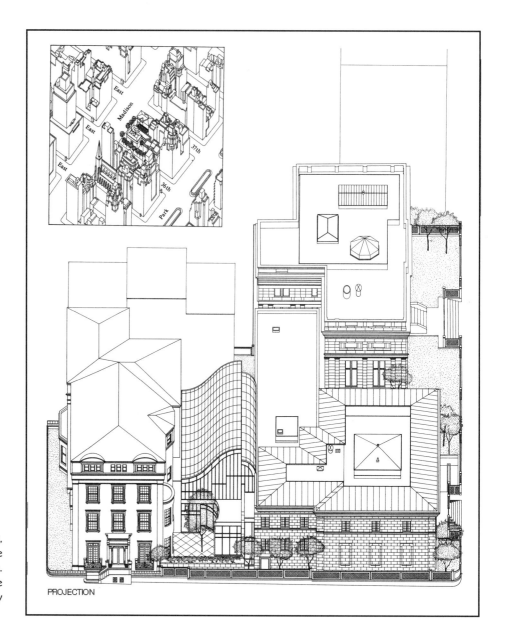

"Projected view" of the original Morgan Library, the annex, Morgan's son's brownstone, and the new glass-roofed atrium linking it to the complex. The inset is an isometric view of the highrise neighborhood surrounding the Morgan Library complex.

Pierpont Morgan Library, Murray Hill, New York, New York

SITE

J. Pierpont Morgan (1837 to 1913) was not only the leading financier of his time but also one the world's greatest collectors. The original Pierpont Morgan Library, a free-standing, one-story Italian Renaissance Style pavillion, was designed by McKim, Mead, and White. The library was completed in 1906, on a lot adjacent to Morgan's own house. It was originally part of a family compound, connected by underground tunnels, which included a McKim designed house for Morgan's daughter (now replaced by an apartment house) and another 1853 Italianate brownstone mansion occupied by his son.

Morgan's son established the Morgan Library as a public institution in 1924. J. P. Morgan's own house was demolished and replaced in 1928 by a new annex in the Renaissance Style designed by Benjamin Wistar Morris. The son's house was later sold to the Lutheran Church in America as its headquarters. The New York City Landmarks Preservation Commission designated the library, the annex, and the Lutheran Church

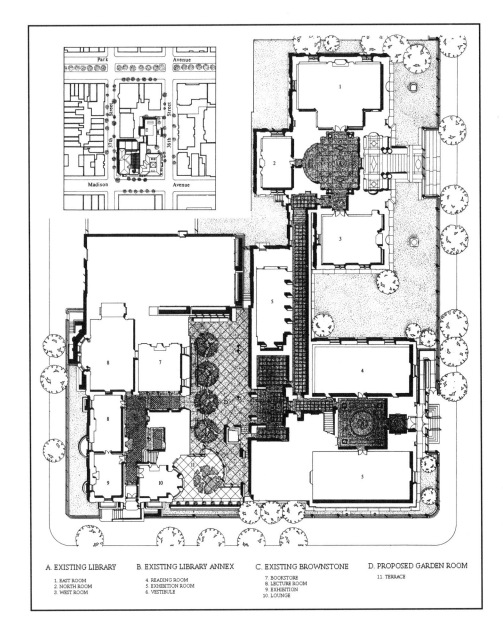

A. EXISTING LIBRARY

1. EAST ROOM
2. NORTH ROOM
3. WEST ROOM

B. EXISTING LIBRARY ANNEX

4. READING ROOM
5. EXHIBITION ROOM
6. VESTIBULE

C. EXISTING BROWNSTONE

7. BOOKSTORE
8. LECTURE ROOM
9. EXHIBITION
10. LOUNGE

D. PROPOSED GARDEN ROOM

11. TERRACE

Main-floor plan showing the relationship between the existing Morgan Library, annex, the Morgan brownstone, and the new garden room. The glassed-in garden court not only links the complex together but also provides barrier-free access by use of exterior and interior ramps and a new elevator. The inset small-scale site plan shows the relationship of the library to its surrounding mix of lowrise townhouses and highrise apartment buildings.

house. The Church, which had wished to develop its site commercially, fought the landmark designation and was successful in having it overturned. Fortunately, they never proceeded to demolish the house. Eventually the library, which was pressed for more space, acquired the house. Voorsanger and Associates Architects were commissioned to link the original library, the annex, and the newly acquired mansion.

PRESERVATION ISSUE

The library's renovation plans called for creating a new exhibition space in the annex building by expanding and relocating the book and gift shop to the ground floor of the newly acquired mansion. The ground floor would also house an education center and seminar rooms for the public. Curatorial and staff offices were to be moved to the second and third floors of the mansion, and the new conservation laboratory was created on the top floor. The most important design question became, how to link the mansion to the existing library buildings. Also, the choice of style became architecturally significant since the mansion is a nondescript 1850s Italianate brownstone and the landmark library annex a light-colored 1928 Renaissance Revival palazzo.

Close-up view showing the new Morgan Library complex garden court and enclosure wall, linking the brownstone mansion and the existing annex, which provides a buffer to the hub-bub of traffic along Madison Avenue.

The architect's solution for the library link was to create a glassed-in garden court. The transparent structure could connect the disparate historic structures without visually crowding them. The sun-filled central court is sparsely planted and provides a peaceful oasis in the midst of the complex and a buffer to bustling Madison Avenue traffic outside the garden wall. It is also a pleasant contrast because the Morgan collection, which consists primarily of works on paper, drawings, manuscripts, and rare books, is displayed for conservation purposes in dimly lit galleries and library spaces to prevent fading.

In the foreground, the Morgan Library's annex; in the background, J. P. Morgan's son's brownstone mansion. Later functioning as the Lutheran Church house, it was acquired for expansion of the existing Morgan Library complex.

SIGNIFICANCE

Many urban cultural institutions are bursting at the seams of their original buildings. Many have expanded beyond the visions of their founders, In the case of the Morgan Library, the building was Morgan's personal treasure house and is as much an artifact as are his collections. It was fortunate that an adjacent small mansion house could be acquired that permitted the expansion and redistribution of the museum's functional needs. The architects have successfully linked the cluster of the three structures without greatly altering the architectural character or scale of the street scape. The preservation of this turn-of-the-century townhouse scale enclave is particularly important since it is now surrounded by highrise construction.

Dumbarton Oaks, Washington, D.C.

SITE

In 1920, in the midst of their distinguished career in the Foreign Service, Mr. and Mrs. Robert Woods Bliss acquired Dumbarton Oaks, a nineteenth-century mansion set on 53 acres, as a permanent home. The original Federal Style mansion, dating from about 1800, was set atop a steep wooded slope rising from the Potomac River. The Blisses were cultivated collectors who moved in the smart upper-class society of their time. They were determined to transform the house and the grounds into a gracious setting for living and entertaining amidst the artworks and treasures they had amassed.

Mrs. Bliss had a great interest in gardening and worked closely with Beatrix Farrand who continued to design and develop Dumbarton Oaks gardens and landscaping until her retirement in 1947. In 1933 Mr. Bliss retired and settled at Dumbarton Oaks. In 1940 they conveyed the house, the gardens, and the collections to Harvard University. They established and endowed the Dumbarton Oaks Research Library and Collection, which is administered by Harvard. Mr. and Mrs. Bliss moved to a nearby house and maintained close ties to Dumbarton Oaks. In 1944 the Dumbarton Oaks Conferences were held in the Music Room. These international meetings led to the drafting of the charter of the United Nations.

PRESERVATION ISSUES

The Mansion. When the mansion was acquired in 1920, it had already undergone in the 1860s a considerable transformation from its original modest Federal Style appearance. Edward Linthicum enlarged the house on every side, added a mansard roof, which contained a small theater, changed the proportion of the windows, and added bracketed cornices. In short, Linthicum changed its appearance to one of fashionable Second Empire Victorian taste. One of the few elements of the early estate structures that has survived through all the renovations is a charming orangery, which was originally a free-standing pavillion but which is now linked to the mansion.

Mr. and Mrs. Bliss called on architect Lawrence White of McKim, Mead, and White to remove the Victorian accretions and to provide a dignified neo-Georgian character to the exterior. The 1870s west wing was enlarged in 1921. The entire interior of the house was remodeled, with the exception of the central hall, which survived throughout the house's many changes. From the beginning the house has reflected a very eclectic taste in its interiors, especially the Music Room added in 1929, the second of several major additions.

Adaptive Use. The shift from the Bliss's residential use to the scholarly, museum, institutional use generated the need for later additions. Dumbarton Oaks functions as research facility related to Mr. and Mrs. Bliss's principal collections, Byzantine studies, the history of landscape architecture, and pre-Columbian studies. Each area has its own library which total more than 100,000 volumes. Resident scholars and fellowships are chosen annually, and each program organizes publications, conferences, exhibitions,

The dramatic vaulted ceilinged gallery retains the architectural stone detailing and columns of the former outdoor Dumbarton Oaks courtyard. The handsome Palladian motif of the doors leads to the 1929 Music Room is now a visual focus of the gallery.

and public lectures. In 1940 at the time of the transfer to Harvard, a new wing to house the Byzantine collection was appended to the Music Room. Two parallel pavilions formed a walled court bringing the extension to the garden wall fronting on a side street and providing a new entry to the complex.

In 1948 Mrs. Bliss started assembling an exceptional library of illustrated books on garden design, plants, and horticulture, with a unique portion of her collection of books by and about women's enduring fascination with the floral and herbal world. In the 1950s she conceived the idea of starting a center for the study of landscape history. The Garden Library had grown so large that in 1963, a special wing was designed by Frederick Rhinelander King to house the collection. Georgian Revival on the outside, it is eighteenth-century French in its interior detail. This addition was appended to the earlier Byzantine collections wing.

In 1963 Philip Johnson was commissioned to design a pavilion for the Pre-Columbian Gallery. Johnson chose to depart from the Georgian Revival aesthetic of the previous additions. Johnson's design is a modern interpretation of a pavilion in Turkish Style, a cluster of nine circular shallow domed spaces. Large curved floor-to-ceiling

Garden view looking from the Dumbarton Oaks mansion down onto the "Turkish-domed" pavilion added by Philip Johnson in 1963 to house the pre-Columbian collection.

glass windows set between heavy round columns is sited in the garden surrounded by lush foliage. It is linked by a glazed passage to the Byzantine Court.

The most recent expansion, completed by Hartman-Cox architects in 1990, has provided additional exhibition space by enclosing the former Byzantine Court. The architects have skillfully integrated the traditional, originally exterior facades of the courtyard into a handsome coved ceilinged, top-lit gallery. The brickwork has been plastered over, but the stone collonades and trim have been retained. The new hipped roof portion visible from the street blends with the standing seam roofs of the flanking pavilions.

The Gardens. The Dumbarton Oaks gardens represent an extraordinary collaboration between Mrs. Bliss and Beatrix Farrand. Much of the coordination had to be carried on by correspondence while the Blisses were on assignment abroad. Because of

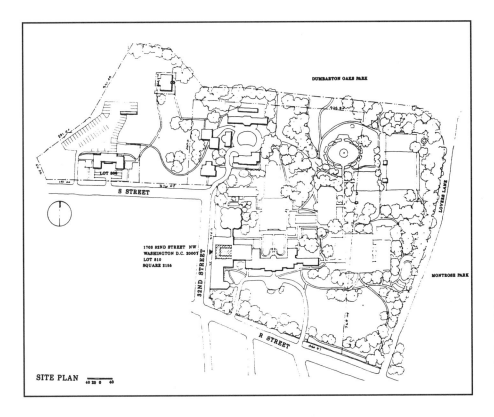

SITE PLAN

Plan of the Dumbarton Oaks 16-acre site. Dumbarton Oaks Park contains the 27 acres formerly part of the original estate, which are now managed by the National Park Service and open to the public. The small hatched area represents the 1990 project enclosing the former courtyard as a gallery.

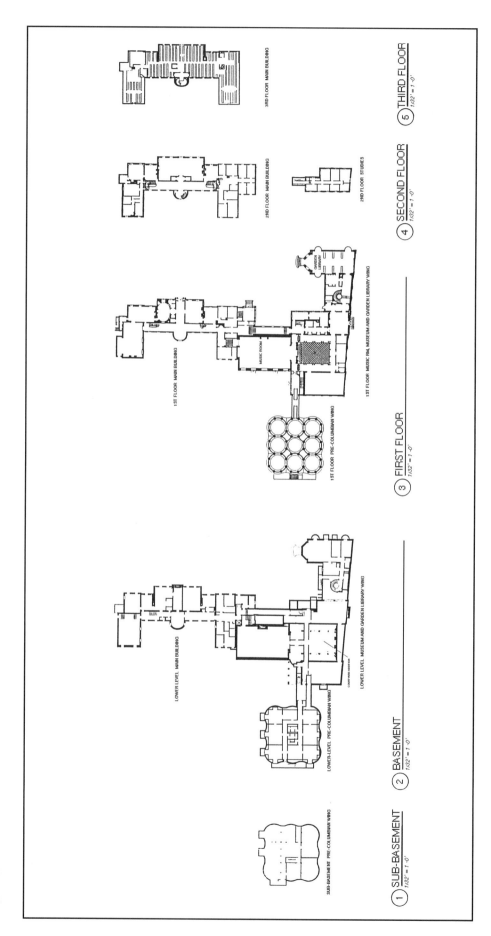

The plans for the Dumbarton Oaks mansion in 1990 show the Bliss's mansion, from the sub-basement to the third floor, with all its subsequent internal modifications and additions.

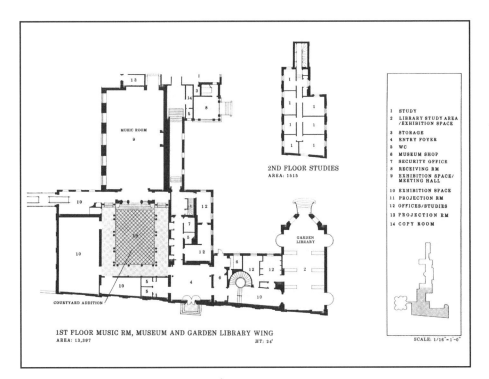

2ND FLOOR STUDIES
AREA: 1515

1 STUDY
2 LIBRARY STUDY AREA /EXHIBITION SPACE
3 STORAGE
4 ENTRY FOYER
5 WC
6 MUSEUM SHOP
7 SECURITY OFFICE
8 RECEIVING RM
9 EXHIBITION SPACE/ MEETING HALL
10 EXHIBITION SPACE
11 PROJECTION RM
12 OFFICES/STUDIES
13 PROJECTION RM
14 COPY ROOM

1ST FLOOR MUSIC RM, MUSEUM AND GARDEN LIBRARY WING
AREA: 13,397   HT: 24'

SCALE: 1/16"=1'-0"

Enlarged plan detail of Hartman-Cox architects' 1990 alterations to Dumbarton Oaks, through which a formerly open garden courtyard was transformed into a new skylit vaulted ceiling gallery space. As shown, the plan also provided for the renovation of existing exhibition spaces and additional study areas for scholars.

their familiarity with European gardens, Mrs. Bliss had very definite ideas on the atmosphere she wished to create. The major construction of the gardens began in 1922 and continued through transfer of the estate to Harvard in 1941. Mr. Bliss died in 1962, and Mrs. Bliss made modifications to portions of the landscape until her death in 1969.

Farrand's scheme for the the gardens involved one large lawn on the North Vista, on the axis with the mansion. The scheme also required cutting terraces into the slope on which she designed a series of enclosed gardens of great variety, progressing from formal to naturalistic. The designs of the garden furniture, gates, piers, walls, and sculpture were all studied and mock-ups prepared for Mrs. Bliss's approval. In 1926 Beatrix Farrand also coordinated with McKim, Mead, and White who designed a loggia and the pool house in a style evocative of the Riviera. Reflecting this eclecticism are three large toolsheds in the Portuguese manner roofed with glazed tiles.

The mansion's site today is reduced to 16 acres, of which 10 are formal gardens. The present garden retains the formal portions that were designed as a series of outdoor

Exterior view of entrance from 32nd Street with the new roof over the courtyard visible between the flanking wings. The hipped roofs, low-scale character, and detailing disguise the institutional nature of Dumbarton Oaks so that it blends comfortably with its residential neighbors.

rooms and some of the naturalistic planting, originally forming the transition to the wooded areas. The remaining 27 acres of planted woodlands, bordering on Rock Creek Park, were given in 1941 to the National Park Service as a public park. After decades of neglect, it has been allowed to grow over and is now somewhat of a romantic ruin with some of its architectural features still evident.

SIGNIFICANCE

Many Washington, D.C., mansions have been preserved as foreign embassies. Mr. and Mrs. Bliss retired from the U.S. Foreign Service and developed Dumbarton Oaks, its collections, and its spectacular gardens to equal any embassy. Through their own entertaining and concerts, the estate made a gracious transition to institutional use. The success of Dumbarton Oaks is the result of Mr. and Mrs. Bliss's involvement in every step of the planning and shaping of the library and research center that would perpetuate scholarly interest in the special areas of their own collections. The mansion has retained its original character through sensitively designed and sited additions, which have permitted it to accommodate the growing needs of the institution.

It also has been a considerate neighbor: By maintaining its superb landscape and formal gardens, as well as by discretely concealing its own 55-car parking lot, it has helped to maintain the residential character of its surroundings. Because of its scholarly purpose and limited number of visitors, Dumbarton Oaks has avoided some of the problems that other publicly accessible house museums have encountered.

Hyde Collection, Glens Falls, New York

SITE

The three Pruyn sisters were the daughters of a prosperous paper mill owner in Glens Falls, New York. The daughters were given adjacent building sites overlooking the logging operation of the paper mill. Initially they were not mansions but rather large houses. The central house in the group was the most distinctive. Charlotte Pruyn (1867 to 1963) met Louis Fiske Hyde (1866 to 1934) while attending school in Boston. Hyde established his law practice in Boston, and they remained there until 1907. They returned to Glens Falls when Henry Hyde took up an administrative position in his father-in-law's paper mill. Widely traveled and influenced by the cultural atmosphere of Boston and New York City, the Hydes became ardent art collectors. Confident in their own superb taste and with sound advice from noted art connoisseurs, they

Recent exterior view of the 1902 Italian Renaissance Style mansion commissioned by Mr. and Mrs. Hyde, which still contains and displays their collections in their original residential setting.

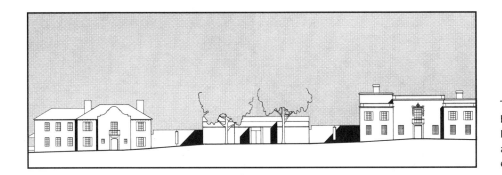

The design study of the contemporary entrance building designed by architect Edward Larrabee Barnes to link the Hyde and Cunningham houses and to provide for much-needed museum expansion space.

assembled a small but exceptional collection of paintings, representing the span in art history from the late Gothic to the twentieth century. They lived surrounded by their treasures in a setting furnished with Italian Renaissance and French eighteenth-century antiques.

They commissioned the Boston architectural firm of Bigelow and Wadsworth to design their house. The refined Italian Renaissance palazzo that Henry Forbes Bigelow designed, features a skylit central courtyard filled with plants and a fountain. It captures on a more modest scale the character of Boston's Isabella Stewart Gardiner Museum, with its central skylit court designed by Edward H. Sears in 1902. In 1919 architect Charles Adams Platt made some minor additions to the Hydes' house.

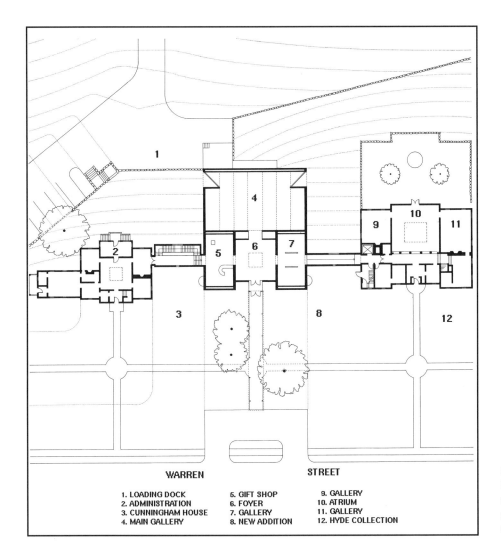

WARREN STREET

1. LOADING DOCK
2. ADMINISTRATION
3. CUNNINGHAM HOUSE
4. MAIN GALLERY
5. GIFT SHOP
6. FOYER
7. GALLERY
8. NEW ADDITION
9. GALLERY
10. ATRIUM
11. GALLERY
12. HYDE COLLECTION

Principal floor plan of architect Edward Larrabee Barnes showing his design for the new addition containing new exhibition and gallery space, and museum shop, as well as the passages linking the Cunningham house and Hyde Collection.

View of the Cunningham house, which now houses administrative offices, and the new entrance pavilion, which serves as the entrance to the enlarged Hyde Collection complex.

View of a portion of the rear of the Hyde Collection, with its top-floor, Italian Renaissance Style loggia and the stone retaining walls of its rear garden terrace. At the right is the intersection of the new passage linked to the central entrance addition.

PRESERVATION ISSUE

After her husband's death Mrs. Hyde hired a curator to help strengthen her collection and prepare the Glens Falls community for an eventual art museum. In 1952 the Hyde Collection was founded as an art museum. Mrs. Hyde's sister's home Cunningham house now serves as the administrative building. The third sister's house serves as headquarters for a local charitable group.

In order to accommodate the growth of the museum's programs of concerts, lectures, and classes, as well as to provide space for changing exhibitions, an addition was needed. In 1989 architect Edward Larrabee Barnes was hired to design the education wing. Fortunately there was sufficient distance between the Cunningham house and the Hyde house to insert the new facility.

To preserve the intimate residential atmosphere of the Hydes' home and its collections and furnishings, the entrance to the museum complex was located in the new wing. All of the commotion of the school groups, visitors, and the museum shop is contained in the new facilities. Barnes has chosen an unabashedly modern architectural expression for the wing. The site slopes downhill at the rear so that the entrance facade will be kept low and in scale with the adjoining houses, to which it is linked by glazed passages. The bulk of the new wing extends toward the rear of the property where it is visible from a street that runs at the bottom of the hill. Much of loading dock and the service and mechanical equipment are discretely nestled into the hill.

SIGNIFICANCE

Today Glens Falls, just as many small American industrial towns, has lost much of its economic vitality. Located in a turn-of-the-century enclave of large Queen Anne and Shingle Style houses, the neighborhood character has changed, and there is now a nursing home facility across the street from the Hyde Collection. The unified ensemble of the three Pruyn sisters' houses and the new education wing are an important visual anchor, preserving the architectural integrity of the houses and permitting the collections to be displayed in their original setting.

CHAPTER 9

Preserving and Adapting Mansions

Much as preservationists would like to regulate the restoration of both the exterior and interior of old mansions, this approach is unrealistic and impractical. Most communities that have preservation ordinances are limited to exterior control only. Through the special permit process that is often required for large acreage estate subdivisions, it is sometimes possible to specify certain restoration goals, including significant interior spaces, as a condition of approving the application.

The result of overrestriction, however, no matter how well intentioned, may actually be greater neglect, abandonment, and eventual demolition. An alternative to legal means for mansion preservation, especially in the case of mansions that have already been seriously neglected or damaged on the interior due to institutional occupancy or fires, is adaptive use strategies, which may be simpler in the long run. Economics, as always, becomes a major factor since the costs of major rehabilitations and the requirements of code compliance may exceed those of comparable new construction.

There is obviously a large inventory of major historic and architecturally significant landmarks that are worthy of preservation as house museums, and many of these preservation projects have been carried out through private or government agencies in various parts of the country. Sadly there are already so many restored houses that they are, in effect, competing with each other for private funds and government grants.

Surviving Mansions and Estates

Those properties that have survived intact are facing greater difficulties than ever before. Most of the great mansions were constructed of the finest, most durable materials, with excellent workmanship and have endured in some cases for a hundred years. Age and natural deterioration have begun to catch up with many properties whose more recent owners have not had the extravagant resources of those who initially built them. This failure of stewardship includes private as well as institutional and governmental owners. Many of the maintenance problems are the same as those of the average homeowner, only on a greatly magnified scale. Mansions typically have large and often complex roofs, dormers, chimneys, and sometimes skylights. These roofs were made of wood shingles, slate, or tile, which are difficult and expensive to repair. In some cases the deterioration is so severe that the entire roofing surface must be replaced as in the case of Andrew Carnegie's 1898 New York City mansion, which houses the Cooper-Hewitt decorative arts collection, a branch of the Smithsonian. The entire copper roof is being replaced while the museum and its precious collections continue to function beneath.

Twenty years ago architects lamented that one could not find the skilled artisans to execute the repairs and restoration work required. This is no longer the case, and amazingly some of the most arcane crafts have been revived. For properties in private or nonprofit ownership, finding the proper artisans is expensive but possible. For institutional and governmental owners who are obligated to choose contractors through the public bidding process, the results are not only frustrating but often disappointing. In the past the National Trust has tried to set up craftsmanship training programs, including a successful workshop on the grounds of one of its historic properties, Lyndhurst in Tarrytown, New York. The training program that flourished for several years has now been discontinued.

Some structural repairs and restoration work will be required to counteract the wear and tear of age or neglect, but if the mansion is to be adapted to museum use or some institutional, commercial, or multifamily occupancy, the existing structural system may need to be reinforced or upgraded. It is difficult to insert or conceal these changes without disturbing existing decorative finishes.

Even if the physical outer shell of the building and its interior finishes can be restored, there is another critical area that compounds the problems of restoring and

Overleaf Clayton, Henry Clay Frick's Pittsburgh mansion, has been meticulously restored inside and out to function as a house museum. To provide barrier-free access for visitors, a lift has been installed at the rear service porch. To conceal the lift mechanism, a wooden enclosure has been constructed replicating the balusters and lattice of the original porches on the house.

adapting mansions of the golden age. The aging mechanical systems, including heating, plumbing, and electrical wiring, are reaching a point where they are not only inefficient but in some cases hazardous.

Rarely did the builders of the great mansions concern themselves with fireproof construction and other life-safety matters that are now mandated by law. Shortsightedness in these construction matters has meant that not only are some mansion structures themselves a cause of concern but the historic furnishings, paintings, and decorative arts unique to the properties are also at risk. In addition, the original owners, who often had several estates in different regions, used them only seasonally, so they did not provide year-round climatization which is essential to sustaining the contents, especially textiles and paintings. In order to introduce more efficient heating, cooling, and humidity control as well as reducing the infiltration of dirt and other pollutants, modern techniques of insulation and vapor barriers are needed, but these cannot always be easily inserted into traditional construction. In earlier building periods, insulation was not employed at all; later on mineral wool, cellulose, or asbestos products were introduced, but, as we have come to realize, these products have serious safety or environmental consequences.

In order to address these concerns with insulation as well as providing fire-detection and security systems, a lot of disruption is required on the interior, which often leads to marring the historic fabric and finishes within the mansion. To conceal the new mechanical systems, the ingenious architect and mechanical engineer will have to seek out secondary space, shafts, ducts, attics, and basements in which to locate equipment. Even though they are highly automated, these sophisticated modern systems require maintenance and operating skills far beyond the capacity of the old-fashioned caretaker. Thus, in rural and isolated areas, it may be difficult to service this type of equipment.

Access

An additional problem now confronting all owners of historic buildings is the enactment by the federal government of the Americans with Disabilities Act (ADA) regulations that require barrier-free access for people who have disabilities. Thus all buildings serving the public, including house museums or houses adapted to other uses, must meet this new challenge.

Prominently located on the main street historic district in the vicinity of Lancaster, Pennsylvania, an access ramp has been discretely installed parallel to the existing entry porch. Having the advantage that there is no operating machinery requiring maintenance or supervision, the principal difficulty of an uncovered long inclined ramp is the nuisance of ice and snow removal, which if unattended can provide a hazard to wheelchair users.

During the great age of mansions and estates, ease of access was never a serious consideration, and entrances, terraces, and level changes were accomplished by steps. No matter how gracious and elegant the interior staircases may have been, they present a serious impediment to handicapped people. The preservation of the original exterior architectural character and appearance of an old mansion makes the provision of ramps, lifts, and new entrances at grade difficult to conceal. The situation obviously varies from case to case, but it can be even more difficult on the interior where there are level changes in different sections or wings of a large mansion. Many of the very large houses originally had service or passenger elevators, but these ancient devices are seldom adequate and may have to be replaced, enlarged, or relocated to satisfy modern requirements. This is particularly difficult for existing mansions adapted and successfully functioning as guest accommodations, conference centers, and catering facilities. The additional costs and complications of satisfying these barrier-free access requirements may further complicate and discourage the preservation of large mansions.

CONCLUSION

"The American country house is a caprice, a whimsy; it is a folly. Certainly there exists the element of too much, of excess, of an image—the house and grounds—straining to look natural, and yet no matter the style, they are human creations of the recent past. Time can add patina and soften the harshness of outline, but ultimately the country house is more image and effect. The country house is in itself a fictional world, time differs, does not stop, but takes on a refracted quality. In a sense the country house allows a freedom not present in the city, the freedom to create one's own world."

Richard Guy Wilson, essay in the exhibition catalog,
Long Island Country House, 1870—1930

Despite my long familiarity with the subject, the process of seeking innovative and successful adaptation of large American mansions and estates has remained a challenge, with no easy resolution in sight.

Several factors are important in determining the fate of these properties. Surprisingly even smaller but exceptional modern residences only 60 to 80 years old have proved even more of a difficulty to adapt to new uses. Significant twentieth-century residences complete with their original furnishings, designed by Frank Lloyd Wright, the Greene brothers, and Walter Gropius, have remained as private homes or are now maintained as house museums. This follows the pattern of substantial houses of the seventeenth through the nineteenth century.

Many of these landmarks of modern American architecture have passed into the ownership of institutions that have not always demonstrated ideal stewardship. As a result many of them have required private fund-raising campaigns and often special appeals to state legislatures to bail them out. In a period of retrenchment and diminished government cultural and arts funding, the historic societies and house museums, in particular, must compete for support against the more dynamic performing arts groups and the large museums, whose highly publicized blockbuster shows and changing exhibitions have attracted public attention and garnered substantial revenues, including corporate sponsorship.

For connoisseurs of art and antiques, knowlegeable collectors, and those intrigued by revisiting the past through sites associated with prominent personages or events in American history, the traditional house museum remains an attraction. Younger adults and families with small children, more accustomed to pseudohistorical theme parks such as Disney World, seek out more interactive and entertaining ways of relating to the past.

The restoration of Williamsburg, the colonial capital of Virginia, underwritten by the Rockefellers, was one of the pioneering efforts to evoke a historic ambiance. All vestiges of the nineteenth- and twentieth-century life were stripped away, and a total restoration—and in many cases reconstruction—accomplished based on archeological findings and considerable research conducted in the 1920s and 1930s. Williamsburg was brought to life by costumed interpreters, townsfolk, soldiers, coachmen, and craftspeople, the visitor could experience a step back into the past—a precursor of the "Magic Kingdom."

Sturbridge Village, in Massachusetts, begun in the 1930s followed a similar theme, but in this case historic structures were moved to the site to recreate an idealized New England village.

More recently at Plimoth Plantation, also in Massachusetts, is a total re-creation containing no historic structures, a site close to the Pilgrims original landing site at Plymouth Rock. Peopled seasonally by townsfolk who actually live in the recon-structed village, who speak only in seventeenth-century English, and who go about their daily life completely immersed in the past. All explanatory placards, historic artifacts, and display cases are concentrated in the interpretive center at the entrance to the site. In a gesture to current preoccupation with multicultural sensibilities, the Native Americans can be visited in their nearby encampment, and they describe to visitors their first encounters with the European settlers. (Many southern mansions including Mount Vernon and Monticello, now include the slave quarters on the tour and provide a more accurate portrait of the original life on these plantations.) Even with this new frankness it is difficult for the authentic historic house to compete with living historical theater.

Williamsburg, Sturbridge, and Plimoth Plantation have been intentionally iso-lated from the intrusions of contemporary life, so that the visitor can step back into time to experience a curatorially correct setting.

The growth of the historic preservation movement in the United States during the 1960s has placed a greater emphasis on restoring individual historic structures and districts as living communities in their original locations. The current philosophy respects the passage of time incorporating later modification and additions to historic buildings, and rejects the former approach of restoring back to the earliest. This involved stripping off later genuine historical fabric for the sake of creating a conjectural restoration out of new materials fabricated in a traditional manner. The new philosophy also rejects the relocation or demolition of historic structures, salvaging paneling and interior elements as background for the decorative arts collections of museums. Winterthur is an extreme example of the historic room or vignette approach, culled from historic houses in many regions of the United States.

It is ironic that many wealthy families of the golden age gave up their estates emptying their contents and donating them to museums, thus setting off the cycle that we are still trying to redress.

The National Trust for Historic Preservation has also had to struggle to garner suffcent funding to manage its far-flung realm of historic and architecturally excep-tional mansions, estates, and formal gardens. The Trust has been criticized for elitism and is under pressure to choose properties more representative of America's economic and cultural diversity. This trend does not offer much promise of assistance for the future preservation of the remaining mansions and estates of the golden age, especially those of primarily architectural interest not associated with historically significant personages or events. The Trust is now encouraging partnerships with local groups in maintaining, operating, and fund-raising efforts. Its involvement with Frank Lloyd Wright's home and studio, in Oak Park, Illinois, reflects this new approach.

Today too much of our American architectural and cultural legacy is at the mercy of the marketplace. Uniquely American artistic and decorative objects have attracted an international audience. Shaker furniture, Frank Lloyd Wright art glass windows, and Arts and Crafts Style furniture are now sought by collectors and museums abroad.

The United States may someday have to enact protective legislation to require permission to export "national treasures."

In the United States there has always been a resistance to increased government control and restriction of individual property rights. Even though more communities large and small have adopted historic preservation ordinances, very few provide any tax incentives, compensation, or special assistance to owners in exchange for the limitations placed on their properties. It is unrealistic to expect that preservation of mansions and estates as well as exceptional buildings can remain a private or charitable burden.

Many of America's most exceptional properties have been spared destruction, either by conversion to museum use or by adaptation to new uses. It is difficult to undo or reverse the lack of sensitive planning which has resulted in many past losses and continues to pit communities against individual owners and developers.

This book has sought to present a variety of examples of mansions and estates which have managed successfully to meet these challenges. There is no simple formula or for that matter any permanent solution. What has seemed an ideal arrangement to an earlier generation has frequently foundered when confronted with changing economic conditions and societal values of succeeding generations.

We cannot expect that our efforts will last forever, so we must continue to adapt to new circumstances, pressures of population growth, and limited resources. We probably would do better to consider our task historic conservation rather than preservation, for we too are trying to come to grips with an endangered species: mansions and estates, relics of an age of extraordinarily creatively constructed habitations and planned landscapes.

BIBLIOGRAPHY

Recent and currently available publications on the general subject of the preservation of American mansions, estates, and gardens are extremely limited.

Gardens and Landscaping

Griswold, Mac, and Eleanor Weller, *The Golden Age of American Gardens,* New York: Harry N. Abrams, Inc./The Garden Club of America, 1991.

Karson, Robin, Fletcher Steele, *Landscape Architect,* New York: Harry N. Abrams, Inc./Sagapress, Inc., 1989.

Ray, Mary Helen, and Robert P. Nicholls, *The Traveler's Guide to American Gardens,* Chapel Hill, N.C.: University of North Carolina Press, 1988.

Tishler, William H., Editor, *American Landscape Architecture, Designers and Places,* Washington, D.C.: The Preservation Press, 1989.

Adaptive Use—Including Mansions

Shopsin, William, *Restoring Old Buildings for Contemporary Uses,* New York: Whitney Library of Design/Watson-Guptill Publications, 1986.

Preservation, American Mansions, Country Houses, and Estates

Shopsin, William, and Mosette Broderick, *The Villard Houses: Life Story of a Landmark,* New York: Viking, 1980.

Shopsin, William, Grania Bolton Marcus, editor, *Saving Large Estates: Conservation, Historic Preservation, Adaptive Re-Use,* Setauket, N.Y.: Society for the Preservation of Long Island Antiquities, 1977.

American Mansions and Country Houses—Historical and Social Background

Aslet, Clive, *The American Country House,* New Haven, Conn.: Yale University, 1990.

Hewitt, Mark Alan, *The Architect & the Ameican Country House,* New Haven, Conn.: Yale University, 1990.

Moore, Charles, and Allen Gerald, *The Place of Houses,* New York: Henry Holt & Co., 1979.

Moss, Roger W., *The American Country House,* Philadelphia: Athenaeum, 1990.

Scully, Vincent, *The Architecture of the American Summer: The Flowering of the Shingle Style,* New York: Rizzoli, 1989.

Wilson, Richard Guy, and Steven M. Bedford, *The Long Island Country House 1870— 1930,* Southampton, N.Y.: The Parrish Art Museum, 1988.

Zukowsky, John, Stimson Robbe Pierce, *Hudson River Villas,* New York: Rizzoli, 1985.

American Mansions and Country Houses—Individual Architects

Curl, Donald, W., *Mizner's Florida: American Resort Architecture,* New York: The Architectural History Foundation and Cambridge, Mass.: MIT Press, 1984.

Morgan, Keith N., and Charles A. Jencks, *Charles A. Platt: The Artist as Architect,* New York: The Architectural History Foundation and Cambridge, Mass.: MIT Press, 1985.

Peck, Amelia, *Alexander Jackson Davis, American Architect, 1803—1892,* New York: Rizzoli, Metropolitan Museum of Art, 1992.

Retaining Family Ownership

Small, Stephen J., *Preserving Family Lands: A Landowner's Introduction to Tax Issues and Other Considerations,* Boston: Powers & Hall, P.C., 1988.

CREDITS

Introduction

The Chalet: photo courtesy of Newport Collaborative, p.1.
Mount Vernon: photo courtesy of William C. Shopsin, AIA, p.2.
Adelphi Hotel: photo courtesy of William C. Shopsin, AIA, p.3.
Westchester House: photo courtesy of William C. Shopsin, AIA, p.3.

Chapter 1

Hillwood: photos courtesy of William C. Shopsin, AIA, pp.5, 9, and 11; site plan courtesy of Hillwood, p.11.

Chapter 2

Santanoni: photos courtesy of Peter B. Olney, pp.13 and 20.
Camp Uncas: photos courtesy of William C. Shopsin, AIA, p.17.
Camp Sagamore: photos courtesy of William C. Shopsin, AIA, p.18.
Kamp Kill Kare: photos courtesy of the Adirondack Museum, p.19.
The Point: photos courtesy of Geoffrey Clifford, pp.21 and 23; site plan courtesy of The Point, p.22.

Chapter 3

Land Trusts: maps courtesy of the Peconic Land Trust, pp.25 and 27.
Mashomack Preserve: photo and site plan courtesy of The Nature Conservancy, Mashomack Preserve, pp.30 and 31.
Kaolin Commons: site plan courtesy of Charles Raskob Robinson, p.34.

Chapter 4

Shelburne Farms: site plan courtesy of Shelburne Farms, p.37; photos courtesy of William C. Shopsin, AIA, pp.35, 36, and 38.
Biltmore House: photos courtesy of Biltmore Estate, pp.41 and 42.
Boston Post Road Historic District: photos courtesy of the Westchester Landmarks Project, pp.48, 49, and 50; site plan courtesy of the town of Rye Assessor's Office, p.49.
Palm Beach, Florida: photo courtesy of Eugene Lawrence, architect, p.53.
Newport, Rhode Island: Lansmere photo courtesy of B. Sterling Benkhart, p.55; Lansmere site plan courtesy of the Newport Collaborative, p.55; Bienvenue photo courtesy of Aaron Usher III, p.56; Bienvenue floor plans courtesy of the Newport Collaborative, p.57; Codman Place photo courtesy of B. Sterling Benkhart, p.58.
East Hampton, New York: photos courtesy of William C. Shopsin, AIA, pp.59, 60, 62, 63, and 64.

Chapter 5

Old Westbury Gardens: photo courtesy of Old Westbury Gardens, Inc., p.65.
Lasdon: photo courtesy of Gannett, p.69.

Wethersfield: photos courtesy of William C. Shopsin, AIA, pp.71 and 72; garden and site plans courtesy of Wethersfield, Homeland Foundation, pp.70 and 72.
Naumkeag: photos courtesy of William C. Shopsin, AIA, pp.73 and 74; garden plan courtesy of The Trustees of Reservations, p.75.

Chapter 6

Dana-Thomas House: photo and floor plans courtesy of Hasbrouck, Peterson, Zimoch, Sirirattumrong (HPZS), Architects, Engineers, Conservators, pp.79 and 80; cross-sectional views (p. 81) courtesy of HPZS/Judith Bromley.
Darwin D. Martin House: photo and plans courtesy of HPZS, pp.82 and 83.
Robie House: photo and plans courtesy of HPZS, pp.85 and 86.
Meyer May House: photos and plans courtesy of Steelcase Inc., pp.77, 87, and 88.
Wingspread: aerial photo and plan courtesy of The Johnson Foundation, p.90; former children's wing photo courtesy of Thomas A. Schmidt for The Johnson Foundation, p.91.
Cole House: photo courtesy of William C. Shopsin, AIA, p.92.
Gropius House: photos courtesy of William C. Shopsin, AIA, pp.93 and 94.

Chapter 7

Blantyre: photo courtesy of William C. Shopsin, AIA, p.95.
Delamater House: photo courtesy of Delamater House, p.97.
Colonnade House at The Greenbrier: photos courtesy of The Greenbrier, pp.99 and 101.
Historic Inns of Annapolis: map courtesy of the City of Annapolis Planning Department, p.102; photos courtesy of William C. Shopsin, AIA, pp.102 and 103.
The Inn at Perry Cabin: photos courtesy of William C. Shopsin, AIA, pp.104 and 105.
Tollgate Hill Inn: plan courtesy of Tollgate Hill Inn, p.106.
John Rutledge House Inn: photo courtesy of John Rutledge House, p.107.
Naulakha: plans and photo courtesy of the Landmark Trust, pp.109 and 110.
Bellefontaine: photos courtesy of Canyon Ranch, pp.111 and 114; drawings courtesy of Jung/Brannen Associates, pp.112 and 113.
Tarrywile: photos courtesy of Roger Pitt Whitcombe, Architect, p.115; plans courtesy of Tarrywile, p.116.
Bragg-Mitchell Mansion: photo courtesy of Holmes & Holmes, Architects, p.117.
McDonald's, Denton House: photos (except period photo, p.119) courtesy of Brian Stanton, pp.119, 120, and 122; plans courtesy of Raymond F. Fellman, AIA, pp.121 and 122.
Constitution Hill: plans and photos courtesy of Holt-Morgan Architects, pp.123, 124, 125, and 126.
Squire House: photos courtesy of Westchester Preservation League, pp.127 and 128.
Maryland's Resident Curatorship Program: photos courtesy of Maryland's Resident Curatorship Program, pp.129, 130, 131, and 132.
The Maples: plan courtesy of Miquelle MZO, p.133; photos courtesy of Alex Beatty, pp.133 and 134.
Ronald McDonald House: photo of model and plans courtesy of Alesker, Reiff & Dundon, pp.135 and 136; interior photos courtesy of Lewis Tanner, pp.135 and 137.
Conyers Farm: plans courtesy of Robert Lamb Hart, Architects & Planners, pp.139, 140, and 141; photos and individual site plan courtesy of Alan Wanzenberg, Architect, pp.138, 139, and 142.
Brantwyn: photos courtesy of Brantwyn, pp.142 and 143.
Swift River Inn: photos courtesy of William C. Shopsin, AIA, p.144; plan courtesy of The Berkshire Design Group, Inc., p.145.
Penguin Hall: photos and plans courtesy of Olson Lewis, Architects & Planners, pp.147, 148, and 149.
Pleasantdale Farm: photos courtesy of William C. Shopsin, AIA, pp.150 and 151; plan courtesy of Allied Corporation, p.152.
Rockledge: photos courtesy of Reggie Jackson, pp.153 and 154.
Ensign House: photos and plans courtesy of Jeter, Cook, & Jepson, Architects, pp.155, 156, and 157.
Cold Spring Harbor: photos courtesy of William C. Shopsin, AIA, pp.158, 159, and 160; plan courtesy of Cold Spring Harbor Laboratories, p.159.

Chapter 8

Aspet, Saint-Gaudens National Historic Site: photos courtesy of the U.S. Department of the Interior National Park Service, Jeffrey Nintzel, pp.161, 163, and 164.
Lyndhurst: photos and plan courtesy of the National Trust for Historic Preservation, pp.165, 166, and 167.
The Mount: photos courtesy of William C. Shopsin, AIA, pp.168 and 169.

Chesterwood: photo of house facade courtesy of Chesterwood, a museum property of the National Trust for Historic Preservation (photo by Paul Ivory), p.170; studio photos courtesy of Chesterwood (photos by Paul Rocheleau), pp.169 and 170.

Yaddo: photo courtesy of William C. Shopsin, AIA, p.172.

Ragdale: photo courtesy of the Ragdale Foundation, p.173.

Sagamore Hill, Glenmont, and Wave Hill: photos courtesy of William C. Shopsin, AIA, pp.175 and 176.

Hackerman House: photos courtesy of Walters Art Gallery (exterior photo by Erik Kvalsik), pp.177, 180, and 181; plans courtesy of Grieves Worall Wright & O'Hatnick, pp.178 and 179.

Evergreen: photos courtesy of David Enders Tripp, pp.181 and 182.

Eastman House: plans and photos courtesy of Eastman House (photos by Barbara Puorro Galasso), pp.182, 183, 184, and 185.

Pierpont Morgan Library: photos courtesy of William C. Shopsin, AIA, p.188; plans courtesy of Voorsanger and Associates Architects, pp.186 and 187.

Dumbarton Oaks: plans courtesy of Hartman Cox, pp.191, 192, and 193; exterior photo courtesy of Harlan Hambright, p.193; courtyard photo courtesy of Peter Aaron/ESTO, p.190; garden view photo courtesy of Dumbarton Oaks, p.191.

Hyde Collection: photos courtesy of William C. Shopsin, AIA, pp.194 and 196; drawing and plan courtesy of Edward Larrabee Barnes/John M. Y. Lee, Architects, p.195.

Chapter 9

Photos courtesy of William C. Shopsin, AIA, pp.197 and 199.

INDEX

ABOUT THE AUTHOR

Wᴵᴸᴸᴵᴀᴍ C. Sʜᴏᴘsɪɴ, AIA, is a prominent architect, preservationist, and a founder of the Preservation League of New York State. A faculty member at Pratt Institute's School of Architecture for more than a decade, Mr. Shopsin has been a lecturer at the Cooper-Hewitt Museum in New York City and has served as preservation consultant for such famous landmarks as the Empire State Building, the General Electric Building, Gracie Mansion, and several others. He was the keynote speaker at the 1989 National Trust for Historic Preservation Conference on Historic Houses, and has authored many popular articles and books, including *Restoring Old Buildings for Contemporary Uses*, *The Villard Houses*, and *Saving Large Estates: Conservation, Historic Preservation, Adaptive Re-use*.